ADVANCE PRAISE for *The Gentleman from Ohio*

"Louis Stokes was an icon in America's political and moral life. He finished writing his autobiography, *The Gentleman from Ohio*, only days before his death at age 90. In precise and vivid prose, and with the wisdom of years, Stokes paints a picture of America's travails and triumphs as the nation made its way from an era of stark racism to one of better hope. Stokes rose from the housing projects in Cleveland to the heights of power in Congress. He was an outsider who became an ultimate insider, but one who never ceased fighting for the poor, the hard-pressed, the exploited, not just in Ohio but nationwide, and not just for African Americans but for all those in need of a champion. Louis Stokes's unique personality and character shine through in this book. Full of humor, graciousness, anger, and glowing optimism, *The Gentleman from Ohio* is an essential read."

—Vernon Jordan

"Two days before the historic 2008 election, my wife Connie Schultz and I had the great honor of standing backstage with civil rights icons Congressman Lou Stokes, Rev. Otis Moss, and Edwina Moss, while more than 80,000 people waited for Senator Barack Obama to take the stage. I listened as three veterans of the American civil rights movement swelled with pride at seeing their generation's hard-won victories make possible the election of our first black president—and I knew this was a profound moment I would carry with me for the rest of my life. Now readers have the chance to experience their own unique glimpses into history through the pages of Congressman Stokes's memoir. His message is an invaluable part of American history, and his wisdom and experiences remain deeply relevant to the continued struggle for equality in America today."

—U.S. Senator Sherrod Brown

"Lou Stokes arrived in Congress with a portfolio under his arm that was filled with triumphs in defending civil liberties. In his 30 years in the world's greatest legislative body, he reached the pinnacle of success. He was a giant of epic dimension in the struggle for civil rights and human rights. His love for life and mankind was conspicuous and contagious, piercing the conscience of America."

—Congressman William L. Clay Sr.

"Lou Stokes, who I was privileged to serve with in Congress, grew up using a big stick to fend off those who had designs on relieving him and his brother Carl of the food that was donated by the church to feed their family. He rose to become a defender of our nation in the U.S. Army and a giant in the U.S. Congress. He effectively wielded a 'big stick' in defense of the poor and dispossessed as a cardinal on the Appropriations Committee of the U.S. House of Representatives. A gentle man in spirit, Lou was the epitome of a gentleman in the House. I was privileged to learn at his knees and benefit from his friendship. It is no exaggeration to say that I stand on the broad shoulders of the gentleman from Cleveland, Ohio, the Honorable Lou Stokes."

—Congressman James Clyburn

"This autobiography of a great and good man will inspire readers young and old. Congressman Louis Stokes takes us on his journey from Cleveland's Outhwaite Homes to his brilliant career as a criminal defense attorney to his extraordinary three decades of service in the U.S. House of Representatives. You are there as he argues a case in the Supreme Court, as he cofounded the Congressional Black Caucus, as he rose to become one of the most important leaders in Congress. We are fortunate to have this fascinating account of the profoundly important legacy of Louis Stokes, told as only he could tell it."

—Barbara R. Snyder, President, Case Western Reserve University

"It is not often that someone comes along who defines an era of a city. The Stokes brothers did that for Cleveland. What is even more telling of Congressman Louis Stokes's character is that he did not just talk the civil rights game, but he walked the challenging roads of ensuring civil rights. He came from the effects of racism and poverty, overcame them, accessed and used power, while never forgetting where he came from."

—Frank G. Jackson, Mayor, Cleveland, Ohio

"*The Gentleman from Ohio* is a consistently fascinating story—some of which I had the pleasure of witnessing firsthand. Congressman Stokes's story is one of utmost importance for believers in how social and political change can defeat inequities in the system. A reading of *The Gentleman from Ohio* is essential for lovers of a good autobiography."

—Congressman John Conyers Jr.

"A book to inspire everyone who believes in a distant dream. Congressman Stokes showed us strength reinforced by generosity. Trailblazer. Sage. A giant oak in the forest. He and his brother honored the callouses on their mother's hands by lighting the path for everyone."

—Diane Sawyer

"*The Gentleman from Ohio* is the story of a life well lived, of respect earned, and of love freely given by a humble gentleman from Ohio who rose like the phoenix from his beginnings on Central Avenue to one of the most powerful men in the U.S. Congress."

—Congresswoman Marcia L. Fudge

"In every respect, Louis Stokes was a man ahead of his time, the 'gentleman from Ohio,' and a great American statesman."

—Marc Morial, President of the National Urban League

"Congressman Stokes taught me so much as my mentor. I learned from him about race and justice, and he influenced my writing and teaching. He will be remembered as someone who believed that he must continue the good fight and pass on our wisdom to the next generation."

—Professor Charles Ogletree, Harvard University

"Lou Stokes was a remarkable leader who applied his penetrating intelligence to the benefit of his constituents and our nation. He tells the inspiring story of his rise from the streets of Cleveland to the halls of Congress, and throws new lights on some of the most important personalities and events of our time. Like Congressman Stokes himself, this book makes a powerful impression."

—Delos M. Cosgrove, MD, CEO and President, Cleveland Clinic

"In a very personal and compelling narrative, Congressman Stokes relates his rise from poverty in Cleveland to being a "cardinal" in Congress where he spoke truth to power. He gives an insider's view of events that shaped America over four decades. It is a book that informs and inspires—one that I will read again and again."

—Grover C. Gilmore, Case Western Reserve University

"A compelling life story of a truly remarkable American, told with warmth and candor by the man who lived it."

—Brent Larkin, columnist and
former editorial director, *The Plain Dealer*

"Congressman Louis Stokes was a pioneer and a leader who served the citizens of Ohio Congressional District 21 with distinction and dedication for thirty years. A founding member of the Congressional Black Caucus, and the first chair of the Health Brain Trust of the Caucus, Lou Stokes had a national impact on a broad array of important issues affecting the health of all Americans. He was the only African American on the powerful health subcommittee of the U.S. House Appropriations Committee. He was effective in securing federal support for many health programs addressing disparities in health status and in access to health care, for America's minorities and the poor.

Lou Stokes was a man of integrity, a gentleman, and a true servant of the people. *The Gentleman from Ohio* is an inspiring autobiography, completed by Lou only a few days before he died. He was a noble warrior who made history and helped to improve the health and the lives of millions of Americans."

—Louis W. Sullivan, MD,
President Emeritus Morehouse School of Medicine,
former U.S. Secretary of Health and Human Services

"This is a riveting story about love, life, family, community, law, and politics. It is a captivating tale of a mother's dreams realized beyond her imagination through the experiences of her two sons, rising out of poverty in a racially divided country to attain international influence. In this book, Louis Stokes paints a vivid picture of his upbringing in a single-parent home with a mother who worked diligently to care for her children and teach them the value of hard work and education. . . . *The Gentleman from Ohio* is a truly inspiring read."

—John Ruffin, PhD, retired founding director of
the National Institute on Minority Health and
Health Disparities, NIH

"This is the story of how a man with courage and integrity was able to bring about change in his town and in his country. I am proud to say that he was my friend."

—Albert B. Ratner, philanthropist

"Congressman Louis Stokes's rise from an impoverished childhood to the pinnacle of political power is well-known in Cleveland, as is the fact that he graduated from Cleveland-Marshall College of Law. Because he was an alumnus, I was privileged to spend considerable time with Lou and to benefit from his counsel during the five years preceding his death. Until reading this book, however, I knew little of the fascinating range of experiences that made up the tapestry of Lou's exceptional life and the scope and magnitude of his influence in Congress. The thirty years during which he served in Congress encapsulated some of the more momentous events in our nation's history, and Lou was profoundly involved with most of them. Through it all, he never forgot where he came from. Lou was not content to be the *first* black congressman from Ohio; his deeply felt mission was to be the *best* representative in Congress for the people who elected him, and for black people across the country struggling to participate in the American dream. He succeeded mightily. This powerful book shares the remarkable story of a man who is as beloved for his gentle and selfless spirit, as he is for the many essential things he accomplished for his constituents."

—Craig M. Boise, former dean, Cleveland-Marshall College of Law,
Cleveland State University

"There are people who are great because of their accomplishments. Other people are simply great human beings. Lou Stokes was both, and he transcended them all. This autobiography conveys the ways he inspired a city and a nation with his warmth, his sincerity, his laughter, and his desire to eliminate life's disparities through his intellect and his enormous heart. I am honored to have been his friend."

—Jay A. Gershen, DDS, PhD, President,
Northeast Ohio Medical University

"Congressman Louis Stokes was a tireless worker for a better America. Lou encouraged us to think more boldly about those segments of our society that need a helping hand. For those segments, and more, Lou's hand and heart were always there. His was a life well lived."

—Morton Mandel, Chairman and CEO,
Jack, Joseph and Morton Mandel Foundation

"Louis Stokes was an extraordinary individual and an important national leader. He has left us a remarkable recollection of his service as an effective public servant and an important record of his involvement with some of the truly significant events of our time, including the congressional investigation of the Kennedy and the Martin Luther King Jr. assassinations. The story of the close bond and political partnership forged between Lou and his brother, Carl— and the pioneering impact of their hard-fought efforts in opening the doors for meaningful minority participation in local, state, and national politics—is also compellingly told, and the impact of their efforts continues to reverberate. Perhaps, most especially, *The Gentlemen from Ohio* provides a much-needed example of how a fiercely dedicated and deeply principled congressional leader can meaningfully advance the causes of his constituents and the nation, while working with and respecting colleagues with radically different viewpoints. In short, now more than ever, Lou Stokes deserves a large audience of listeners."

—R. Thomas Stanton, former chairman,
Squire, Sanders & Dempsey

THE GENTLEMAN FROM OHIO

The GENTLEMAN *from* OHIO

LOUIS STOKES

with David Chanoff

Foreword by
CONGRESSMAN JOHN LEWIS

TRILLIUM, AN IMPRINT OF
THE OHIO STATE UNIVERSITY PRESS
COLUMBUS

Copyright © 2016 by The Ohio State University.
All rights reserved.
Trillium, an imprint of The Ohio State University Press.

Library of Congress Cataloging-in-Publication Data
Names: Stokes, Louis, 1925–2015, author. | Chanoff, David, author. | Lewis, John, 1940 February 21–
    writer of foreword.
Title: The gentleman from Ohio / Louis Stokes with David Chanoff ; foreword by Congressman
    John Lewis.
Description: Ohio : Trillium, an imprint of The Ohio State University Press, [2016] | Includes index.
Identifiers: LCCN 2016017093 | ISBN 9780814213124 (cloth ; alk. paper) | ISBN 081421312X (cloth ;
    alk. paper)
Subjects: LCSH: Stokes, Louis, 1925–2015. | African American lawyers—Ohio—Cleveland—Biogra-
    phy. | African American legislators—United States—Biography. | African American civil rights
    workers—Biography. | United States. Congress. House—Biography. | Cleveland (Ohio)—Politics
    and government.
Classification: LCC E840.8.S835 A3 2016 | DDC 328.73/092 [B]—dc23
LC record available at https://lccn.loc.gov/2016017093

Cover design by AuthorSupport.com
Text design by Juliet Williams
Type set in Adobe Caslon

♾ The paper used in this publication meets the minimum requirements of the American National
Standard for Information Sciences—Permanence of Paper for Printed Library Materials. ANSI
Z39.48–1992.

9 8 7 6 5 4 3 2 1

To the memory of my mother, Louise, for the blessing she was, for the sacrifices she made, and for her spiritual strength through which she taught us to become what we became.

To my brother, Carl, whom I loved with all my heart, who gave me the inspiration for my political life and who set an example for black Americans across the nation.

To my beloved wife, Jay, who has been the bedrock for me through all the years in all I have been able to do. The best wife a man could have. The best mother to our children. In memory of the complete and fulfilled life she gave me.

CONTENTS

Photographs follow page 100.

ACKNOWLEDGMENTS

IN WRITING this book, I benefited greatly from friends and colleagues who graciously shared their memories of people and events that were important to my life story. Bill Clay, my longtime friend and fellow representative, embodies the institutional memory of the Congressional Black Caucus, which he and I helped bring to life at the beginning of our tenures. His recollections stimulated my own and on several occasions corrected errors and illuminated situations that we had both been involved in but that had dimmed somewhat in my own memory. Dr. Louis Sullivan, former secretary of the Department of Health and Human Services, did likewise for our partnership in bringing significant health-care legislation into law and in addressing the shameful disparities between the health of mainstream and minority Americans. I treasured his friendship and support through the years, as I did Bill Clay's. Dr. John Ruffin is another colleague whose perspective on health matters helped give our discussion here both breadth and depth. For twenty-four years John was the director of the National Institutes of Health's Institute on Minority Health and Health Disparities, which began life not as an institute but as a far less influential NIH "office." John guided the institute's growth expertly. In the course of that history he and I collaborated closely and formed a fast friendship. Ron Lancaster and Dale Dirkes were also closely involved in our efforts to bring equal health care to minorities, and they too gave freely of their insights and recollections.

I owe them lasting gratitude for that, as I do to Daniel Dawes, executive director of government relations at the Morehouse School of Medicine, who shared with us his extensive research on my participation in health-care legislation. Lodriguez Murray, senior vice president at the Health and Medical Counsel of Washington, contributed to our health-care discussions and also smoothed the path on occasion for our efforts to gather congressional information. My old friends and former staff members Joyce Larkin and Joanne White were also helpful in facilitating our research, as was Lia Kerwin at the Library of Congress and Ann Sindelar at the Western Reserve Historical Society, which houses my archives along with my brother Carl's. My good friend Susan Hall also helped considerably with our research there. Representative John Lewis is another colleague whose support and warm friendship meant so much to me over the years. I'm especially grateful to him for providing the foreword to *The Gentleman from Ohio.*

My oldest daughter, Shelley Stokes-Hammond, is a writer and researcher herself. Her memories of our family life from a child's point of view added greatly to this book, as did her detailed knowledge of the Ludlow Association, which maintained the integrated and racially harmonious neighborhood we lived in during a fraught period of white flight and black influx. My other children, Angie, Chuck, and Lori, were also available any time I wanted to talk about subjects that touched on our lives as a family. They have my gratitude, as they know they have my love. Lori, our youngest, did the immense job of culling my photographic archives for the display incorporated in this book, ably assisted by graphic designer John Rodriguez. In his position with the National Science Foundation, my grandson Eric Hammond was helpful in locating information on some of my congressional activities involving that organization. Another of my grandchildren, Brett Hammond, an assistant district attorney in Cleveland, spent time with me discussing the *Terry* "Stop and Frisk" case, which I argued before the Supreme Court. Those discussions helped focus me on the details of that landmark case.

The Gentleman from Ohio is, among other things, a family story. In terms of family, my wife, Jay Stokes, provided comfort, support, and companionship during the entire writing process and, more than once, a gentle correction when my memory had gotten something wrong or where my tone might have made an unintended impression. It's a cliché to say that a wife's love and moral support made the writing possible. In my case that happens simply to be the truth.

The book would have found a far more difficult course had it not been for the foundations that provided such generous support. Here I would like to express my gratitude to the Cleveland Foundation, the George Gund Foundation, the Sherwick Fund of the Cleveland Foundation, the Mount Sinai Health Care Foundation, Cleveland, the Steven and Dolly Minter Fund of the Cleveland Foundation, and the Treu-Mart Fund of the Cleveland Foundation.

I also want to express my deep appreciation for the help provided by President Barbara Snyder of Case Western Reserve University. Steve Minter was instrumental in our endeavor to bring funding together, and Craig Zullig, the director of research administration at Case Western Reserve University's Mandel School of Applied Social Sciences, managed the grants expertly. I also need to thank the Mandel School's dean, Grover "Cleve" Gilmore, who helped verify information having to do with my fifteen-year faculty tenure there, but more particularly for being such a warm and supportive friend to me and my accomplished writing collaborator, David Chanoff.

FOREWORD

Congressman John Lewis

IT IS NOT too much to say that Louis Stokes and his brother Carl helped
lead the way in establishing a place for African Americans in the world of
mainstream American politics. In doing that they helped rearrange our country's political landscape. It was a historic achievement.

In *The Gentleman from Ohio,* Louis Stokes tells his story, but the book
does a great deal more. It opens up a panoramic view of American life in
an essential era of our recent history, and it does so from a perspective that
most Americans will find fascinating, moving, and, very possibly, disturbing.
Moreover, Congressman Stokes has done this with the warmth, incisiveness,
and humor that marked his unforgettable personality.

Louis Stokes's brother, Carl, was the first black mayor of a major American city, Cleveland, Ohio. In that position he demonstrated that blacks had
the talent and leadership skills to take charge, not only in their own communities but in mainstream government as well. He showed that African
Americans were up to the task of serving the overall community without
neglecting the interests of their black constituents. In doing this he served as
a model for the black mayors, governors, and congresspeople who have come
after him.

Carl's story and Louis's were inexorably linked, from their childhoods in
black Cleveland through their rise to national prominence. The entwined
stories of these two remarkable men is one of the subjects Lou Stokes covers

here so well, but *The Gentleman from Ohio* inevitably focuses on its author's own rich and accomplished life, as well it should.

Lou Stokes was the first black congressman in Ohio's history. In the House of Representatives he carved out a path for African Americans to achieve power, by establishing themselves as players on the committees that mattered.

Lou Stokes was elected for the first of his fifteen terms in 1968. When he arrived in Washington there were only six black members in the House, but Stokes came in as part of a historic cohort. His election, along with that of Shirley Chisholm and William Lacy Clay, brought the black House numbers up to nine, a critical number as Stokes saw it, the most African Americans to ever serve in the House at the same time.

Stokes and Clay together pushed for the formation of a formal black power block that could act in concert on the issues vital to their communities. With guidance from the departing Adam Clayton Powell, they organized what became the Congressional Black Caucus, the membership of which has grown to forty-five as of this writing. Stokes served as the second chairman, and under his leadership caucus members committed themselves to focusing their efforts on gaining power through the committee system and placing minority issues on the agenda of every committee they served on.

That was a visionary decision made with the long-view perspective that characterized Stokes's approach as a legislator. What he saw was that most black legislators came from districts that would continue to elect them as long as they did their work honorably and well. That meant that over the long run they would wield considerable power via the House's seniority system. "Those of us in the Congressional Black Caucus," Stokes writes, "succeeded in establishing an understanding that black legislators were every bit as capable and dedicated as white legislators. I have no doubt that we changed perceptions in that regard. Over time we were no longer regarded as strange and semi-foreign anomalies in the world of political power, but as a normal part of governance."

Stokes's own accomplishments as he rose to leadership positions in the House were legendary. He served as chair of the House Select Committee on the assassinations of President John F. Kennedy and Dr. Martin Luther King Jr. He was chair of the Ethics Committee during Abscam, the House page scandal, and the Geraldine Ferraro investigations. He chaired the Intelligence Committee during Iran-Contra. The health care legislation he sponsored changed the way the health establishment treated those who most needed help. He became, perhaps most significantly, a "Cardinal" on the

House Appropriations Committee, overseeing and directing the expenditure of many tens of billions of dollars.

With all his political achievements, Louis Stokes was not at heart a politician. He got great fulfillment from his life in Congress, but his first and last love was the law. As a twelve-year-old newspaper delivery boy in Cleveland he read about the Scottsboro Boys, lynchings, and other racial cruelty in the South and dreamed of becoming a lawyer who could defend his people from that kind of injustice. He knew his family would never have enough money to send him to college—his father had died when he was three and his mother made a meager living as a domestic—but the dream persisted anyway. When he was drafted in 1943 into the segregated army, he met and was inspired by African American men who had bachelor's and even master's degrees, and when he was discharged after the war he used the GI Bill of Rights to go to college and law school.

Stokes practiced as a criminal defense attorney and also as head of the Cleveland NAACP's Legal Redress Committee. Stokes's legal career took him in front of the U.S. Supreme Court three times, including the famous *Terry* "Stop and Frisk" case that determined the legal parameters for police stops on the street, still in effect and still controversial.

Stokes was an advocate, a fierce fighter for the principles he believed in. But he also treated even his adversaries with respect and fairness. He left Congress after serving thirty years. Carl, his political confidant, had died by then, which greatly diminished the enjoyment he got out of his congressional work.

Louis Stokes died at the age of ninety very shortly after finishing this autobiography. He was an icon in Ohio; his body lay in state at the Cleveland City Hall rotunda. He was beloved by all who knew him. He was a unique man, a person of huge accomplishment, steel character, but also great humility, all of which comes through in *The Gentleman from Ohio*, which so poignantly documents his life and legacy.

John Lewis
Representative
Fifth Congressional District
Georgia

CHAPTER 1

~◦

Poppin' the Rag

WHEN I WAS TWELVE years old my paper route took me all through the area around Sixty-Ninth and Cedar in the heart of Cleveland's black neighborhood, where my younger brother Carl and I lived on the first floor of a rickety old house with our mom, Louise, and our grandmother, Fannie Stone. We were poor as poor, and we knew it. We wore hand-me-down clothes given to us by the wealthy white employers for whom my mom worked as a maid—though she never called herself that. She was, she said, "in service." Her meager salary, eight dollars a day, wasn't enough to support us, so she had to go on Aid to Dependent Mothers welfare, too. Carl and I would bring home food supplies, dried beans and peas, sugar, and flour from the Shiloh Church distribution center in our wagon, looking out to defend ourselves from any sudden attack by someone who might think we were easy targets. One of us would be pulling the wagon, the other brandishing a big stick. We weren't the only ones hungry; by the time I was seven, in 1932, the Depression was in full swing.

To help bring in money Carl collected bottles and other glass to turn in for cash. I shined shoes, poppin' that rag as loud as I could, hoping for a big tip, or any tip. In addition, I had the paper route. I got the route from Caldwell Gaffney, a kid a couple of years older than me who lived across the street. Caldwell and his brother George had more or less cornered the market on paper routes in our part of town. They came from an entrepreneurial family—their father had a painting business, one of the few black-owned businesses we were aware of. We used to see him driving off each morning in his white cap and painter's outfit, sometimes taking Caldwell and George along, wearing their own white caps.

Caldwell hired me to take on part of his route. He and George had bikes. They'd hang two heavy bags of papers from either side of their handle-bars, and off they'd go. Without a bike, I'd lug around my own bag full of papers, the *Cleveland News* Monday through Saturday and the *Plain Dealer* on Sundays. Many of the houses in the ten-block area Caldwell assigned me were two-family homes, like ours. I learned to fold the papers into a square and sail them up onto the upstairs porches or into hallways if an outside door was open.

My ten-square-block route was a lot of walking, and I began thinking about what I could do with a bike myself, if only I had one, how much easier it would be. If I had a bike maybe I could even get my own route directly from the newspaper company. I liked Caldwell and George. They were good guys, but with my own route I could make more money to help Mom.

Finally I decided to ask her. A bike cost a lot, about thirty-five dollars, but I'd be able to make that back, and much more besides. As I waited for her to come home from work one day, I sat on the swing on our front porch, going over in my head how I was going to convince her. I'd tell her what a good investment it would be. That was my main talking point—a good investment that would enable me to bring in more money for the family. Obviously a good idea. How could she say no to that? I could already picture myself flying around the neighborhood on my new bike, whizzing those papers up onto the porches.

Before long she came toward the house from her streetcar stop, walking slowly after another hard day, but her face lit with a smile when she saw me. As she climbed up the porch steps I jumped off the swing and hugged her. "Can you sit down with me?" I said. "I need to talk about something important." We sat on the swing together. I explained about the bike, why I needed one, how much more money I could make for us if I had one. It cost a lot, but it would be an excellent investment. She looked at me, hurt in her eyes. "Billy," she said. My nickname from birth. "Billy, I'm sure it would be an excellent investment, but I can't afford to buy you a bicycle. We just don't have the money." She saw my crestfallen expression. "Maybe after you work a while longer we can figure out a way. Let's see."

I was so sure I could convince her, and now my hopes were dashed. I felt worse for her, though. I knew our circumstances. I knew we couldn't afford it, but I had forced her to say it out loud, to admit to me how poor we were. I felt bad, but I had made her feel worse, after she had come home tired from another long day washing floors, doing laundry, and looking after someone else's children. But Grandma Fannie saved the day. When she heard about it she took me to her room and got out a little white bag, where she was saving part of her social security money. Untying the strings, she fished out thirty-five dollars. "For your bike," she said.

So I got my bike, and I got my own paper route. I delivered the papers, but I also read them, the *News,* the *Plain Dealer,* the *Call and Post,* Cleveland's black newspaper, and the *Pittsburgh Courier,* the closest thing there was to a national black paper. They had all sorts of stories, about what was happening in Cleveland and all over the country. But the reports I was most drawn to were the ones about lynchings down South, where my mother had come from.

Carl and I had heard stories from her and Grandma. They had both grown up as sharecroppers near the old Oliphant plantation outside Wrens, Georgia. They didn't talk about it much; they didn't like to dwell on their past in Wrens. But Carl and I understood that if you were black, bad things could happen to you down there. We had the clear idea that the South was not a place you wanted to be, a place where there were no opportunities, where white people were mean and could do anything they wanted to you. And here in the newspapers were exactly those stories about what *could* happen to you.

When I was twelve and had started my newspaper reading career, the story of the Scottsboro Boys had flared up again, even though the nine black teenagers had originally been arrested and sentenced in Alabama six years earlier. But the case had gone through appeal after appeal and had become a national fixation. Reading about it mesmerized me. Nine black boys accused of raping two white women while all of them were riding a freight train to Memphis, Tennessee. Almost lynched in Scottsboro, they faced all-white juries and bigoted judges and were, all but one of them who was thirteen, sentenced to the electric chair, the usual fate for blacks accused of raping whites.

But the Communist Party had fastened on the case as an example of American racism and hired lawyers for appeals, which had reached up through the Alabama judicial system all the way to the Supreme Court of the

United States. Big constitutional issues were involved, about the exclusion of blacks from juries and the right to a fair trial. At age twelve I'm sure I didn't understand all the nuances, but the newspaper reports talked of frame-ups and racist police and judges, all of it an eye-opener for me.

Reading about what had happened to the Scottsboro Boys upset me. It made me angry. But I was also struck by the fact that the lawyers who came in to represent the Scottsboro Boys were white—Samuel Leibowitz, a famous defense attorney from New York, and other white lawyers. That seemed to happen in other cases I read about, too. In Detroit Clarence Darrow had defended a black doctor in a famous case where the doctor was accused of murder while he was defending his home against a mob.

My imagination began to work on these things. I thought a lot about what was happening to black people in the South. I didn't feel threatened by that kind of thing myself—not where I lived, anyway. But I identified with what was going on in the South where black people were subjected to hatred and violence and couldn't even get fair trials. I imagined myself as a lawyer traveling around from city to city to defend black people who were accused of crimes they didn't commit. I would represent them in front of white juries and judges and win my cases by the power of my arguments for justice and what was right. I made up my mind then that when I grew up I would become a defense lawyer, like Leibowitz and Darrow, only I would be a black lawyer defending my own people.

That image lived in my mind; it was my dream. Reality was a different story. You had to go to college to be a lawyer, and I knew I wasn't going to college. Mom would never have the money to send me. We didn't even know anybody who went to college. So the fact was that whatever my dreams were, there was no way I was actually going to become a lawyer.

The best that I was going to be able to do was graduate from high school. That was what Mom wanted desperately for me and Carl, that we would earn our high school diplomas. It was her dearest wish. She herself had only gone through eighth grade, which was why she had to make her living the way she did. If she told us once she told us a thousand times, "Get something in your head so you don't have to work with your hands like I have to." It was a refrain we both remembered forever, even if we didn't appreciate the depth of what that meant to her when we were kids.

I guess I thought of it more as just an expression then anything else—"get something in your head"—something any working mom might say to her kids. Until one night when I was about thirteen. Mom was almost never sick, which was why it was so upsetting when she came down with something that put her flat on her back, groaning with pain. I went into her bedroom to see if I could comfort her in some way—we had recently moved from the old house on Sixty-Ninth Street into the newly built Outhwaite Homes Projects. The room was pitch dark. I sat by the bed; it was almost unbearable listening to her, she was in so much pain. I reached across and took her hands in my hands. Her hands were cold—hard, callused hands that had scrubbed people's floors for years so that Carl and I could get an education and look forward to having something better in life. And it hit me for the first time what she was trying to get across when she kept telling us to get something in our heads so we wouldn't have to work with our hands, the way she did. Feeling those hard, callused hands in mine, I understood.

Carl and I were our mother's hope in life, her boys. Our father had died when I was three and a half and Carl was two, so we never knew him. I had no memory of him at all, and Carl was just a toddler when he passed. But we knew that Mom had loved him. She talked so romantically about him, what a wonderful person he was, how he was so handsome, how he always had a smile for her, how he conducted himself as a man. You couldn't help but know that she adored him. We heard that from her, and we heard bits and pieces from relatives whenever his name came up in conversation. The same kind of thing, what a fine person he had been, how tragic it was that he had died so young, at age twenty-eight, only five years after they married—of what our relatives said was "acute peritonitis."

He had come up from Georgia, too, probably with even less formal education than she had. They hadn't known each other down there, but in Cleveland they met, fell in love, and married. The two of them were part of the Great Migration that took place in the early twentieth century, when millions of African Americans left southern towns and farms to look for a freer life in the North, where there were jobs available so you could make a decent living and where you didn't have to experience the constant humiliation that went with being black in the South, a place where you would never be recognized as a full human being or given any opportunity to better yourself.

Our father, Charles Stokes, "Charlie" to everyone who knew him, had worked in a laundry. Years later, when I was campaigning for Congress, a lady came up to me after a speech and said, "I want to tell you, I knew your father. I worked with him in the laundry. I remember him talking about his two sons. He was so proud of them. He said they were going to grow up to be great men." I treasured that, as I treasured all the little pieces of information we picked up about him along the way.

My father's middle name, if he had one—we weren't clear on that—was Louis. In any event, he and my mom named me Louis, though to relatives and old friends I'm Bill, or Billy. Apparently when my mother was pregnant with me, she and my father would talk, as married people do, about the baby moving around inside her belly. And not having chosen a name for the baby yet, they called me "Billy." "Billy certainly is active today." "Billy's really kicking in there tonight." When I was born they named me Louis, which is on my birth certificate, but they kept calling me Billy. There are people in my family today who, if you call me Louis, don't know whom you're talking about. They've always known me by Billy. It's the same case with Carl. Carl was named Carl Burton Stokes. But everyone called him "Brother." So we were not Louis and Carl, we were Billy and Brother.

Carl and I were close, and having no father drew us closer. It forced us to rely on each other even more than we might have otherwise. Mom's work often called for her to live in, which meant she'd be away all week and come home weekends, so we were on our own more than most kids.

During those times Grandma—"Aunt Fannie" to friends as well as relatives—took care of us. After our father died, Mom had sent money to her down in Georgia to come up and help her with her two babies. Grandma Fannie lived with us. As far back as I remember she always seemed old, a matronly, gray-haired lady in a long, black, ankle-length dress, always with an apron around her waist that reached down to the tops of her shoes.

Grandma Fannie was the idol of the family. Everybody loved her. They wanted to come by and see her, and they all wanted her to cook something for them. They would especially drop by on Sunday morning, which was when she would cook a big breakfast, fried chicken and grits and pork brains, sweet potato biscuits with butter slathered on them, all of it so tasty that as often as not there would be a small crowd around the table.

Grandma's voice was low. She had a soft-spoken manner about her, which went with her sweetness. She loved Carl and me, but she was strict with us. And though she was sweet, she could also be tough as nails. She would only take so much of our fussing and fighting before she'd stop talking and smack us. If we really got out of hand she'd call her son "Doc" to administer the discipline, a consequence Carl and I didn't want to precipitate if we could help it.

Doc's real name was Poughsley. He wasn't the kind of person anyone wanted to mess with. The story was that back in Georgia he had gotten into it with a white man and had done something—we were never told what—that made it necessary for him to get out of there fast.

Doc wasn't tall, but he was strongly built and had a quick temper. He lived a block away, on Sixty-Eighth, where he ran a pool hall and drinking joint. Rough characters frequented that place, and he might have been the roughest. We weren't allowed in there, but we'd hear stories about him whacking some unruly patron with a gun butt. I once saw federal agents pouring barrels of beer over the balcony of his house into the street.

If Carl and I didn't cease and desist from whatever we were doing, we'd hear Grandma say the dreaded words, "Okay, now I'm calling your uncle Doc." She knew that would catch our attention because when Doc came through that door he would already be reaching for his belt.

Doc was not the kind of uncle who might take you fishing or to a base-ball or football game. He wasn't someone you could sit down with to talk over problems and get advice and counsel. Neither Carl nor I would ever have thought of calling him a father figure. In fact, there was no one in our lives who might have filled that role. Other than Uncle Doc, the only men who visited were some of my older cousins who came mainly to see Grandma and our mom.

Mom was only in her mid-twenties when our father died and very pretty, but she hardly dated at all. During the years when Carl and I were grow-ing up there were occasions when some man would show up attempting to court her. But the kind of life she lived—often gone all week sleeping at her employers' houses—wasn't conducive to forming relationships. Carl and I probably weren't conducive, either. When we got to be teenagers we'd do everything we could to intimidate any prospective suitor. We were tall and well built, especially Carl. When someone came to the house, Mom would introduce us and we'd give him a hard handshake and a look he couldn't have interpreted as friendly, which was really unfair because she was entitled to have some type of male companionship, being the young woman she was.

But there weren't many potential boyfriends coming around—I can only really recall two or three. They would come to take her out on occasion, but she never had any man stay there. She would never have subjected us to that kind of thing. Jack Hinkle was one who spent more time with her than any of the others. He seemed like a good guy, fun to be around, and he played bridge, as she did. She loved bridge, and sometimes on weekends she'd have a bridge party. In our small living room she'd set up three tables, and she and Jack Hinkle would be partners. But when the bridge party was over Jack went home.

Our house on Sixty-Ninth Street had two bedrooms, a living room, din-ing room, bathroom, and kitchen. Grandma slept in one bedroom. As she grew older and more frail she needed a room for herself. That meant Mom, Carl, and I slept in the other, all three of us sharing the one bed the room could accommodate.

Our Sixty-Ninth Street house was heated by a big pot-bellied coal stove that sat in the living room. We'd feed it coal from the coal bin in the basement—fill up the coal bucket there and bring it upstairs to the stove. At night we'd have to bank it for safety, and in the bitterly cold Cleveland winters the heat was never enough to keep the bedrooms warm. We wore socks to bed and bundled up. The place was drafty, with holes in the floors where rats would come up and scurry around. Carl and I covered the holes as well as we could, nailing down tin can tops over them.

As it was, Carl and I were out on the streets as much as we could be, running with the other kids on the block. A few of the local adults took an interest in us, with the idea that we should be doing something constructive. A lady down the block, Mrs. Dixon, organized a little band, with used instruments she managed to dig up somewhere. The *Call Post* even wrote an article on us. We had an old piano, a drum set, a tambourine. I played the spoons.

Carl and I also learned to box down there on Sixty-Ninth Street. Later Carl became a very good Golden Gloves boxer. I didn't have his interest or talent, but I learned. A neighbor who had been a professional fighter taught a group of us. We'd go down to his place, and in his backyard he'd give us boxing lessons. We'd fight each other with the gloves on. He was tough on us; when he was showing us something he'd bang us hard.

I did that for several years, and I'm glad I did because when we were older Carl would come home some nights and say, "Bill, let's fight." I had to be able to do something just to defend myself. And of course there was a lot of fighting in our neighborhoods—gang fights, the guys from our street versus gangs from other streets. These weren't gangs the way we think of them today, just guys from one block squaring off against guys from another. On Sixty-Ninth Street we took pride that we never started a fight with anybody. But if somebody started one with us, we knew how to handle ourselves.

That was the time when Joe Louis and Hammering Henry Armstrong were the great black champions. In 1937, when I was twelve, Armstrong won twenty-two bouts in a row, twenty-one by knockout. He went on to hold three different weight division championships at the same time. But as great as he was, the big spotlight was on Joe Louis. Every young black kid coming along then wanted to be Joe Louis, just as later we all wanted to be Jesse Owens. Most African American boys knew they weren't going to college. They weren't going to go into the professions. But if they could be as good at fighting as Joe Louis they could make some money. There was at least some hope in that.

Cleveland's Majestic Hotel stood on the corner of Fifty-Fifth and Central, less than a mile from our house. The Majestic was the city's black hotel, the place where visiting African American entertainers and other celebrities stayed since even in the North, downtown white hotels were off limits. There were no segregation laws as there were in the Jim Crow South, but it was understood where you could stay and where you couldn't, where you could eat and where you couldn't.

The Majestic stood among the smoke shops, bars, pool halls, and barbershops on Fifty-Fifth where old men sat outside playing checkers or chess, joking, telling stories, and enjoying each other's company. On Joe Louis fight nights a bedlam of celebration swirled around the hotel. On those nights practically every black family in Cleveland and everywhere else in the country gathered around their radios listening breathlessly to the ringside action. The moment Joe knocked out his opponent, which is what usually happened, Cleveland's black neighborhoods exploded with joy and thousands of people made their way down to the Majestic hollering and dancing and singing. His victories meant so much, especially if he had knocked out a white guy. That was Joe getting even for the rest of us.

In 1938 we moved from Sixty-Ninth Street to the recently built Outhwaite Homes. Outhwaite was the first low-income public housing in Cleveland, and one of the first projects in the nation. The rent was $4.87 a month.

Mother had told us something about what to expect, but that didn't lessen our awe when we saw it. Our new home was clean and freshly painted. Downstairs there was a living room, kitchen, dining room—all small, but big enough for us. The kitchen was especially wonderful. Hot and cold running water in the sink, a real refrigerator instead of the old icebox we had on Sixty-Ninth Street, a washing machine. No holes in the floor and no rats. Upstairs was even better—three bedrooms, which meant Mom could have her own room for the first time while Carl and I had separate beds in our room. And the radiators kept us warm, the first time in all the winters I could remember that we didn't need to bundle up at night and look to each other for a little body heat.

Outside was a small but neat backyard and beyond that a grassy play area. Even more enticing was the Portland Outhwaite Recreation Center less than a block away, which had a basketball court, ping pong tables, a boxing ring, even a swimming pool. Carl had been an outstanding student in elementary school, but after we moved to Outhwaite he seemed to spend more and more time in the recreation center playing ping pong and boxing, and out on the street, learning hustling skills that Mother would not have been happy with had she known. "Get something in your head!" was still her refrain, especially if she thought we were slacking off. "Be somebody! You have to be somebody!"

I was trying. After graduating from Giddings Elementary School I enrolled at Central High School, which was then both a junior and senior high school famous for at least two of its graduates: John D. Rockefeller, who founded the Standard Oil Company, and Langston Hughes, the great poet of the Harlem Renaissance. I was good at school, especially in history and English. I had learned to read early and at Central my English teacher, Mrs. Fitzgerald, took a personal interest in me. She had us reading Shakespeare's plays—*Romeo and Juliet, Julius Caesar,* and others. We memorized speeches and I loved getting up and reciting the poetry. Marc Antony's "The evil men do lives after them / The good is oft interred with their bones." His ultimately sardonic "And sure, Brutus is an honorable man."

Jim Thrasher, Eugene Shepherd, and Walter Cox had been through elementary school together with me. By the time we got to Central Walter was drawn toward art, but Eugene, Jim, and I took the academic courses together. The three of us were serious students; we reinforced our mutual desire to do well. We were in one class together where the teacher started off by saying, "I don't give A's. The man who wrote the book is the only one who'd get an A here. I teach it, so I get a B. The best you can do in this class is a C." Hearing that we said to ourselves, "That's ridiculous, let's the three of us get A's." And we did.

One teacher who made a great impression on me was Miss Chestnutt, who taught Latin. Her father was Charles Chestnutt, an eminent essayist, fiction writer, and activist. Miss Chestnutt not only taught Latin—she had written the textbook we used. Not many students took four years of Latin, which brought you up to reading Virgil's *Aeneid.* But Eugene, Thrasher, and I did. We were in the Latin Club. I wasn't totally in love with Latin, but I did love challenges and I mostly rose to them, even in Latin with its seven often-confusing cases. But it was tough for me. Eugene, on the other hand, just sailed through it. Of the three of us he was by far the smartest, even though Thrasher ended up valedictorian. The three of us buddied our way through Latin, as we did in other courses, which helped make high school more fun than it would have been otherwise.

Miss Chestnutt was black though very light skinned, one of only three or four African American teachers at Central, whose student body was almost a hundred percent black. Miss Thomas was another black teacher. We liked her, even though she was especially strict, all business all the time. One day I got a message that Miss Thomas wanted to see me after classes. I had no idea what it was about. I hadn't done anything to get myself in trouble, at least that I was aware of.

When I walked into her classroom at four o'clock, she said, "Louis, some of us here have been talking about where you might be headed after graduation. We're wondering what your plans are for college. We hope you're thinking about that."

"Miss Thomas," I said, "I'm not going to college. My mother has no way of sending me. She's looking forward to me getting my diploma and going to work to try to help her."

"I'm sorry to hear that," she said, but that was it. Our discussion didn't last much longer. There was no follow-up, no talk of what kind of scholarships or aid might be available or any suggestion about how I might work around our lack of tuition money. That kind of discussion would definitely take place today, but this was 1942. The United States was in the middle of a two-ocean war, and it's possible there just weren't any scholarships or aid available.

I felt good, though, that she thought I was college material and that she and other teachers had been discussing my future. That gave a little kick to my self-confidence, even if I wasn't going to college.

Given our circumstances, I shut the idea of college out of my mind and tried to think about what I actually would do. What was I going to make of my life after I got my diploma? Maybe a haberdashery shop, I thought. I liked dressing sharp. A suit, shoes shined to a gleam, a properly creased hat. When I was a kid I had only had one pair of hand-me-down pants that I could wear to school. When I got home I'd take them off and put them under the mattress so they'd be pressed for the next day. But I had been working steadily ever since my paperboy jobs and had managed to buy myself a couple of items of clothing so I could make a good appearance. I was interested in clothes; a haberdashery shop might be just the right thing.

That thought grew on me because by my senior year I actually was working in a clothing store, Outdoor Sportswear at 801 Prospect, in the heart of downtown Cleveland.

Charles "Satch" Page had gotten me that job. Satch, one of my best buddies, had a knack for finding jobs for himself, and as he moved up to something more appealing he'd let me or one of his other friends know about the one he was leaving. Charles had gotten me my first shoeshine job a couple of years earlier, at a shoe store that gave away a coupon for ten shoeshines with every pair of shoes purchased. I was the one who did the shining, every afternoon until the store closed at six.

I had arranged my class schedule so I could get out of school early, get down to the shoe store, and work until closing time. The arrangement was that customers who had bought shoes were given a coupon card, which I punched each time they came for a shine. The store didn't pay me, but whatever tips I earned were mine to keep. The problem was that this store was in one of Cleveland's ethnic enclaves, a poor neighborhood originally settled by Polish immigrants. The combination of a poor neighborhood, cheap shoes, and free shines was almost guaranteed not to produce much in the way of tips. The customers got their shines and I popped the rag as loud as it would pop, but the tips were meager and far between.

So I quit that and got another shoeshine job, this one at a newspaper and confection store on the corner of East Twenty-First and Prospect. The tips were better there, and after a month or so another opportunity opened up. One of my regular customers was a Mr. Greaves, a heavy tipper. I really made the rag sing for Mr. Greaves, and after one shine he motioned for me to step outside to talk. "How much money do you make here?" he asked. When I told him, he said, "Listen, how would you like to come and work for me?"

Mr. Greaves owned a company called Instant Whip that made pressurized cans of whipped cream. I would operate a machine there that injected gas into the cans. The job sounded okay, a lot better than shining shoes on other people's feet all day, and the pay was better. So I took it.

Mr. Greaves had three employees operating the machines, two white boys and myself. I was happy enough, but one day while Mr. Greaves was out to lunch my two coworkers approached me about going out on strike with them for a higher wage. Something like that never would have occurred to me, but the prospect of a higher wage sounded good, and I agreed. When Mr. Greaves came back from lunch he found us sitting by our machines not working. "What's going on here?" he asked. "We're striking," one of the white boys said. "We need more money."

Mr. Greaves's normally pale face blazed red. "You ingrates!" he yelled at the white boys. "And you"—he turned to me. "I pulled you out of a shoeshine parlor where you were making next to nothing! I gave you a decent job, and now you're doing this to me? Get the hell out of here, all of you! You're fired!"

That was my first lesson in labor relations, maybe the best one I ever got.

My next job was as what they called a "pot and pan man" at the old Colonnade restaurant on Euclid Avenue, one of Cleveland's most popular eating places. I soon found out that a pot and pan man had status. A pot and pan man was a step above the ordinary dishwashers. Exactly why I couldn't have told you. Scrubbing grease off of pots and pans in a crowded noisy kitchen didn't have a lot of romance in it. Which is why I was happy when after a month or so Satch Page called me again. Would I be interested, he asked, in a porter's job at a store downtown?

The name of the store was Outdoor Sportswear. When I walked through the door a large, heavy-set man asked if he could help me.

"Yes," I said, "My name is Louis Stokes. I've come for the porter's job."

"Good," he said. "Sit down with me for a minute and I'll tell you what your duties are. But before we do that why don't you tell me a little about your school, and your family."

There was something I liked about this person immediately. He had a quiet, fatherly way about him. He actually seemed interested in me.

His name, he said, was Isadore Apisdorf. I could call him Izzy. I would be working for him. He was the store manager, but this store and two other army-navy surplus stores on the block were owned by a Mr. Kaplan. My job would be to sweep the floors, help him put up stock, make deliveries, and wash down the sidewalk in front with soap and water and a broom. I would be expected to learn the inventory, how the shelves were organized, where things were in the back—everything I needed to know so that if he or the clerks needed something I'd know how to get it for them.

After I had been working for a week or so he sat me down with him again. "Louis," he said—*Louis*, with an emphasis on Louis. He could say "Louis" more emphatically than anybody I have ever heard say it.

"*Louis*, I have an idea. While you're doing your duties as a porter I'd like to teach you how to be a salesman. There's no reason a black person shouldn't be able to operate as a sales clerk in a store like this. They ought to be able to sell to white people the same way white people sell to black people. So when you're not doing your stock work I'm going to teach you how to sell."

In 1942 this was revolutionary. In 1942 there were no black salespersons in downtown Cleveland. In terms of Cleveland's customs, what Isadore Apisdorf was talking about was groundbreaking. There were no laws; it was just clear that you were not welcome to do certain things or go certain places. At that time blacks couldn't even go to restaurants downtown. It was a major event when the first restaurant opened that welcomed blacks as well as whites.

"Now *Louis*," Isadore Apisdorf said, "if this doesn't work out, I don't want you to hold it against me. But I believe it can work."

I wasn't quite sure what he meant by "if it doesn't work out." Did he mean that I might not be up to learning the job? Or that customers might make trouble and not accept being served by a black person? Whichever, it sounded like a great opportunity. Being a salesperson would be a step up, a decent job with a little prestige attached. As a trained salesperson I'd have a regular job waiting for me when I graduated.

So Isadore—Izzy—trained me. He taught me cloth. He taught me about the different fabrics and qualities. He taught me how to measure a man's pants, how to measure the inseam. He showed me how when you're putting clothes on the person you have to make sure they fit properly. You have to be able to measure the shoulders on the shirt, the sleeve length, the neck.

I watched his demeanor when he was talking with customers. He'd ask if he could help. He'd listen, then he'd say, "I know exactly what you want. Let me get it for you. I'll just be a moment." Then he'd come back with the item. "How is this? Is this what you're thinking of? Now let me tell you about the quality of this shirt. This is a gabardine shirt. Here's the difference between this and a standard cotton shirt."

I listened to all of this, and I learned how to be a salesperson. Eventually he hired a white kid for me to train as a porter and he put me on the floor, selling.

At Outdoor Sportswear we carried a lot of military clothing and gear—pants, shirts, equipment, like the army-navy stores Mr. Kaplan owned. But we had regular clothing also, as well as camping and fishing items. Our customers were a mix of military and civilian. If somebody wanted something we didn't have, we could often say, "Oh, we can get that for you." Then I'd dash across the street to one of Mr. Kaplan's army-navy stores and get it.

In an alley just off Prospect Avenue was a place called Max's tailor shop. If a customer needed to have his pants taken in or let out, shortened or lengthened—I was the person who ran down to Max's shop, took the items, and told Max what we needed. Then I'd go back to pick the clothes up when they were ready.

Things worked out well for me as a sales clerk, with only one incident during the time I worked there. A white man came into the store and started looking around. I left him alone for a bit, as Izzy had taught me, then I approached him and said, "May I help you, sir?"

He looked at me, not pleasantly, and said, "No—*you* can't help me." I just stepped back.

Izzy saw it. He walked over to me. "Louis. What did that man say to you?"

"I asked if I could help him. He said, 'No, *you* can't help me."

Izzy was probably in his fifties. Heavy set, something of a stomach. Five foot ten or eleven, over two hundred pounds. He walked with a bit of a rolling gait, side to side. He'd stand there sometimes with his arms a little out from his sides, as if they were a bit too big to hang properly from his shoulders. He was a very strong guy, and he gave that appearance.

Izzy walked over to the customer and took him by the shoulder. "If Louis can't wait on you," he said, "we don't want your business."

Then he took him by his collar and pants, walked him to the door, and put him out.

After that I knew that Izzy was behind me all the way.

He had a sense of humor, too. He'd say to me, "Louis, you know what a *mensch* is?" "Louis, you know what *oy vey* means?" "Louis, you know what a *gannif* is?"

"No, Izzy, I don't. What does it mean?"

He'd laugh and tell me. He'd explain it.

"It's Yiddish, Louis. A *mensch* is a human being, a good human being. Now repeat it." And I'd repeat it. Izzy had fun doing that. He took pride that I was developing at least some minor Yiddish vocabulary.

Izzy meant more and more to me the longer I worked there. He took time with me. He took an interest in me and my life. He counseled me. If I had a decision to make, I'd ask him. "Izzy, I'm not sure what to do in this situation." He'd hear me out and give me his advice. I had no one else to do that, other than my mom. No older man. That was just a vacant area in my life. I never had a father or anyone who tried to fill that role for me. Izzy Apisdorf was the first man I could sit down with and talk with like that.

I worked for Izzy full time from January 1943, when I graduated high school, until I was drafted into the army in August of that year. I knew it was coming. All around me my friends were either volunteering or being drafted. Almost every day someone else was leaving.

I didn't relish the idea of being drafted. I didn't know where they were going to send me, where I might be involved in danger, but immense violence was going on all over the world, and I knew there was a real possibility that I would never come home. I was also painfully aware that black soldiers were being subjected to all kinds of indignities. They were segregated in the army, the same as blacks were segregated in the South. So I would be going from the nonsegregated North into a segregated army. That wasn't a pleasant prospect. I knew that black soldiers weren't being allowed into combat units. I was going to be subjected to those indignities and wouldn't even be permitted to fight. That was offensive, galling. I mulled that over a lot.

When I told Izzy I had gotten my notice, he said, "Louis, remember, when you come out, you've got a job right here."

The day I was inducted, he went with me down to the Terminal Tower train station. He saw me off that morning. Nobody was there but him. My mother was working. I'm not sure where Carl was. But Izzy was with me.

CHAPTER 2

Becoming a Lawyer

THE TRAIN took us to Columbus, Ohio, where we were processed and issued uniforms and gear. From there we were off to Jefferson Barracks outside of Saint Louis for basic training. We didn't know much about what training would be like, but we did know that Jefferson was supposed to be one of the toughest boot camps in the country.

On the train we were separated, blacks from whites. At Jefferson Barracks we lived separately from the whites, we ate separately, we trained separately. But the training itself was exactly the same, the marching, the shooting, the combat skills. In August the weather in Saint Louis was excruciatingly hot. The instructors would get us out of bed at 4 a.m. to march us and run us. They taught us how to fire M-1s and carbines. They instructed us on grenades and how to throw them. We had bayonet drills, we learned how to stay balanced, use footwork, block, parry, and thrust. We learned how to patrol, we mastered the basics of hand-to-hand combat. "You've got two purposes" the drill instructors yelled. "Kill the enemy and don't get killed yourself." "Don't give him a chance; he's not going to give you one. Go after him with no holds barred."

By the time our eight weeks of basic were up we might not have been killing machines, but we were prepared. We were ready to fight. Except that we weren't going to. The white recruits were going off into combat units. But we were detailed into support units—construction, field medicine, supply, and others—to service the white soldiers instead of fighting alongside them.

I got my first taste of the humiliation involved on our way from Jefferson Barracks to our first posting, Camp Stuart, Georgia. On the way there the train stopped in Memphis, Tennessee, where they got us out of the cars to eat at the train station. We were led past a big dining room filled with white soldiers eating lunch, then into a second room crowded with German prisoners of war still wearing their German uniforms. Passing through the tables we listened to the babble of German and drew stares from the POWs. On one side of the room was a black curtain. We were taken through that curtain into another room where we were seated for lunch.

I was thinking, German prisoners—white German prisoners, Nazis, the people we had just been trained to kill. White soldiers, then white POWs, then us. Separated from all the whites, German and American both. How could it be that these people were being treated better than we were, wearing the uniform of our country? I didn't think I was naïve, but that drove home what it meant to be black in the U.S. Army. I had already experienced the separation of black and white units during our basic training. But although we were separated, we were experiencing the same things in the same ways. We were trained the same. That was separate, but at least in terms of training it was equal. Now looking at the whites, the Germans, and ourselves, it sank in that there was no kind of equality in this place.

I began thinking about what this meant to me, and it was not a good feeling. I was a young black kid coming out of Cleveland, and I had never really felt segregated. We didn't hang with whites in Cleveland. There were places you knew were not hospitable to blacks—restaurants, hotels, neighborhoods. But inequality had just never made much of an impression on me, until now. I deeply resented being treated like this. These people thought I was inferior because of my skin color. It was hard to take that in. Black kids from the South had experienced this from the day they were born. The perception of their inferiority was a condition of life where they came from. This was my introduction to it.

Before I left, my mother had given me a little lecture. She knew the South. "Bill, they're probably going to send you down there. Don't forget, it's not the same as Cleveland. You can't just go anywhere you want. Places are off limits to black people. They're dangerous. Stay out of trouble. Don't go in those places. You should really just stay in your camp."

She was worried about me. I didn't know the mores there; I was innocent, naïve. It would be so easy to get in trouble. Emmett Till's murder wouldn't take place for another twelve years, but that demonstrated what could happen to a northern black kid unaccustomed to conditions in the South. "Bill, you stay in that camp. When you get leave, get yourself to the train or airport and come straight home." She knew what the South was like. She had gotten out of there because of it.

At Camp Stuart every morning trucks picked us up and took us down to the white area of the camp. There we were handed sticks with nails embedded in the end and told to police around the barracks of the white soldiers. They were out training, and we were relegated to this kind of demeaning duty. Policing up the white barracks. Trained for combat and picking up litter.

A group of us decided we were just not going to do it. We were better than that, more intelligent than that. We had been toughened up at Jefferson Barracks. We were ready for combat. As far as we were concerned, it was the white soldiers' job to police their own barracks. We policed ours. Let them police theirs.

We talked it over and decided we weren't going to clean up after white soldiers. No one was supervising us. We were just dropped off to pick up the refuse. The trucks would be back to get us at noon. Camp Stuart had a library that just happened to be across from the white barracks. We put the sticks up under the barracks and went off to read in the library. At quarter to twelve we came out, got the sticks, and milled around until the trucks came.

We did that every day for a week or so. They didn't really seem to care about us. We weren't being monitored. As far as we could tell no one checked up afterward. But eventually somebody complained that the barracks weren't being policed properly. The litter was piling up. So one day we were all in the library as usual when jeeps full of MPs suddenly screeched up outside.

We scattered. I went out one of the windows and ran. But I was caught. We were all caught. I'm not sure where we thought we could escape to; we were on an army post. The MPs took us to the Camp Stuart jail and locked us up. Even that place was segregated. Toilets for white prisoners, toilets for black prisoners. Water for whites, water for blacks.

They kept us there for two or three hours then took us back to our own barracks. "You people are being punished," the sergeant barked at us. "You will march back and forth in front of your barracks each day for the next week with 50 pounds of rocks in your backpacks. You will be an example for others who might want to be insubordinate."

We did that for a day. We loaded our backpacks with rocks and marched in the hot Georgian sun like that, back and forth, back and forth, back and forth, all of us getting hotter, sweatier, and more resentful by the minute.

We hadn't obeyed orders to clean up around the white barracks, but this was more punishment than it should have been. Those white soldiers should have been policing their own barracks anyway. So we agreed among ourselves that we were not going to do it. We would appeal to Major Gentry.

The group chose me as our spokesperson. "Major Gentry," I said. "We trained at Jefferson Barracks. We trained hard, and you know what kind of a place Jefferson is. We're here to serve our country and do what's right. But it's not right to take us to do these kinds of nonmilitary, demeaning duties for people who should be doing them for themselves. We felt we were right to do what we did. We know we disobeyed orders. We're willing to take some punishment for that. But this is too much. It's way out of line with what we did."

This could have gone very badly. We were in the army. We were in the South. Major Gentry was white. But we lucked out. The major wasn't entirely a hard case. He listened. He thought about it. And he allowed us to take off our backpacks. We still had to march, but at least without the rocks on our backs.

I was eighteen years old and I had never been subjected to segregation and discrimination in my life. I didn't like it, and I was determined not to give in to it—to the extent that was possible. I had no intention of just peacefully going through this. And I was with some other guys who felt exactly the same as I did. I ran with another kid from Cleveland—he had been a track star at East Tech, the school that Jesse Owens came out of. He and a kid from Chicago and I found ourselves together, more or less leading these insubordinations. All three of us didn't mind fighting or doing whatever we had to do to show that we were not people who could be taken advantage of. We stuck together. We reinforced each other. We had an attitude.

One day a black sergeant from Chicago—Sergeant Meadows—took the three of us aside.

"I don't think you boys understand that you're in the South now."

"Well, what does that mean?"

"What it means is that you can't do in the South what you've done in the North. You've got to adjust to the way things are here. I'm telling you this for your own good. Smarten up."

We listened to him, but we didn't accept it.

My experiences at Camp Stuart were repeated at other postings. Waco Army Airfield was a pilot training center. Every morning at five we were driven out to the airfield to gas the planes that white pilots would be flying. We didn't have a chance to fly; only they did. My job as a U.S. soldier was to gas planes for white boys. It was outrageous. It ate at you. One night a group of us got so angry about the way we were being treated that we just tore up our barrack, destroyed the furniture, broke the windows—we tore that place up. The next morning early they shipped us out.

They got us out of Waco as fast as they could. They didn't want any more of our type of revolt. We were aware that incidents like this were happening all over the country, and in Europe too. We were also aware that there was a political leader in New York named Adam Clayton Powell who was fighting for the right of African Americans to join in combat, to be officers, to be treated as United States soldiers, not as black soldiers. The *Pittsburgh Courier,* the *Chicago Defender,* and the *Cleveland Call and Post* editorialized in support of Powell's efforts and carried articles about these things. Someone would come back from leave with newspapers, someone else's mother would send some with a care package. We read them. We were aware.

We knew that Powell was putting up a big fight. We knew too that a black fighter squadron had been formed, in Tuskegee, as a test we understood. Late in the war we heard about several other black combat units. That wasn't going to be happening for us, though. We loved this country as much as anybody. We felt it was our country, too, despite the awful way we were being treated.

The anger back then was widespread. The white officers, many lieutenants especially, were brash and arrogant and abusive. When you did see a black officer he generally was a chaplain, and he wasn't being treated as a regular officer, either. They had commissioned and noncommissioned officers' clubs on these bases, but blacks who were officers of any sort couldn't go in. They were segregated, too.

Camp Shelby in Hattiesburg, Mississippi, was vast; to get from our area to the commissary in the center you had to take a shuttle bus. And even on this U.S. post, black soldiers had to ride in the back of the bus. Riding in the back of that bus behind white soldiers and civilian employees I was constantly asking myself: How can this be? How can the United States do this to its own servicemen? When black soldiers are just as willing to give their lives fighting as white soldiers are? How can they treat people in this way? What in God's name was going on in the minds of white people to take prejudice and segregation to this end?

Camp Shelby was directly adjacent to Hattiesburg, but I never went into town while I was there. I remembered my mother's warnings, and if Mississippi wasn't the worst place in the South, it had to be close to it. But one night we heard that some of the guys in our unit had taken the bus to town.

In the bus was a sign: "Colored to the Rear," and one of our guys had bent the sign. Maybe he wanted to tear it off, I don't know. What we heard was that he bent it. The bus driver took issue with that and ended up shooting him. That caused a tidal wave of anger. I couldn't think of anything else. How could this be done to us? American soldiers! This kind of indignity! This kind of hatred! They moved us out of there the next day, too.

My brother Carl was also in the army; he went in a year after I did. In his autobiography he wrote, "What I learned in the army was a white hot rage against white people." My reaction wasn't the same. I didn't hate whites, but I felt a deep indignation at the demeaning and derogatory treatment.

One thing that helped me psychologically was that even though I just had a high school education, there were a number of fellow soldiers in my various units who had bachelor's and master's degrees. One had just finished law school and there was another with a PhD. A number of guys had been teachers before they were drafted. I tried to associate with them as much as I could. I loved being included in their conversations. I learned so much. I had put college out of my mind long before, but I began to feel that I wanted an education, like they had.

Alvin Coleman was the PhD. I spent a lot of time with him. He explained to me about getting his master's and doctorate. For his thesis he had done some sort of scientific experiment that had been published. He had gotten calls all the way from Germany about the work he had done. He talked about education to me. He inspired me.

Many of the southern soldiers educated me about black achievement. They had much more exposure to African American history than I had. Coming out of Cleveland, in all my high school courses I had never been taught any black history at all. But that had been part of the curriculum in their segregated schools in the South. I felt embarrassed that I didn't know these things, that I didn't know my own history.

They knew about events and people in black history that I had either never heard of or had only the faintest familiarity with. They knew about the W. E. B. Du Bois, Booker T. Washington debates—Washington's philosophy that blacks should go into the trades as opposed to the arts and sciences, Du Bois's insistence that all the arts and sciences, all the professions, should be available to blacks, that the "talented tenth" could lead blacks to equality in America. They knew about Crispus Attucks and Harriet Tubman, about the black regiments that fought for the Union during the Civil War. They knew about George Washington Carver and Mary McLeod Bethune and Paul Lawrence Dunbar. The importance of these figures had been instilled in them. I had hardly heard of any of them.

All this was a learning experience for me—actually a revelation. I was embarrassed by my ignorance. But at the same time I found to my delight that I could discuss subjects with these college graduates on something like an equal basis. I could sit with them and discuss and argue; I could keep up with them. I began to think that if I was able to enter into these intellectual discussions as a high school student, how much better it would be if I had a college education.

These thoughts grew on me and came to a kind of climax when I was assigned to Fort Ord in Salinas, California. At Fort Ord we were occasionally given three-day passes to go into town. For those three days we were free to do whatever we wanted. A three-day pass gave you an opportunity to work and make some money or do whatever. I played a fairly good game of pool, not like Carl who had developed into a shark, but well enough to make some money at the local pool halls.

But pool, or my pool anyway, wasn't all that lucrative. You could make much better money hiring yourself out to work for the three days. With the war going on workers were in short supply, and the Salinas factories were soaking up whatever labor they could get. A few of us went to work at a food processing plant helping unload gondola cars filled with sweet potatoes. With the bottom hatches open, the potatoes should have just tumbled out themselves, but often they would get jumbled up and clog the openings. Standing on the load of potatoes you could hold yourself up by clasping the sides of the car and kick the sweet potatoes out through the bottom doors. It was good to have the extra money, but I'd be kicking those potatoes eight hours a day and thinking the whole time that this was absolutely no way to make a living.

Then one day they took me off the gondola cars, gave me a broom, and put me in the basement of one of the plants as a cleaner. A few minutes after I started sweeping I looked up and saw just across from me an elderly white man doing the same thing I was. Pushing a broom. And I thought—this is a white man, a white man without an education, and this is what he's reduced to doing, cleaning out a basement with a broom. I said to myself, Man, whenever I get out of here I have got to find me a way to get an education. I just cannot live the rest of my life like this.

A three-day pass also gave me a chance to get to San Francisco to hear Howard Thurman preach. I had learned about him from a couple of guys in our unit. They said that Thurman was a preacher's preacher, famous for his intelligence and depth, as far as you could get from a fire-and-brimstone type. He had apparently met with various world leaders, including Mahatma Gandhi. He had been a professor and dean at Howard University, but they heard he was now in San Francisco, where he had helped found something called the Church of the Fellowship of All Peoples, a racially integrated, interfaith church. I had never heard of such a thing before. The churches in Cleveland were either black or white, and the southern white churches wouldn't even let a black person in the door. I wanted to see how this worked, but I was even more eager to hear Thurman speak.

Just walking into that church was a revelation. Thurman was in the pulpit, presiding over a mixed but predominantly white congregation. I sat down thinking, this is what America should be, all these different people sitting with each other, worshipping together. Thurman was a presence with his long face, high forehead, and deep-set eyes. His voice was low, his speech slow, but the congregation was hushed, hanging on every word. There was something mesmerizing about his voice and his demeanor, the way he pronounced each word so distinctly. He seemed almost like a mystic, speaking to God and the congregation at the same time. I had never seen anyone like him. "No race or tribe has standing here," he said. "All swept away by the ceaseless streaming of infinite light." Exactly the opposite of what I had been experiencing ever since I was drafted.

In the first week of August 1945 we were shipped to Seattle, Washington, where they issued us light clothing and gear. We were sure that meant we were going someplace hot, someplace in the Pacific. Germany had surrendered several months earlier, but Japan was still fighting, so we speculated that maybe we were going to be part of the force that would invade Japan. "It looks like we're going overseas," I wrote my mom. "To some warm climate."

We were in Seattle for about a week when word came about a giant bomb that was dropped on Hiroshima, then another one on Nagasaki. Not long after we heard the Japanese had surrendered. There wasn't going to be an invasion. We had been speculating about going to Japan; we knew it was going to be awful. But suddenly the war was over. We weren't going to Japan—we were going back home where we could hug our mothers and resume our normal lives, where we could start thinking about our futures.

After V-J Day we knew we were going home. I couldn't wait. I had heard about the GI Bill of Rights, and by then I knew that I absolutely needed to go to college. I had the image in my head of that elderly white man pushing a broom down in the factory basement. I knew I had to better my condition. The only way to do that was to get an education, and what better opportunity for a poor boy who didn't have the money than to take advantage of the GI Bill of Rights?

Demobilization began almost immediately. We were going to be sent home in order of how much time we had served. I had been in for thirty-one months, so my own demobilization came pretty quickly. I was sent to Indianapolis and honorably discharged from there at Camp Atterbury. By the beginning of September I was back in Cleveland.

Seeing Mom again was joyous. We had missed each other terribly. Our happiness wasn't complete, though, since Carl was still in and we longed to have him back home with us. Mom had a surprise for me, a thousand dollars she had saved from the allotment I had sent her out of my pay each month. She was still doing domestic work, making the same meager wage, but she wanted me to have something to start off with when I came back (she had done the same thing for Carl). I could only shake my head in wonder at this extraordinary woman whose sole desire in life was to see that her children had the chance to get ahead and do well.

The first friend I hooked up with was Jim Thrasher, my high school buddy who had been our valedictorian. He had just been demobilized himself. As smart as he was, I assumed he'd be planning on college, too. Maybe we could even go together. When I told him we could use the GI Bill of Rights for tuition, he said, "Bill, I'm not going to college. I've gotten a job at an electric company."

That was a bit of a shock. "Why not?" I asked. "You were our valedictorian."

"Well, I know myself," he said. "I know I'm not about to work the way I did in high school. I'm just not going to do it."

The fact was that none of my group of immediate friends wanted to go to college. They admired me for planning to go, but their general thought was—no, we're just not going to worry about it.

But I had been influenced by those guys I had hung out with in the army who had degrees. They had really inspired me, and all of our discussions had given me confidence that I could handle it, that if they could do it there was no reason I couldn't.

If I was going to go to college, I thought I should go to the top college, which in Cleveland meant Western Reserve University (which later became

Case Western Reserve). So I took myself down to their admissions department and filled out an application. But when I told my mother, to my surprise she wasn't too happy about it. "Bill," she said, "you can't go to school. I
need you to get a job and help me."

That pulled me up, but I agreed with her. She was right. She was entitled
to have all the help I could give her. My role all through high school was to
help, to work while I was getting that high school diploma she wanted so
badly for me. Also, Carl had actually dropped out of high school, which had
just broken her heart. She had written to me about it while I was in the army.
So that added to my sense of obligation. I didn't fight it.

I knew that Western Reserve had something called Cleveland College,
where people went to school part-time at night. So I thought—that's what
I'll do. I'll work days and go to school at night.

When I was still in high school I had taken a typing course and had
become a pretty fast typist. In the army I had eventually brought my typing
ability to the attention of my unit's officers, who had put me to work at clerical and then administrative jobs. I liked the work, and it enabled me to show
that I was capable. So clerical work had become my military specialty.

Since I could type, I looked at the government clerical jobs that were
available in Cleveland. There was an opening at the Treasury Department
that I qualified for, so I took that. Since I was going to start going to school
at night I wanted something light, something I could do without too much
thought. The Treasury job—typing checks all day—could bore you to death,
but it fit the bill. I worked for Treasury for a while, then went over to the
Veterans Administration as a file clerk.

I attended Cleveland College at night for a little over two years, and during that period I met a fellow college student, Mildred Sharpley. After a brief
courtship we married. A year and a half later our first child was born.

Becoming a father churned up emotions that had always been just under
the surface for me. I had never had a father. I had no memory whatsoever
of my father—only little bits and pieces of information our relatives would
drop on occasion. When other boys talked about their fathers taking them
fishing or to ball games, I listened avidly, enviously, thinking what that would
be like. As I grew older, deep in my recesses I yearned for the day when I
might have children myself, particularly a little boy I could take to football
and baseball games and do all the other things my friends had done with
their dads. It wasn't that I had anything against girls, but the idea of going
to the games with my own little buddy had taken root in my head.

Our first child, though, was a girl, the prettiest little girl I had ever seen in my life. I looked at her and felt an instant bond. At that moment I thought, okay, a boy can wait. I was sure this beautiful new being was special, and I thought she thought I was special, too. We named her Shelley Denise.

Our second, born three years later in 1953, was also a girl, a tiny, delicate baby, so angel-like in both her body and her demeanor that we named her Angela. Our third, born in 1954, was, finally, a boy, whom we named Louis Charles, Louis after me, Charles after my father. Not Louis Junior (I had no middle name myself) but Charles, which gave us the nickname Chuck, or Chuckie, as we called him. I had always had a nickname, and now he did, too.

While I was studying at Cleveland College I joined Kappa Alpha Psi, a national fraternity that emphasized achievement, which spoke to me since that was what I aspired to. A fellow worker at the VA, Herman Frank, was a member and talked often about the fraternity and how I should definitely join. Carl also was a member and made the same suggestion. Not many years before this I had never even thought about the possibility of going to college, let alone joining a fraternity. But more than a few of the Kappa brothers had gone on to do great things. I admired them. And after Herman introduced me to Girardeau Spann, a Kappa who was to become a distinguished law professor at Georgetown and a leading affirmative action advocate, I was convinced that this was something I needed to do. So I did join, and I became as active in the fraternity as my time allowed for, which put me in touch with people whose own academic striving stimulated me even further and gave me friendships that were to last for many years.

In my second year at Cleveland College I learned about a special program at Cleveland Marshall College of Law. If you had two years or more of undergraduate credit and had kept a B or above average, Cleveland Marshall would allow you to apply. A bachelor's degree wasn't necessary.

This was ideal. I had the credits; I had the average. I didn't need to wait another two years before I could apply to law school. By this time I was twenty-three years old. Time seemed of the essence. I applied, and they accepted me.

Cleveland Marshall was exactly the right place. Three years earlier two proprietary law schools had merged, the Cleveland Law School and the John Marshall School of Law. Both had been night schools, and the new entity, Cleveland Marshall, was as well, which meant I could continue working days and studying at night. Cleveland Law School had been the first in the state to accept women, and Cleveland Marshall was the second to accept black students.

The school was housed in an abandoned factory building at 1240 Ontario Street. The place looked derelict, dilapidated, and forlorn, with broken windows and other signs of decay. But every evening the building came alive. The second floor had been divided into classrooms and administrative space. There, at six in the evening, the students and professors showed up and turned the place into a beehive of teaching and learning, the whole presided over by Dean Wilson V. Stapleton, a man who took education seriously.

Dean Wilson V. Stapleton was all about scholarship. He himself was Phi Beta Kappa. He was a big man, always in a three-piece suit, with his Phi Beta Kappa key dangling from his vest.

If you went to see him about something the conversation would wait until he had apprised himself of who you were and what kind of student he had in front of him.

"Dean Stapleton, I'm Louis Stokes."

"Just a minute."

He'd buzz his secretary. "Bring me the Stokes record." He'd get the file, and you'd sit there until he had satisfied himself about your status and grades. "All right," he'd say then. "Now let's talk."

Most of Dean Stapleton's students were as committed as he was. They were from poor or working-class families, bound and determined to get law degrees and make careers for themselves. A number of my fellow students were African American with backgrounds similar to mine. They had been in the service; either their college educations had been disrupted and they had gone back to school after the war, or they had taken advantage of the two-year admissions policy, as I had. Like me, they had lost three or four years of their lives and were eager to make up for it.

Inside this derelict space a determined student could get an unusually good law education. Many of our teachers were sitting judges or practicing lawyers, among them some of the most prominent names in the Cleveland area. Some had written the books we were studying. They would share with us what was happening in court, cases they were currently arguing or hearing from the bench, many of which were in the news. They described what was going on, what their objectives were, how they were approaching the various problems. Law studies at Cleveland Marshall were text-based and theoretical, but they were also vividly alive.

How exciting to have the man who wrote the book on pleadings teaching us about pleading. Giving us illustrations from the great decisive cases, but also the hows and whys from his own experience and from cases we were reading about in the daily newspapers.

We had a great trial lawyer there—Professor Marstellar, who taught evidence. A little short fellow, dumpy, but he bounced around excitedly at the front of the class and he talked as if he had a train to catch.

Professor Marstellar would have us recite cases and discuss them. He had called on me one time and as I made my way through the case, attempting to explain its salient features, he said, "Stokes, you'll-never-make-an-argument-in-the-United-States-Supreme-Court. They-only-give-you-thirty-minutes. You'll-never-make-it." In that machine-gun staccato of his. Twenty plus years later when I was arguing the *Terry* case in front of the Supreme Court, I caught myself thinking, "See that, Professor Marstellar. You were wrong. I *am* doing it."

Dean Stapleton took pride in his students, and he took pride in his school. Cleveland Marshall, the scrappy local night school, felt itself in direct competition with the Western Reserve School of Law, a nationally prestigious private law school. That competition is still in the air today. In recent years Cleveland Marshall students have passed the bar in larger numbers than their counterparts from Case Western Reserve. The school doesn't boast, but they're proud of it.

For four years, from 1949 to 1953, I worked during the day and went to school from six to ten every night. As tired as I might have been, I came to most of my classes full of excitement and anticipation. I couldn't wait to get to criminal law especially. I knew as a practical matter that most of my business would come as a criminal defense lawyer. One reason for that was that black lawyers were simply not accepted into white law firms with their wide-ranging practices. White firms didn't even interview; there wasn't a single black lawyer in all of Cleveland's major law firms. While I was in school black lawyers couldn't even rent office space in downtown Cleveland. That meant that black lawyers all practiced in the black neighborhoods and depended on the black community for their business.

I knew I wanted to defend people in criminal cases. That had been my aspiration when I was twelve, my fantasy at a time when I never dreamed that some day I might actually be in law school. So I couldn't wait to get into that criminal law class. I wanted to learn everything there was to learn about criminal justice.

Pleading was another subject I knew I needed to master. If I was going to be a trial lawyer I had to know how to plead and how to file pleadings. Evidence was going to be important. What I needed to know about autopsies, gunshot wounds, gunpowder residues, and forensics generally—how you utilize that evidence in court, how you keep evidence out of a case, how you get it into a case, how to try a case in front of a jury, how and when to use outside resources, technical experts, psychologists, and others.

I wasn't particularly interested in courses that dealt with commercial paper, real estate law, or corporate law. But I loved constitutional law. I couldn't get enough of it. I thought maybe that would be my specialty. I knew I was going to be active in civil rights, and the debilities blacks were suffering under largely involved constitutional issues. If I was going to do that, I had to know the Constitution and all the case law derived from it. I fell in love with the Constitution. I loved all the areas of the law that I knew were going to be important to me.

In terms of civil law, one of our professors, Ellis Rippner, was considered the top probate person in the state. He knew probate law backwards and forwards; he had written the book on it. I studied with him: I was sure that at some point I'd be dealing with wills and other death issues. And once I graduated I did run into those situations from time to time. On one convoluted estate case I got involved in, the judge called Rippner in to consult on it. The will had been in probate for years and the lawyers working on it were keeping the case open and milking the estate for all it was worth. As a young, idealistic lawyer, and not knowing any better, I filed suit in probate court to close the case out. When the judge found out what had been going on all these years, he was irate. To help dispose of the matter he called in Ellis Rippner, and I got to work with him, my former professor who had helped train me. That was a proud moment.

As my studies progressed at Cleveland Marshall I was aware that I was experiencing a kind of mental or intellectual metamorphosis. The fact is that there's nothing quite like the law. You can talk about medicine, teaching, any profession. But to me there's nothing like the law, and as a student I was already beginning to understand that. I wanted to learn everything I could in order to know how to represent clients, how to go into a courtroom and argue, how to be a complete lawyer.

Not only did I want to be a lawyer, I wanted to be the best lawyer anybody could have. I still had those same thoughts I had as a twelve-year-old boy: I wanted to be able to go anywhere in the country and represent people in front of any jury. But to do that I had to be the best, I had to have the background.

As a result I not only accepted the intellectual challenges, I welcomed them. I tried to learn as much as I could from all the top lawyers. If I had a day off from work—by now I had moved from the VA to the Ohio State Highway Department—I would go down to court and watch Norman Minor, the great trial lawyer who was fast becoming my idol. I watched how he tried cases, how he approached juries; I tried to embed in my own mind what he did and how he did it. I told myself, This is how I'll handle cases when I become a lawyer.

I understood that I wasn't simply absorbing knowledge, learning cases and principles—my mind was being trained to a way of thinking. I was absorbing a certain kind of logical, philosophical approach to processing and presenting information. I was seeing how you apply law to facts, how you sort out the more persuasive from the less persuasive points in order to outthink your opponent and achieve your ends. I wasn't adept yet, I was only a student, but I was already feeling the satisfaction of being able to think like this. I knew I was becoming a different person from who I was previously.

I graduated from Cleveland Marshall in June 1953 and passed the bar exam a little while later. There were not that many black lawyers all told, and those of us coming out with me were something of a new wave. We were going to break ground; I felt that and I know my peers did also. We saw that the challenge was not just to become lawyers, but to become lawyers with a high standard of excellence. In a way this was a daunting prospect. We were not going to be joining the white firms with the kind of training they afforded young lawyers and the level of expertise demanded by highly sophisticated clients coming to them with a wide variety of complicated cases. We were entering a profession where we were regarded as inferior not just by white lawyers but even by many in the black community. You would hear black people make comments like, "I don't want a black lawyer representing me. Those white lawyers have lunch with the judges."

Within this constricted horizon, pretty much the only way for a newly minted African American attorney to get started was by looking for an opportunity in the office of an older black attorney. Building a career from that start meant that it could take time for the new lawyer to develop anything like a decent income. My own situation was a little easier. It was my good luck to have a close friend named Tommy Robinson, a real estate salesman who worked for John Carmack, president of Carmack Realty, the biggest black real estate firm in Cleveland. Carmack had an in-house counsel who was about to leave for another position, and Tommy, who was very close to Mr. Carmack, said he'd see if he could get me the job. The upshot was that Mr. Carmack hired me—with a salary.

The understanding I had with Mr. Carmack was that whenever I wasn't engaged with company business I could do private work. That was great. It gave me a chance to start building my own practice. The other good thing was that Mr. Carmack agreed to teach me the real estate business. I didn't know much about real estate law, so this was an opportunity for me to add to my stock of legal knowledge.

John Carmack was a big player in what were then called "land contracts." Under land contracts people would purchase a home, often from the realtor, on an installment plan. They would pay a monthly fee but wouldn't receive the title until they had paid off half the land contract loan. At that point they would have enough equity to secure a regular mortgage. Land contracts weren't regulated the way ordinary mortgages were. They were an avenue to home ownership for people who might not qualify for a regular mortgage from a bank or might not be able to afford required minimal down payments.

Land contracts could include complicated provisions, and though Mr. Carmack was not a lawyer, he knew these contracts inside out and was intimately familiar with real estate and financing procedures in general. It was an education to watch him and the deals he made. He took me with him on many occasions, and eventually I became quite proficient myself in real estate law and in contracts related to real estate law.

But as convenient as it was to be a real estate lawyer, I was champing at the bit to get started as a trial lawyer in criminal and civil cases. That was where I was headed, and the quickest way to get some trial experience was to find some criminal clients. As a young black lawyer that meant going down to Twenty-First and Payne Avenue, where the same building housed the municipal court and the city jail.

CHAPTER 3

Criminal Defense

THE MUNICIPAL COURT and the city jail, and the common pleas court just down the street, were where a young black lawyer hustled business. Arraignments and misdemeanor trials took place in municipal court. Defendants in criminal cases were bound over to the grand jury or the Court of Common Pleas. These places were where the action was, and this is where I was every morning, along with every other criminal defense lawyer looking for clients.

The clerk's office was up on the second floor at Twenty-First and Payne, as was the municipal courtroom itself. I'd go up there and hang around in the hope that somebody would walk up to me and ask, "Are you a lawyer?" If that happened I would quickly say, "Yes, I am," thinking that my day's earnings might just have said hello to me.

Other young lawyers were also loitering in the hallway, talking to people—to police officers, court personnel, bail bondsmen, talking to each other; so catching cases was largely a matter of luck. A person would come up to you, or sometimes an entire family would. Maybe a husband or a father or some other relative had been arrested and charged. They're having trouble finding out anything from the police. They've been told they can't see the arrested person. They might have been informed what he was charged with, or maybe not. They're at a loss as to what to do or how to do it.

You see them walk out of the clerk's office frustrated. They know they need a lawyer, but they don't know any lawyers. They see you standing there wearing a suit. And they say, "Pardon me, are you a lawyer?"

"Yes," you say. "I am."

"Can I talk to you about my brother's case?"

That's when your heart gives a little jump for joy. You've just caught a case.

Those encounters were random, and as a recently graduated lawyer new to the system myself, that was what I got: random cases. But as I spent time around the court I got to know people who could be helpful—the bail bondsmen, for instance. Striking up a relationship with a bail bondsman was win-win. If I had a client who needed bail, I'd call my bondsman. He'd return the favor. If somebody approached him to do a bond, he'd say, "Do you have an attorney?"

"No, not yet. Do you know somebody?"

"I think I saw Mr. Stokes over there earlier. He might be available. Let's see if he can talk to you."

I went about establishing friendly relationships with probation officers and others in the clerk's office. People would go in and out of there, making bonds, asking for information, direction, advice. And often they would say, "I guess I need a lawyer. Do you know anyone I could get?" "Well," they'd hear. "Mr. Stokes is a lawyer."

Then there were guys who just hung around the courts. Familiar faces. Lots of them, some of them bondsmen, some working for bondsmen, some just low-level fixers, looking to connect anyone who needed connections with someone else who wanted connections. Over time I got to know these people, some of them right out of Damon Runyon. I remember one character, a short individual with a big cigar, who talked out of the side of his mouth like a racetrack tout. He was a former boxer, well known locally. He or one of the others might well throw you a little business now and then.

My fee would be whatever I thought I could reasonably get, the market rate. In that day and age, a DUI case might be two to three hundred dollars. Most often the client would give me a down payment. They'd pay the rest over time, some of which I might actually collect. But I always had to have at least fifty dollars down. That was considered fair. Of course the better I was at getting them off, the more they were likely to tell their friends, "You're in trouble? Mr. Lou Stokes is the person you need to see."

This was hustling, plain and simple. You started off completely on your own, then you developed a network, and you worked your network. Most of the things you were handling in the first building were municipal type cases—traffic violations, DUIs, misdemeanors of all sorts. But that's the way you did it. It put you in the system. You were in and out every day, making friends, talking, cajoling, kibitzing. And next door, if you had a felony case, that's where you represented some client who might have been charged with anything from simple assault to murder. That's where you got real trial experience, where people were facing serious charges with serious penalties, for serious crimes.

I'd spend part of my day with the real estate company and part of my day in court working to build my practice, up against everything a sole practitioner was up against. Cases of any significance were hard, especially civil cases where a major law firm was on the other side. They could bring in four or five lawyers, researchers, administrative staff, whatever they might need, which of course I couldn't. I was lucky to have the real estate company where at least I could get some secretarial help from time to time. I knew how lucky I was to have Mr. Carmack behind me.

Most all my clients were black, and most of the judges and juries were white. Occasionally a jury would include some minority person, but not that often. If you did have one, any minority, you were glad, because that person might be more receptive to the facts you were presenting, although he or she might just as easily want to go along with the majority in order to avoid making waves. But by and large you had to go into the courtroom and try the case in front of a white judge or a white jury. They are white, your defendant is black, and so are you, which put a big premium on your ability and your training.

To my great good fortune, my training included the fact that I had been assiduously watching Mr. Norman Minor ever since my law school days. Any time he was expected to make a closing argument, especially in some sensational case—which many of his were—I would make it a point to be there, drinking in not only his arguing techniques but the way he approached the jury, his gestures, the way he used his voice. Norman S. Minor was in my opinion the greatest trial lawyer Ohio has ever known. He was the first black assistant county prosecutor, an office he held for seventeen years. He tried over five thousand cases and rarely lost. In legal circles and beyond, Norman Minor was a legend.

Minor's courtroom presence was mesmerizing. He had a finely nuanced ability to modulate his voice in accord with whatever the moment might require. Loud, soft, angry, sarcastic, assertive, humorous, he played on the jury's sensibilities. He was blessed with a photographic memory. He never took a note, no matter how many weeks a trial might last. And he was brilliant. During recess periods he'd operate a little clinic. Lawyers would come over and ask, "Why did you do this?" "Why did you do that?" "Why didn't you do this or that?" And he would take time to tell them, to explain his reasons. It was a law school class, right there in the corridor. I studied him. I wanted to be like him, not just a lawyer, but a great lawyer.

In those days Ohio didn't have a public defender's office. Instead, when defendants were unable to afford legal representation, the court would assign an attorney. In major felony cases the court would assign two.

At one point after Minor had left the prosecutor's office for private practice, he and I were assigned to the same rape case. My head was spinning. For me to be assigned to a case with Norman Minor? The man whose cases I sat in on, whose tactics I memorized? I was a couple of years out of law school then, so I was no longer a complete novice. But to be arguing a case together with Minor was beyond anything I might have dreamed.

I was second chair in that case; he was first. He allowed me to participate in parts of the trial; I examined some witnesses, I cross-examined some. But the shocker came after all the evidence was in and all the examinations were over. We were ready for closing arguments, and Minor said, "All right, you are going to do the closing."

I looked at him. I was stunned. The closing! I heard myself saying, "Okay." And I stood up to make my case. At some point while I was speaking I glanced around and noticed that Minor was no longer sitting at our table. He had gone off somewhere.

When the jury left the room to deliberate Minor appeared again. He had been in the vestibule, where he could hear the arguments without my feeling that he was scrutinizing my performance. Sitting there at the table he began asking me questions. How long had I been practicing law? Where had I gone to law school? Where was my office? How long had I been defending criminal cases?

Then he said, "Listen, I'm going to be away for the summer. I need someone to work for me to get a continuance on whatever comes up. I don't want you to try the cases for me, just get a continuance. If you'd like to do that for me over the summer, I'd like to have you do it."

It was an effort to keep my feelings under control. "Mr. Minor," I said, "I will be glad to do that."

That summer Minor's office called whenever a case came up and I'd go down to the court and get a continuance. Then one morning something unexpected happened.

"Your honor, I'm here representing Mr. Norman Minor who is this defendant's attorney. On his behalf I'd like to request that the court continue this case."

"Oh no," said the judge. "This case is not going to be continued. It's been continued too many times already. It's going to be tried this morning. Are you ready for trial?"

"No, your honor, I'm not ready for trial. I'm just here to get a continuance."

"Mr. Stokes, this case is going to be tried now. Are you going to represent these people or not?"

I took a beat. "Yes, your honor. I am."

My thoughts were crowding in on me. When Minor came back how could I tell him I had left his client without representation? He would understand if I was forced to defend the client with no preparation. But he wasn't going to understand if I just left his client without representation—which meant that he himself would have left the client without representation. His client.

The judge gave me a little recess period to sit with the client and get the facts. Then we went to trial. I cannot now remember what the case was about, but I remember very well that whatever it was, I got the client acquitted. That was an important moment for me—how important I would find out before too much time passed.

By this time I had left Carmack Realty and opened an office of my own. Then in 1956 Carl graduated from Cleveland Marshall Law School. In June 1957 he passed the Ohio bar, and as soon as he did we set up a firm together, Stokes and Stokes. Our office was three small rooms on the second floor of a building at 10604 Saint Claire Avenue in the heart of one of Cleveland's black neighborhoods. I couldn't have been prouder or happier. I thought that Carl and I practicing together could build a black law firm powerful enough to compete against any firm, black or white. That was my hope, my aspiration.

Having Carl with me was something I could hardly have imagined. What made it even more satisfying was that Carl's life had not unfolded in a way that ever gave promise of his becoming a lawyer. When I was in the army my mother had written to me, "Brother's dropped out of school. He's gotten a job at Republic Steel." It had crushed her heart when he did that. All she wanted from us was that we would get our high school diplomas, and here was Carl quitting school in order to push a broom in a steel plant.

Knowing Carl, he left school because he wanted to hang out on the corner with his boys. He had turned himself into a pool shark and street hustler, and considering the life he was living, high school didn't offer much of an attraction. A job put at least a little money in his pocket while he was pursing his real interests.

As close as we were growing up, over the past years we hadn't been able to keep up that well with each other. Carl had been drafted as soon as he turned eighteen, and while we were in the service it had been impossible to talk—long-distance calls were just too expensive. After my discharge I was working days and going to school at night, so I hardly had a moment to myself. But our bond was still strong, and when Carl got out he saw that I was in college and decided that he needed to go as well. At the age of twenty-one he went back to high school, got his diploma, then enrolled at West Virginia State College, a black school outside of Charleston, West Virginia.

Our mom hadn't confronted him about that as she had me when I told her I had decided to go to college. Carl was her baby, and she had always been a little more indulgent with him. She was happy at least that he had earned his diploma, and she reconciled herself to the fact that he was now going away.

Carl stayed at West Virginia State for two years. He was extremely popular there, as I knew he would be. That was Carl. He was smart, handsome, and a fighter on the boxing team. He was charismatic wherever he was.

He might have stayed at West Virginia, but there was a professor there who took a liking to him and saw that this was a young man with serious potential. He sat down with Carl one day and said "Carl, for a southern black kid to come up to West Virginia State to go to school—that's progress. But for you to leave Cleveland where there's a Western Reserve University and come down here for college—that's not progress. You need to consider moving back up there. You can get the kind of education at Western Reserve that will take you where you want to go."

Carl took his professor's advice. He came back and enrolled at Western Reserve. But he was still at loose ends, without a clear idea of where he wanted to go in life or what college was going to do for him, besides which the only money he had was from a part-time job in a liquor store and some residual pool hustling. He needed to make a living, so after a year he dropped out of Western Reserve and got a job as a state liquor enforcement agent.

As a liquor agent Carl's assignments took him all over Ohio, to Canton, Toledo, Dayton, and other cities. In these places he would hit the bootleg joints and gambling dens that were selling booze illegally. These were not friendly establishments and Carl was involved in some rough situations. He was no shrinking violet in any sense. He loved to fight. And his anger sometimes would get the best of him, which gave him an opportunity to let people know that he would take them on and whip them. He wasn't afraid to be in enforcement work. It wasn't easy, going in and out of those places, finding people who were violating the law, people who did not want to go to jail and didn't mind confronting law enforcement officers. But if you confronted Carl, you got what you wanted. He was not the kind of person who was going to back off. In a couple of instances he even had to shoot people, though fortunately he never killed anyone.

Carl worked as an enforcement agent for a couple of years, but some of his lawyer colleagues at the liquor board encouraged him to go to law school, which sounded like a good idea to him, a step up. With that in mind he enrolled at the University of Minnesota to finish up his bachelor's degree (he was friends with Walter Mondale there), then he went on to law school, first at Minnesota, then at Cleveland Marshall.

When we set up our firm together my dream was to build it into a power. I was more in love with the law than ever, and that was where I saw my future. Even as we began working together, though, Carl was already harboring a different set of aspirations.

At 10604 Saint Claire Avenue we had a reception area for our secretary and two small adjacent offices for Carl and me.

One afternoon while Carl was out the secretary buzzed me.

"Yes."

"Mr. Norman Minor is here to see you."

I thought she must be kidding. "Right," I said.

"No. I'm serious. Mr. Minor is here to see you."

I walked out and there he was. "Hello, Lou," he said. "Let me see your place."

That took a minute, then we sat down in my office. Minor mentioned the case I had handled for him while he was away, the one I had won an acquittal on. He said how much he appreciated what had happened there. Then he said,

"Do you think you and your brother would like to practice law with me?"

I was taken aback. Shocked. Norman Minor was asking us to come practice law with him.

Now there were some very fine black civil attorneys in Cleveland. But no one with anywhere near his reputation as a trial lawyer, both when he was a prosecutor and when he came out into practice. He handled all the most notorious cases. Invariably people involved in high-profile or especially difficult criminal matters would get Norman Minor to represent them, whites as well as blacks. Once they got indicted they tended to come straight to him. Norman Minor was the Johnny Cochrane of his day.

Minor was the type of lawyer about whom stories abounded in the black community about what he had done in the courtroom. Some exaggerated no doubt, maybe even some made up. But he was held in such esteem that he had become legendary.

There was a case when he was prosecuting a very notorious criminal. The story—a true one—was that when it came time for closing arguments, Minor brought out two suitcases and put them down in front of the jury. "If you release this man"—he pointed to the defendant. Then he pointed to the suitcases—"If you release this man, I'm leaving this town."

That was a highly prejudicial thing to say to a jury. I think it might have made the case reversible. But those were the kind of stories that grew up around him. "Minor's suitcases" became a catchphrase: "If Minor brings his suitcases, you are going away."

One of the things Minor was known for was that the young black lawyers he took into his office were considered as having a very bright future. The cream of the young crop, so to speak. One, Merle McCurday, had just left Minor's firm to become an assistant county prosecutor, as Minor himself had been. As an assistant prosecutor McCurday quickly became known for his razor-sharp mind and skill at argument, similar to Minor himself. On occasion he and Minor found themselves as adversaries in cases, one prosecuting, the other defending. When that happened the courtroom would fill to overflowing with lawyers and others eager to witness a battle of two courtroom masters. Later President John F. Kennedy appointed McCurday the first black DA in Ohio's history.

In any event, McCurday's departure meant there was a vacancy in Minor's office, which he was now asking Carl and me to fill. I told Minor I thought we'd be interested. I'd talk to Carl and we'd get back to him.

Of course we decided to go with him. We weren't making a lot of money. We were hustling. It was tough. We had our hopes and dreams about this— or at least I did, and we had confidence, but building a practice is a long, hard endeavor, and the opportunity to work with Norman Minor wasn't something any aspiring lawyer was going to turn down.

I worked with Minor for eight years, second chair to him on some of Cleveland's most famous criminal trials as well as more mundane cases. For a young lawyer still learning the ropes, those years were a blessing. Sitting with him you couldn't help but learn, if only by osmosis. But it wasn't just osmosis. Minor took the time to teach me why he did the things he did. I got to understand his mind, his approach, his tactics. I also got to see the tricks of his trade.

In one of our cases the prosecutor brought in an unexpected witness. We didn't know about this witness—we hadn't seen him before. But we suspected he had a criminal background and it was important for us to be able to discredit him.

In the middle of the trial we weren't able to run out and try to get the police records. But when it came time to cross-examine we had the right to ask him if he had ever been convicted of a state or federal crime. We did that. His answer was "No," and we had no way of either corroborating or disproving it.

I watched as Minor went up to the stand with a sheaf of papers in his hand, put them down, and began shuffling through them. He asked a couple of more questions, then went back to his papers, as if he were looking for something in particular. Everyone's eyes were on him as he took time to do this—the jury, the prosecutors, the judge as well. Judges always paid close attention to Minor. They never knew what he was going to do next, as likely as not something they had never seen before.

The witness watched nervously as Minor searched through his papers, then suddenly appeared to find whatever it was he had been looking for.

Minor looked up at the witness.

"Now," he said, "Let me ask you again," then louder—"*Have you ever been convicted of a crime against the state?*"

The guy was in a sweat. "Yes," he said. "I have."

"Please tell the jury," said Minor, "what it is you have been convicted of. Tell the *jury* what *you* have been *convicted* of."

The jurors were all ears. They wanted to know. Now their attention was focused on what he was convicted of instead of his testimony, devastating as it was, but now utterly discredited.

That was the kind of performance that enlivened conversation at Lancer's Steak House, where the younger black attorneys often went for dinner or drinks. Lancer's was a gathering spot for all kinds of people: doctors, lawyers, schoolteachers, politicians, policy dealers—you could never tell who might be sitting at some nearby booth or table. It was one of the places where stories got heard and passed around, where they became common knowledge, and more than a few of those stories were about Norman Minor.

Fleet Slaughter was the owner of Lancer's, a debonair man, suave, as smooth as they came, the kind of person who would always appear at exactly the right moment to light a lady's cigarette. Fleet worked the room every night, together with his attractive wife, Beulah, talking with patrons, joking with them, shaking their hands and slapping their backs, making them feel special, the epitome of the genial host. But beneath his amiable exterior Fleet was as tough as they came. If he told an unruly patron it might be time for him to leave, that patron didn't stop to argue cases.

Sports stars like Jim Brown and Ozzie Newsome of the Cleveland Browns would eat at Lancer's. Don King, the future fight promoter, was known to come by. King in those days was a big, flamboyant numbers dealer involved at one time or another in struggles over control of the black numbers business. He was in fairly regular trouble with the police then. They had a penchant for busting up the black numbers houses while leaving the white bookies free to ply their trade. King had killed someone who was trying to rob one of his policy houses—the verdict on that was justifiable homicide. He killed someone else too, in a debt argument. The verdict there was non-negligent manslaughter and he was sentenced to four years. It was while he was in prison that he decided to get out of the rackets and do something more productive with his life, which of course he did.

King was one of Minor's clients. On those occasions when Minor wasn't able to be present at a court appearance, he would send me down to represent King, mainly to get continuances. I was really just assisting Minor then, but later on when I was in Congress, King would on occasion come to speak with the Congressional Black Caucus. "Lou Stokes over there is my lawyer," he'd say, laughing.

Working alongside Minor and constantly learning from him I became increasingly proficient as a criminal defense attorney, and as my reputation developed I found myself representing a wide variety of cases. Two of the men I represented were considered to be the top pimps, Chuck Pugh and Kenny Jones, both of them colorful figures in the community. Pugh and Jones were close friends. One came to me first, then recommended me to the other. In that capacity I represented the women who worked for them, their "stables." All the women had my name and number in the event they were arrested, which of course they were regularly. When that happened they would call my home, usually after midnight.

I was divorced and had remarried by then (more about this later) and my wife, Jay, would take their names and tell them she would give me the message and that I would be down to see them in the morning.

The next morning the police would bring the women into court and I'd be there to represent them.

"Your honor, I represent the defendant. We'd like to request a continuance."

Or more often, "You're honor, we're ready for trial. We plead not guilty."

I was always ready for trial when it was clear there would be no witnesses to the offense. Most of the time the police officer himself did not see the exchange of money or the act; the arrest came afterward, so the officer couldn't testify. And the johns were almost never arrested, just the girls. Many of the johns were white men from the suburbs, good upstanding citizens who were not about to show up in court, which would let their wives and families know what they had been up to. If there was a question about that, I'd get their information from the police sheet and subpoena them. The moment I did that they'd tell the police, "Listen, I can't come down there." And the police would drop the case.

Many of the prostitutes were tough; they'd been through a lot in their lives. I remember one girl named Billy who had been arrested many times. One night apparently one of the johns had attacked her. Kenny Jones, her pimp, told me that the john had been wearing a leather jacket and that "Billy cut that jacket right off of him." That's how tough she was.

I got to know Billy. I got to know many of my clients. I knew they had faith that I could get them off or get their sentences reduced, and I wanted to live up to their expectations as best I could.

Strange as it may seem, a lot of those people had character. Marvin Cox was a client I represented in an armed robbery case. He was accused of having robbed Jack's Bar on Cedar Avenue. Witnesses said he had jumped up on the bar, waved a gun, and shouted, "Give me all your money." Marvin had enough money to retain me, but not enough for a trial. But he told me beforehand that regardless of what happened he would pay my fee. He was a disabled veteran and received a social security check. "Lou, even if I'm convicted I'll pay the fee from my social security."

We tried the case. The jury was out a long time, but they finally came back with a guilty finding. Marvin did wind up in prison, but he kept his word. Every month he'd send me a check from the penitentiary. That was unusual. Most of my defendants, if they were convicted and they went off, that was it.

I represented another armed robber who had been convicted before and had done time. I was sitting talking with him about what he had done and why he had done it. He said, "Now Mr. Stokes, I can do time. When I do my time and come out, I don't ask anybody to give me anything. I'm entitled to the opportunity to work. I try to get work. But I can't get work. And if I can't, I'm going to take it. I see these other people with it, so I'm going to take it. I can *do* the time."

You had to try to understand a man who thinks like that. So part of the reputation I was able to build was that I took time with people and cared about them. I saw them as human beings. I took an interest in them and tried to defend them with an understanding of why they did the kinds of things they had.

Despite Norman Minor's prominence, all the black lawyers in Cleveland, and around the country for that matter, labored under the general white perception of their inferiority. They hadn't gone to the right schools, they were not as well equipped, they weren't as well prepared. Besides, they just looked different. They didn't fit. In Cleveland there were no black lawyers in any white firm; they were excluded from working alongside white lawyers, not by law but by universal custom.

Functioning in that environment you are constantly aware of how people think, and it affects you. Back in school it was important to show that just because you were black it didn't mean you weren't as smart as whites, or smarter. It was important to you that they not be able to look down on you as being inferior to them.

Attorneys practiced in that same deeply prejudicial atmosphere. We resented the fact that black lawyers couldn't practice in downtown law offices, that they couldn't even have their own offices downtown. Building owners would not rent the space. We resented the fact that white attitudes toward blacks even infected blacks. In those circumstances it was essential to me to function as a lawyer such that no white lawyer opposing me in a courtroom would think he was superior to me. He might come in thinking that, but I was determined that he would leave thinking differently.

In that respect, I made up my mind that if I was going to be accepted as a lawyer, not just as a black lawyer, then I not only had to be skillful in court, I also had to make a place for myself in the professional associations. The legal community had to know me at that level and respect me at the same level as they respected me in the courtroom.

In Cleveland we had two bar associations, the Cleveland Bar Association and the Cuyahoga Bar Association. I joined both. I'd go to meetings, where I'd find myself one of a very small group of black attorneys (it's still that way today). Eventually, though, I was elected to the board of the Cleveland Bar along with John Bustamante, a black Harvard law graduate who had arrived in Cleveland at about the same time I completed law school. On the Cuyahoga Bar Association I became chairman of the criminal law section and wrote a publication for them on criminal law.

I also joined the American Bar Association along with Jay White and Jim Willis, two other top young African American criminal lawyers from Cleveland. At one ABA meeting outside Chicago the three of us helped found the National Association of Defense Lawyers in Criminal Cases, which became a national organization.

In that organization I was associating with the top criminal lawyers in the country. Notwithstanding that they were white, we were with them, we were recognized. We got to know each other. We respected them, and they respected us. If a matter came up in Ohio that some Texas lawyer was involved in, he'd call one of us. "Lou, what do you think about this?" That to me was functioning as a lawyer and being recognized at the level I thought was important.

In 1967 I gained a great deal more national visibility around a case I took on that seemed at first a relatively ordinary felony situation. A man I knew slightly called me from the Cuyahoga County jail. He and a friend had been arrested for carrying concealed weapons. Could I possibly come down to see him? I said I would. I had no way of knowing that John Terry's case would become a landmark in American criminal and constitutional law that would have me arguing in Washington, D.C., in front of the U.S. Supreme Court.

CHAPTER 4

⁓

Stop and Frisk

TERRY'S CALL was the kind I received regularly. A cold call. "I've been arrested. I'm in jail. Would you please come see me?"

I did know Terry, though. He was one of a group that hung around with a client of mine named Billy Cox. Billy Cox was a tough guy in Cleveland's underworld scene, an alleged hit man. His hangers on, including John Terry, weren't exactly a crew, but they looked up to him and liked to congregate at his house. Many of them had been in trouble with the law, and on occasion Billy would call me to defend one or another of them. Terry himself, though, had never been my client.

By way of background, Billy Cox was a sometime associate of Shondor Birns, a Jewish mobster who oversaw Cleveland's black numbers operations and at one point unsuccessfully tried to blow up Don King in order to resolve a business dispute. When that didn't work he sent shooters to ambush King, with an equal lack of success.

I'd been involved peripherally in a federal case with Shondor Birns that had gotten a lot of publicity. When the jury couldn't reach a decision and the jurors were polled, one of them said that when he took the juror's oath he had had his fingers crossed behind his back, which he believed absolved him from trying the case honestly.

That upset the judge, who sentenced the juror for contempt of court, and the juror's family retained me to represent him. When I researched the law

I saw that in order to sentence someone for contempt in a federal court the judge had to first conduct a hearing on it, which he had not done. I filed a motion for the court to reconsider, giving the judge a chance to reverse himself, which he eventually did.

Shondor and Billy Cox had a long association, and, as I mentioned, Billy was my client. I represented him in a number of cases, including two where he had been picked up "on suspicion." The Cleveland police had a particular modus operandi where they would apprehend people "on suspicion" and hold them for three days without charges.

But "suspicion" is not something a person can defend himself or herself against, and in fact there was no legal justification for the police practice. Another attorney had won a ruling on that, and if any of my clients were detained on suspicion I would threaten to file a writ of habeas corpus, which was enough to get them released. That's what I had done on Billy Cox's "suspicion" arrests.

As I began talking to John Terry at the jailhouse it struck me that his arrest, which had been initiated due to an officer's "suspicion," was likely to have been legally questionable. The more I learned about the circumstances the more I was convinced of it.

At the jail Terry told me that he and a friend, Richard Chilton, had been arrested on a charge of carrying concealed weapons. There was a third man with them who was stopped but not charged with anything, a man by the name of Carl Katz.

The three of them had been downtown around Thirteenth and Euclid, the business and commercial district. They hadn't been doing anything, Terry said, just standing on the pavement talking when a policeman walked up and arrested them.

"Well," I said, "you must have done something. Had you committed a crime?"

"No. We were just standing on the street in the middle of the afternoon and a cop came up and arrested us. Both of us had guns. But they weren't even our guns. We had just found them. We had been walking through an alley when we saw this paper bag that turned out to have guns in it."

While Terry's gun story was more or less preposterous, it just didn't seem logical to me that a police officer could see them standing on the street, with no knowledge of a crime having been committed, and would be able to make a valid arrest. If they weren't doing anything, the arrest had to have been based on "suspicion." My own suspicion about this was heightened when Terry told me that Katz was white. Terry and Chilton were both black, and I was sure that this pavement discussion between two black men and a white man was what had attracted the policeman's attention. An association like that must have struck him as unlikely. In this cop's mind something improper must have been going on.

The Fourth Amendment clearly states that you have to have probable cause to arrest a person. If a person is committing a crime, that's probable cause, but not if people are just standing on the street talking. The guns had been found subsequent to the arrest, which suggested that they were evidence obtained as a result of an illegal arrest, which would mean that the guns would be inadmissible in any trial.

Of course I didn't have all the facts, only what Terry and Chilton were telling me; I hadn't yet seen the police report. So after talking with them I decided to file a motion to suppress the evidence. That would force the court to inquire into the circumstances that caused the arrest and produced the evidence. That way I could find out all the facts, and not least I'd be able to interrogate the police officer.

The first thing I discovered as I began preparing for the suppression hearing was that the arresting officer was Martin McFadden, a plainclothes detective assigned to the downtown area. McFadden had been on the force for thirty-nine years, almost all of it spent catching shoplifters and pickpockets. I had actually heard of him; many Clevelanders had. McFadden was semifamous for his numerous arrests of the city's notorious pickpocket, Louis Finkelstein, aka Louie the Dip. Over the years the *Cleveland Press* and the *Plain Dealer* had written many articles about McFadden's encounters with the Dip. McFadden had joined the force back in 1925 when it was more or less standard procedure for police to arrest anyone who seemed to be loitering or who piqued their curiosity otherwise. McFadden used to arrest Louie the Dip pretty much on sight, regardless of whether he was actually picking somebody's pocket. In an interview he gave later on, he said that all he had to do was see Louie in a crowd of people and he'd throw him in jail. That suggested to me that McFadden might certainly have been prone to making arrests on suspicion. But he apparently had no experience at all at arresting people like Terry and Chilton, who had committed no crime and weren't known criminals, or weren't known to him anyway, unlike Louie Finkelstein.

Judge Bernard Friedman was going to be on the bench in this case, which gave me some assurance. I had tried a number of cases before him previously and I thought he was one of the top common pleas judges, absolutely fair and a stickler for the law. I knew that if the facts didn't fit the law, Friedman had the guts to call it like it was, whatever the reaction might be. Here were two black men caught with concealed weapons, but if Bernie Friedman thought the law was on my side he would release them. Whatever was required under the law, I had confidence that he would do the right thing. He was exactly the kind of judge I needed in this case.

As I studied the case I could see the constitutional questions emerging more and more clearly. The policeman had approached Terry and the others, asked their names, then frisked Terry. Why did he have the right not only to stop them but to frisk them, which is a violation of the individual? The moment you put your hands on me you've violated my constitutional right to be free, particularly if you're a police officer. If you're a police officer I have no freedom of action once you put your hands on me. Police had no right to arrest someone on mere suspicion and no right to demean them further by patting their bodies and exercising dominion over them.

This was 1967, when black men in particular were being stopped for "suspicion" or simply for no reason at all on streets all over the country, as they still are in many places today. I had been stopped myself going to a Boy Scout meeting when I was thirteen or fourteen. Police had gotten out of a squad car and stopped and questioned me. What was I doing here? Where was I going? Where was I coming from? Then, "All right, get on down the street," brusquely, angrily.

This was the treatment many black men experienced, an ongoing humiliation and violation of rights. Now, in this case the police happened to find two guns. But what about the thousands or tens of thousands or hundreds of thousands of times people were stopped and there were no guns or illegal contraband? The case I had in hand here had the potential to strike at a problem that existed on the streets of every major American city. If I could establish a ruling on this in Cleveland, it was going to affect the stopping and frisking of black men all over the country.

I was, I believed, squarely within the Fourth Amendment here. This was an illegal arrest and frisk; the guns were the so-called fruit of the frisk and therefore should be excluded from evidence. I also knew that this was going to be a difficult case. Even if I was right, the court was going to be confronted with the fact that both men had been found with concealed weapons, a felony. To release them on the basis that the guns were the fruit of an illegal frisk and therefore could not be admitted as evidence was going to put the court in a tough position. So I knew I had to walk a very thin, ticklish line. I'd be asking the court something that had never been asked under circumstances that had never been presented to them before in a case where a felony had actually been committed. A delicate situation, to say the least.

Judge Friedman was going to preside over the hearing on my motion to suppress the evidence. If my motion to suppress was overruled, then I was going to waive a jury trial and try the case directly in front of him. Going before a jury, I'd have several problems. The jury would be mostly white, maybe all white, trying two black men. The chief witness would be a white police officer, so they'd be predisposed to believe him. Equally to the point, I was raising constitutional questions regarding the Fourth Amendment that as far as I knew had never been raised before. The Fourth Amendment protected citizens against arbitrary arrests. It guaranteed that people would be secure in their persons against unreasonable searches and seizures. There was a better-than-even chance that the legal arguments would get lost in a jury trial, whereas Bernie Freidman would have a firm grasp of the constitutional issues.

Interestingly, the county prosecutor assigned to this case was Reuben Payne, a black attorney who had graduated from Cleveland Marshall along with me and was active in the NAACP. He and I weren't social friends, but we knew each other well. Reuben Payne was smart and knowledgeable, an outstanding lawyer. The more I thought about how this might unfold, the more I recognized that all of us involved here—Judge Friedman, Reuben, and I—would be aware that we were trying a case that had profound implications and that might very well end up before the Supreme Court. We were all going to be exceedingly careful here. I had no idea what the state might do if the decision went against them, but I was certain they knew that if I lost I'd be appealing it up as far as I could.

As I prepared, my suspicion that race was an issue here didn't diminish. I thought that McFadden had initially stopped Terry and Chilton at least partly for racial reasons, that he had profiled them. But in the end I decided to leave the race question out of it. There was plenty going on here as it was. Given the guns, I was already skating on thin ice. I was about to test the Fourth Amendment. That test would best be made by itself, without adding a different sort of issue, which might be equally portentous.

Additionally, the climate was good for a Fourth Amendment case. The Supreme Court under Chief Justice Earl Warren was in the process of extending to state cases the constitutional protections that technically applied only to federal cases. In fact, the first such case had taken place in Cleveland only a few years earlier, *Mapp v. Ohio.*

Mapp was Dollree Mapp, an African American woman whose name had come up in a bombing investigation as someone who might be harboring a suspect, and who also, incidentally, was thought to be keeping numbers slips in her house. In fact, the bombing in question was Shondor Birns's attempt to blow up Don King during their numbers dispute. Three police-men had come to Mapp's house and demanded to come in and look around. When it turned out they had no search warrant, Mapp refused to let them in. At that two police went off, leaving their colleague at the door. Not long afterward the two returned, bringing several more police with them. They waved a piece of paper at Mapp, telling her it was a warrant, but when she insisted on seeing it they shoved their way through the door. Mapp man-aged to snatch the piece of paper—which turned out not to be a warrant at all—and put it in her blouse. The police struggled with her to get it back, then they handcuffed her and searched the house. They didn't find either the bombing suspect or any numbers slips, but they did find some pornographic material in a trunk in her basement. She was arrested, charged with posses-sion of obscene material, and convicted in state court. Eventually the case made its way to the Supreme Court, which found that the right to be free from unreasonable searches and seizures applied in state as well as federal courts and that evidence seized in violation of the Fourth Amendment was inadmissible.

The *Mapp* case was a landmark. I knew it well, and I knew the lawyers who had argued it in front of the Supreme Court. I thought about the prec-edent it set. There had been a couple of other similar cases as well. It was clear the Court was moving toward being much more expansive in its inter-pretations of the Fourth Amendment together with the Fourteenth, which guaranteed that no state could deprive any person of life, liberty, or property without due process.

So I argued to suppress the evidence in front of Judge Friedman. What had taken place was that at about 2:30 in the afternoon of October 31 on a normally busy downtown street, McFadden had seen Terry and Chilton talking together. As he watched, each of them had strolled up and down the block several times, each time stopping for a moment to look into a particular store window—from where he was standing McFadden couldn't tell whether it was the United Airlines office or the jewelry shop next to it. A white man had stopped to talk with them a bit, then had moved on. After ten or twelve minutes the two men had walked several hundred yards down the street where they were joined by the same white man. It was then that McFadden approached the three of them and identified himself as a police officer. Given that Terry and Chilton had stopped and looked into the store window a number of times, he suspected they had been casing the place for a stickup.

After McFadden asked their names, he grabbed Terry, turned him around so that they were both facing Chilton and Katz, and frisked him. It was then that he felt a gun in Terry's topcoat pocket. Once he removed the gun, he ordered the three of them into the store they were standing in front of and told the storekeeper to "call the wagon"; then, frisking Chilton and Katz, he found a gun on Chilton as well.

My argument was that the frisk itself was illegal since there were no reasonable grounds to think that a crime had been committed. My position was that at the moment McFadden put his hands on Terry, Terry was under arrest. But no crime had been committed, therefore he had no right to proceed further in terms of searching Terry.

I argued, citing case law, that under the Fourth Amendment, suspicion does not ripen into probable cause. Under the amendment, unless a crime is being committed or has just been committed, the only other reason for accosting someone as McFadden did would be probable cause. Suspicion is not probable cause. So even if you see suspicious circumstances, you do not have the right to stop and frisk.

That was the position I took.

In his cross-examination Reuben Payne's argument was that McFadden was justified in frisking the suspects. "Why did you pat them down?" he asked McFadden.[1]

"I suspected them of casing a job," he said. "I patted them down to see if they had guns."

"In your thirty-nine years of experience as an officer," Judge Friedman asked, "have you ever had experience in observing the activities of an individual casing a place?"

"To be truthful with you," McFadden answered, "no."

"The problem arises," Judge Friedman said, "whether or not in the circumstances surrounding this situation an officer is justified based on what he saw to stop and frisk an individual.

"Another question that comes to my mind," he said, "is whether or not stopping and frisking is a search or whether there isn't a different meaning between stopping and frisking and searching."

---

1. All quotations are from John Q. Barrett, "Appendix B: *State of Ohio v. Richard Chilton* and *State of Ohio v. John Terry*," *St. John's Law Review* 72, no. 3 (1998), article 34.

Payne argued, also citing case law, that since a police officer has the right to inquire into suspicious activities, "it follows as readily as night and day that he has the right to do what is necessary to protect his own life"—that is, to frisk for weapons. "I think that there must be a distinction made," he said, "between a frisk or patting down and a legal search and seizure as set forth under the Fourth Amendment." "The security of public order," he argued, "and the lives of police officers" had to be weighed against what he called "the minor inconvenience" of being frisked.

"I realize," I said in response, "that the Court is in a difficult position given that these two men were on the street with loaded guns. But we have to look at what the law is, and what our Supreme Court justices have said about situations like this.

"The law says that a police officer cannot arrest for a felony unless he has reasonable grounds to believe that a felony has been committed. The prosecutor was talking about one which is anticipated and therefore has never occurred, and that is not Ohio law, which we have to apply if we are to follow the search and seizure rules.

"The syllabus of this case," I said, "is the following. A search is either legal or not. It isn't made legal by what it turns up. That is the Supreme Court speaking. The Supreme Court has also maintained, 'That law enforcement may be made more difficult is no justification for disregarding the constitutional prohibition against unreasonable searches and seizures.' The Court has also said, 'The forefathers, after consulting the lessons of history, designed our Constitution to place obstacles in the way of a too permeating police surveillance, which they seemed to think was a greater danger to a free people than the escape of some criminals from punishment."

The following day Judge Friedman rendered his opinion.

"Can it be said," he asked, "that the frisking of a person by an officer for the purpose of his own safety violates the Fourth Amendment? This court believes that such conduct would not be held as a violation. At the same time a police officer cannot be permitted to stop and frisk an individual simply because he has a suspicion, unless there are reasonable circumstances justifying a frisk. This Court believes that there is a distinction between stopping and frisking and search and seizure. There was reasonable cause in this case for Detective McFadden to approach these individuals and pat them . . . for his own personal protection. By doing so he discovered the concealed guns. The guns are the fruit of the frisk, not of a search.

"I have stated," said Judge Friedman, "and I repeat again, there is a distinction between a frisk and a search and seizure. This matter is of great importance and great concern, and I certainly hope counsel will endeavor to have this question determined by the Appellate Court, for it is most desirable that we have clearness with respect to this problem and that police know what they may do and can do in a stop and frisk matter. The motion is overruled. It is so ordered."

So I lost on my motion to suppress the evidence. The search and seizure wasn't illegal because it was not a search and seizure, it was a stop and frisk, a different animal according to Judge Friedman. And evidence turned up in a stop and frisk (the fruit of the frisk) was admissible. But at the same time the judge formally acknowledged my right to take exception to his ruling and appeal, which I most certainly intended to do.

A few days later we proceeded with the trial itself. With the guns admitted as evidence, the chances for acquittal were minimal, to say the most for them. But I still wanted to make my case as strongly as I could, first to help my clients to what might possibly be a lighter sentence, but also, especially, to buttress the appeals court argument I was planning to make.

When Reuben Payne placed the guns in evidence, I objected.

"If your honor please, may I show an objection to all questions pertaining to this gun, a continuing objection."

"Let the record show it," said Judge Friedman, then he overruled me.

On my cross-examination of Detective McFadden, I undertook to show that it was highly unlikely any robbery was going to happen. It was, after all, broad daylight on a downtown commercial thoroughfare.

He agreed, it was broad daylight and there were indeed people around.

I tried to draw him out on what excited his suspicions in the first place.

"Now, when you first saw these two men, there was nothing unusual about two colored men standing on the corner talking. Was there? . . . At what point did you consider their actions unusual?"

"To be truthful with you," he said, "I didn't like them."

I questioned him to the effect that not only was it unlikely they were going to pull a robbery in that place at that time, but that they were conducting themselves absolutely normally when he accosted them.

"The three of them were just standing there talking?"

"That's right," he said.

He didn't know anything about any of the three—nothing at all that might have suggested to him that they were criminals or robbers?

"I had no information whatsoever," he said.

"When exactly did you arrest them?" I asked.

"After I got the first gun and got those men in [the store]," he said.

"What were Chilton and Katz being arrested for?"

"Association."

"At that point they were being arrested for 'association'? . . . Do you know of any charge under Ohio law entitled 'Association'?"

"As far as I know," he said, "I don't know."

"During your tenure as a police officer," I asked, "during your thirty-nine years as a police officer, how many men have you had occasion to arrest when you had observed them and felt as though they might pull a stickup?"

"To my recollection," said Detective McFadden, "I wouldn't know. I don't know if I had—I don't remember any."

I endeavored as well as I could to discredit McFadden as a reliable observer. I wanted to drive home the point that he had made the arrest on mere suspicion, which was not probable cause as understood by the Fourth Amendment and the subsequent case law. I interrogated him about other aspects of the arrest as well—the witness statements he took, the representation allowed or not allowed the defendants at first, the validity of the statements. But in the end it came down to the evidence, and Judge Friedman was allowing the evidence.

When the prosecution rested, I moved to renew all my objections regarding the evidence that had been overruled. I moved for a directed verdict of acquittal. My motion for acquittal was denied, as I knew it had to be. My renewed objections were also denied, though again Judge Friedman explicitly acknowledged my exceptions to his ruling.

Then I rested.

Before Judge Friedman rendered his verdict he volunteered a gratifying commendation about how both Reuben Payne and I had argued our cases. "I am sure," he said, "that Justice Potter Stewart of the Supreme Court, if you would argue the same way, he would commend you in the same manner." "Don't take it so nonchalantly," he said to us. "I am sincere in saying it."

I was ready to move ahead with the appeal, though I did not have any faith that the appellate court would overturn Judge Friedman's closely considered opinion. But I did have some hope that in the end the Supreme Court would accept a motion to hear the case. *Terry v. Ohio* was a test of the search and seizure law that, to my knowledge, had never before been made.

I did appeal to the appellate court, which as I expected sustained Judge Friedman's verdict. I then appealed to the Ohio State Supreme Court, and they upheld him as well.

When that happened I filed a writ of certiorari with the Supreme Court, requesting that they hear the case. I had no assurance that they would accept my writ; they received many thousands of these requests every year and heard only eighty cases. On the other hand, *Terry v. Ohio* was a test of one of the most fundamental rights enshrined in the Constitution, and this particular Supreme Court was deeply involved with issues of constitutional rights. In 1954 they had decided the *Brown v. Board of Education* case, which had ruled the "separate but equal" doctrine unconstitutional. Earl Warren had been chief justice then, and he was still chief justice.

A writ of certiorari incorporates a brief giving the facts of the case, the history, the importance, and the reasons urging a Supreme Court hearing. In order to prevail in the competition for the Court's attention, the brief needs to be as clear, concise, cogent, and persuasive as you, the appellant, can possibly make it. I had never filed a Supreme Court certiorari. It was a challenge to get it exactly right, but I was fortunate to have very expert help.

Jack Day, a good friend of mine, was an unusual person and an unusual lawyer. Jack was a professor at Case Western Reserve Law School and a distinguished criminal defense attorney. Although he was an expert in criminal law and also labor law, his true passion was civil liberty and the rights of citizens. Jack was the founding president of the Ohio ACLU and had fought to protect the rights of people charged with disloyalty during the McCarthy period. I knew him from the National Association of Criminal Defense Lawyers, and he was on the NAACP Legal Redress Committee, which I had chaired earlier. Jack had participated in a number of Supreme Court cases—including *Mapp v. Ohio*—and was often consulted on constitutional issues.

Jack and I were talking one day and he asked me about the *Terry* case. He had been keeping an eye on it. He knew I had lost in front of Judge Friedman, the appellate court, and the Ohio Supreme Court. Was I working on a U.S. Supreme Court certiorari?

I told him I was. He asked how I was supporting all of this. "I'm doing it at my own expense," I told him. "The defendants are indigent. But the principles here are too important not to pursue."

"Lou," he said, "I think so, too. I'd like to offer to pay half the costs. I'll also do half the brief work."

So Jack and I wrote the brief together. This is a question the Court has never before decided, we said. It is a fundamental test of the Fourth Amendment.

The justices saw it that way, too. They were at the same time considering certioraris regarding two similar Fourth Amendment cases, but ours was the one they chose to hear.

The morning of the arguments I felt nervous, no doubt like most lawyers arguing before the Supreme Court for the first time. The august surroundings, the nine robed justices, each of them a famous legal name, a number of them institutions, really, in their own right. Chief Justice Warren, Potter Stewart, Byron White, Hugo Black, William O. Douglas, Abe Fortas, William Brennan, John Harlan, and, most moving for me, Thurgood Marshall.

Marshall was the famed, beloved, brilliant lawyer and judge whom I idolized. I had followed his career as an NAACP trial attorney, where he had traveled all over the United States, trying cases and defending African Americans. He shaped so much constitutional law in the nineteen cases he argued before the U.S. Supreme Court, of which he won fourteen. Thurgood Marshall was the epitome of what I wanted to be. He defended the rights of those I most wanted to defend. He embodied the excellence in the law that was my own highest aspiration.

It occurred to me that not only would I be arguing in front of Thurgood Marshall for the plaintiff, but Reuben Payne would be arguing for the defense. Two black attorneys arguing in front of the first black Supreme Court justice, which invested the proceedings with an additional historic dimension, at least for me, and I was sure for Reuben as well.

That morning, when all of the lawyers arguing cases that day were oriented to the court procedure, we were advised that we would be seated at a table. When we were asked to present our case we would stand at a lectern in front of the table. On the lectern we would see three lights. A green light would come on signaling us to begin our presentation. We would then have thirty minutes to argue our case. In twenty-five minutes an amber light would come on, signifying that if we wanted to reserve five minutes at the end for rebuttal or closing, this was the time to do it. The red light meant that you had reached the thirty minutes and had to stop.

I began my presentation with a prepared argument. I had spent two weeks in the Library of Congress researching additional legal points and writing my presentation. I went to the lectern, the green light came on, and I began my argument.

I had thirty minutes for this. I had prepared a thirty-minute presentation on the facts, the law, and the importance of limiting stop and frisks to instances where police had probable cause, the Fourth Amendment standard. My recitation of the facts was interrupted several times by brief questions asking me to clarify, but I was moving along fairly well, reading from my brief. The incident had taken place in broad daylight, I told them. The officer had no knowledge that the men were criminals, he had been initially attracted because, as he said, he didn't like them, he had no experience of ever having seen men casing a place, and he had never arrested anyone for casing a place. I told them that although the court of appeals had upheld the verdict that the frisk was legal, even though there might not have been reasonable grounds to arrest, that it also had opined that "in all probability this would lead to abuses by the police."

At that point Justice Fortas asked me if McFadden wouldn't have been concerned with his safety the moment he walked up to Terry and the others, and he and Justice Brennan began a colloquy with me on that subject, suggesting that McFadden might not have had probable cause to arrest them at this point, but that he had probable cause to think they might be carrying guns and that his life might be in danger.

I argued back that he had not interrogated them; he had gotten ahead of himself and did not at this point have the right to lay his hands on Terry and spin him around. He had no probable cause to do that under the meaning of the Fourth Amendment, and the evidence he seized was seized improperly as per the *Mapp* decision, that to think differently would be to nullify or at least relax the Fourth Amendment and overturn their own decision in *Mapp*.

In short order Justices Black, Warren, and Thurgood Marshall joined the discussion, which became fairly lively—not in any antagonistic way, but the justices were determined to understand whether under these circumstances the frisk was a legally permissible search, as the previous courts had decided, or an impermissible search, as I was arguing.

I was so caught up in this back and forth that I failed to notice that the green light on my lectern had turned to amber. By now my prepared brief had been left far behind and I wasn't looking down at my lectern at all. I was engaged in a debate that was absorbing every bit of my attention and reasoning ability. But just before we came to the end of time I was able to tell the justices that I wasn't actually so concerned about Terry himself. It was through Terry that we had to look at all the many people walking on the streets day by day who might find themselves observed by a policeman who might think, "to tell the truth, I just don't like them," and then might want to go further and lay his hands on them. "And at that point," I said, "I think we're subjecting all of the people who have this inviolate right of privacy to this type of activity on the public streets throughout our nation."

At that moment my light turned red, which I did notice, and I quickly said, "I would like to reserve five minutes of my time," which was not how we had been told this was supposed to work. Did they give you any leeway in this? I didn't know, but I did know I wanted those five minutes.

When Reuben Payne got up to make his case, the justices piled right in on the question of the difference, if any, between probable cause and reasonable suspicion. They wanted to know if reasonable suspicion was equivalent or different in degree or different in essence from probable cause. Assuming for a moment that Detective McFadden had reasonable suspicion, to what degree were his actions permissible under the Fourth?

Again the discussion was friendly and respectful but intense. Laughter broke out when Justice Marshall asked Reuben where McFadden might have gotten his casing-the-joint expertise from, given that all he'd done in his career was catch pickpockets and shoplifters. By being a member of the force for forty years, Reuben said, he was sure McFadden would have picked it up by osmosis. "Oh," said Marshall, "now we're getting intuition by osmosis," which everyone thought was funny except Reuben.

He recovered quickly, though, and went on to make his case that when McFadden put his hands on Terry and turned him around it was not an arrest, it was a "temporary detaining," not a "seizure" but "an interference with his person," that did not need to be justified by the probable cause amendment, but was justified by the policeman's obligation to protect public safety and the policeman's right to defend himself against bodily harm. And since what he had done was legal in those senses, the "fruit of the frisk" was obtained legally and was therefore permissible evidence.

Jack Day was sitting with me at my table as my co-counsel, and as Reuben finished an individual handsomely attired in tails and white tie came over to me. This person leaned down and said to me very brusquely and authoritatively, "Mr. Stokes, you do not have any more time."

As he walked off Jack leaned over to me and said, "Lou, what did he say to you?"

"Jack, he said I don't have any more time."

"Oh, to hell with him," said Jack. "You get back up there."

When Reuben Payne concluded his argument, Chief Justice Earl Warren looked at me, hesitated a moment, then said, "Mr. Stokes, your time has expired. But this is an important case. The court would like to hear further from you. You may have three more minutes to finish."

"Thank you, your honor."

"Your time had expired."

"Thank you very much."

I was about to begin my precious three minutes, so graciously bestowed on me, when Justice Black spoke up with another question about whether I thought a police officer had a right to interrogate people and get an answer unless he had probable cause.

I answered, "I am saying that where a police officer chooses . . . to interrogate or to investigate further with respect to citizens lawfully in the street, that in order to exercise dominion or custody or control over that citizen and thereby deprive him of his rights under the Fourth Amendment, that he must have, before approaching him, that probable cause which this court had made reference to in its decisions."

"Supposing he [the officer] wants to do something short of arresting him?" said Justice Black.

"Then I don't think he has that right."

"Then the man can go on off, not answer the question, because the officer . . . doesn't have at that time a sufficient amount of evidence to make a case of probable cause?"

"That is precisely what I am saying. Because otherwise the Fourth's inviolate right to privacy is being invaded."

"I thought that was it," said Justice Black.

"Yes, sir," I said.

"Very well," said Chief Justice Warren. My three minutes were up.

"Thank you," I said, and went back to sit down with Jack.

It wasn't at all clear to me in which direction any of the justices had made up their minds either after reading the briefs or listening to the arguments, or if any of them had. I didn't get a sense from their questions if one or another was looking at this positively (from my point of view) or negatively.

We argued the case on December 12, 1967. It wasn't until six months later, on June 10, 1968, that the verdict came down. When it did, the decision was eight to one against me. Justice William O. Douglas was, perhaps, the only one I had fully persuaded. I say "perhaps" because many years later at a Saint Johns Law School seminar on the case, some of the participants, who had clerked for Thurgood Marshall back then, said that afterward Marshall felt he had voted wrongly. In fact, I was surprised when the opinion was handed down to learn that Marshall was with the majority. I had heard rumors that he himself had been stopped on the streets, and I believed he would be better prepared to understand my reasoning than most of the others.

I wasn't happy about losing my case. But the Court's opinion, written by Chief Justice Earl Warren, did not simply say that McFadden's actions in that situation were legal. It was far more nuanced than that, in a way that established rules for what was permissible in stop and frisk situations and what was not.

Reuben Payne had argued that Detective McFadden's grabbing Terry, spinning him around, and patting him down did not constitute search and seizure as defined by the Fourth Amendment and therefore were not governed by the probable cause requirement. A "frisk" was not a "search," he maintained, and it was justified by the need to protect the officer from danger and for the security of the public. And because it was justified, evidence produced by the frisk was legally valid and permissible in court.

The Warren decision emphatically rejected the idea that Terry had not been "searched and seized." "Whenever," the court said, "a police officer accosts an individual and restrains his freedom to walk away, he has 'seized' that person. And it is nothing less than sheer torture of the English language to suggest that a careful examination of the outer surfaces of a person's clothing all over his or her body . . . is not a 'search.' Moreover it is simply fantastic to urge that such a procedure performed in public by a policeman while the citizen stands helpless, perhaps facing a wall with his hands raised is a 'petty indignity.' It is a serious intrusion upon the sanctity of the person, which may inflict great indignity and arouse strong resentment."[2]

But though the justices said that "stop and frisk" was indeed "search and seizure," as defined by the amendment, they said in addition that "where a reasonably prudent officer is warranted in believing that his safety or that of others is endangered, he may make a reasonable search for weapons." In other words, the Supreme Court in its *Terry* decision carved out an exception to the Fourth Amendment. Where an officer reasonably suspected a person might be armed and dangerous, he did not need to have probable cause in order to stop that person and frisk him.

---

2. Quoted in Paul Butler, "A Long Step Down the Totalitarian Path," *Mississippi Law Journal* 79, no. 1 (2009): 21, 22.

The Supreme Court decided *Terry v. Ohio* almost fifty years ago at this writing. Since then the so-called Terry Rules have defined the boundaries of what the police may do when it comes to stopping and searching citizens on the streets. When police investigate someone whose conduct is suspicious, they have the right to search that person, not for the purpose of obtaining evidence, but in order to protect their own safety if they believe the person might be armed. They do not have the right to simply stop and search people indiscriminately.

Since the decision came down, the *Terry* case has been taught in every law school, and the Terry Rules have been taught in every police academy. Today every policeman in America knows those rules. Police profiling of blacks and Hispanics is regularly challenged as a violation of the Terry Rules. New York City's police tactic of indiscriminately stopping and searching young black and Hispanic men, which has caused such anger there, has led to high-profile court cases, all of them governed by the *Terry* decision.

I didn't feel good having lost the case. But I did feel good that I had been able to get the Supreme Court to carefully consider the factual circumstances of police stops like these and define the workings of the Fourth Amendment. The Court specifically upheld the principle that probable cause is required in order for police to conduct a search; it had only carved out a limited exception. And for this exception I had been able to get them to establish rules. So in that sense I hadn't lost but won. That was significant.

I also cherished the experience of arguing in the Supreme Court, something few lawyers in their careers get a chance to do, and particularly in a case that became a landmark, a case that is listed as being one of the twenty-five top constitutional law cases in the history of the Supreme Court.[3]

-----

3. Justice William O. Douglas's dissent from the *Terry* decision has achieved its own fame among constitutional scholars. I considered him among the finest minds the Court has had and I was honored to have him with me. His dissent, I believe, is still very much worth contemplating.

> To give the police greater power than a magistrate is to take a long step down the totalitarian path. Perhaps such a step is desirable to cope with modern forms of lawlessness. But if it is taken it should be the deliberate choice of the people through a constitutional amendment. There have been powerful hydraulic pressures throughout our history that bear heavily on the Court to water down constitutional guarantees and give police the upper hand. . . . Yet if the individual is no longer to be sovereign, if the police can pick him up whenever they do not like the cut of his jib, if they can 'seize' and 'search' him in their discretion, we enter a new regime. The decision to enter it should be made only after a full debate by the people of this country. (*Terry* 392 U.S. at 335–39, quoted in Butler, "Long Step Down," 23)

CHAPTER 5

NAACP Attorney

I DEFENDED my first criminal case in 1953, shortly after passing the Ohio bar. By the time the Supreme Court heard *Terry v. Ohio*, I had been a working criminal defense lawyer for fifteen years. But for most of that time I had pursued a parallel legal career as well. Not long after I finished law school I joined the Cleveland branch of the NAACP. By 1958 I was chairing its Legal Redress Committee.

I was twenty-five when I passed the bar, thirty-one when the Cleveland branch asked me to take on its legal work. In those years I was a young lawyer fighting to build a career, still catching cases at Twenty-First and Payne and learning the trade from Norman Minor. But I was also caught up in the turbulence of an exploding civil rights movement. As I was finishing law school, Thurgood Marshall was arguing *Brown v. Board of Education*. Shortly after I graduated the Supreme Court agreed with him unanimously and threw the separate but equal doctrine into the dustbin. The next year down in Mississippi, fourteen-year-old Emmett Till was brutally murdered and the three murderers were acquitted by an all-white jury, to the outrage of African Americans around the country. Not long afterward, Rosa Parks refused to give up her bus seat and Martin Luther King Jr. launched the Montgomery bus boycott. In 1957 Arkansas governor Orville Faubus blocked nine black students from entering Little Rock's Central High School, and President Eisenhower had to federalize the Arkansas National Guard and send in the 101st Airborne to protect them. One historic event followed the next: lunch counter sit-ins; freedom bus rides; Selma; the University of Mississippi, where rioters killed two people while protesting James Meredith's enrollment; Birmingham, Alabama, where Bull Connor's fire hoses and police dogs became daily fare on national television.

For much of the country's white population, at least in the North, the hatred and violence were a revelation. But I had seen the South up close. I had felt the demeaning and despicable nature of segregation as a young man in the service of my country, wearing the uniform of the United States. I hadn't suffered it for a lifetime as blacks in the South did, but for three years I had lived it. I didn't need any demonstrations in order to understand what it was.

When I began practicing law I wanted to be part of striking down discrimination and segregation any way I could; I wanted to help eradicate it, so it was natural for me to get involved with the NAACP. Early on I joined the board along with two contemporaries of mine, Harold Williams and Clarence Holmes. We were junior people, but I think the branch wanted youth, fresh ideas, and energy. They thought: these young guys are motivated; let's let them do it. Clarence soon took on the chairmanship and Harold became executive director. They asked me to head the Legal Redress Committee.

Harold Williams was bright, articulate, and fearless. It was a pleasure to watch him in action. He mastered issues quickly, and once we decided on a direction he stood firm as a rock. Clarence Holmes was quieter, thoughtful, always focused, and to the point. We were living in volatile, challenging times, and the three of us were about to engage in a number of events that would make the Cleveland NAACP one of the most active branches in the country, and one of the most successful.

But for me, it wasn't just the times that were challenging. My personal life was also going through difficulties. By 1958 Mildred and I had been married for ten years. We had three wonderful children but the marriage itself had broken down, and in 1958 we divorced.

When we separated I moved in with my mother. By then she was long out of the Outhwaite Projects. With money she had managed to save from her work as a domestic, augmented by the help Carl and I were providing, she had bought a nice home on East 149th Street in the Mount Pleasant area, a majority black but still (at that time) integrated neighborhood.

By then Shelley, our oldest child, was nine, Angie seven, and Chuckie five. I was absolutely determined to have them with me. My mother had been the most wonderful parent to Carl and me, someone we could always talk to, someone who gave us all the love and security she could in the midst of her own hard existence. But the fact that I never had a father had stayed with me in more ways than one. For many years I thought about what it would be like to be a father myself, to have children and give them the care I knew my father would have given me had he lived.

When Mildred and I married and began having children it fulfilled something in me. Now that we were divorcing I simply could not envision Shelley, Angie, and Chuck growing up without me being present to raise them. Having custody was something I wanted badly, something I needed. I wanted so much to provide for them, partly, I knew, because of what I myself had never had.

At the end of the divorce proceedings the court did award me custody. So there I was, a thirty-three-year-old single father with three young children, most fortunately living with a mother who was as loving a grandmother to my children as she was a loving mother to Carl and me.

Not long afterward Carl and Shirley, his wife, came to live with us. Now we were seven in the house, Carl, Shirley, Mom, myself, and the three children, a large, sometimes raucous, but loving extended family. A year and a half later the family in Mom's house grew by one, when I married Jay Francis, a former model who was then working at the Cleveland Board of Education.

In December 1960 Jay and I had been introduced on a blind date by a fellow attorney and close friend of mine also named Jay, Jay White. The young woman, my friend Jay said, had an engaging personality and was, not insignificantly, exceptionally beautiful. She and his girlfriend, Elmira, were best friends. The two girls were planning to see an early play at the Karamu Theater on East Eighty-Ninth Street. We could meet them afterward. Jay was sure I would like her.

The Karamu Theater was a unique institution, the oldest black theater in the country, the place where Langston Hughes had developed and premiered many of his plays. The theater was part of the Karamu Settlement House founded and run by two white Oberlin College graduates, Russell and Rowena Jelliffe. The Jelliffes were revered in Cleveland's black community. They had established the settlement house in Fairfax, one of the city's poorest, most crime-ridden neighborhoods, believing that the area's kids would benefit by being exposed to the arts, including acting and playwriting. The theater had grown out of that initial idea and had become famous for nurturing African American actors and playwrights, a number of whom went on to become nationally prominent.

I had a late meeting that day, so I wasn't able to attend the play myself, nor was my friend Jay, so we arranged that we would all meet at the theater after the show. As people left the Karamu Jay and I were standing a little apart, and when his girlfriend and my blind date came out Jay's girlfriend, Elmira, pointed across the way at me and said, "There he is. That's him, your date." I heard later that my date took a look and said, "Why in the world would you want to introduce me to a bald-headed old man?"

I wasn't actually bald then, just balding, and I was thirty-five, not exactly an old man, though it turned out that Jay Francis was only twenty-two, so it was likely I might have seemed ancient to her. But when we went out for drinks at the Carnegie Hotel it turned out that despite our age difference, she and I had a lot to talk about. Right off I was attracted to her warmth and intelligence, as well as her beauty, and it seemed as if she liked me, too. For me, that first date was it. I was going to pursue this gorgeous young lady whose company I had enjoyed so much.

I courted Jay for nine months. I was deeply in love with her. Despite our obvious mutual attraction, when I finally asked her to marry me I was more than a little surprised to hear her say "yes." I was extremely happy to hear it, though I could hardly believe that she was willing to marry a divorced man, thirteen years older and caring for three energetic youngsters from a prior marriage, while she herself was in her early twenties, with years of opportunity still ahead of her.

But she said that none of those things were a problem for her. She loved me, and she loved the children, with whom she had bonded early on in our courtship. She didn't see any difficulty either with them or with our age difference. So that August we were married at Jay's church, East Mount Zion, by her pastor, William Downs, and Jay moved in with all the rest of us at Mom's house on East 149th.

For a while Jay continued working at her school department job. But it was getting to be too much for my mother to be raising grandchildren, and I thought that, really, I was a lawyer making my way; I should be able to earn enough money to provide decently for us. So after discussing it, Jay left her job and became a full-time mother to the kids.

The children, of course, were front and center in our minds. We thought about where the best place would be for us to live and in particular where they would have access to the best possible schools. It was important to us that they grow up in a diverse neighborhood, where they would have white friends as well as black, where they would be exposed to different family cultures and come to respect other people's ways of living and doing things, not just those of ourselves and our own people. In those days the Cleveland suburb of Shaker Heights had one of the top school systems in the country. It also turned out that the Ludlow area of Shaker Heights had formed a neighborhood association that was taking a revolutionary approach to integration.

Ludlow was adjacent to a black neighborhood in Cleveland, and as black families began to improve their circumstances and look for better housing and educational opportunities, they had started buying homes in Ludlow. As typically happened in that kind of situation, when blacks started moving in whites started getting out, the changeover in population abetted by realtors and banks that had learned how to profit from neighborhood racial transitions. As more black families moved into Ludlow, tensions flared; in 1956 a bomb exploded in the garage of a black lawyer who was building a new house in the neighborhood. But instead of precipitating even more antagonism and flight, the bombing led to the formation of a biracial community group that dedicated itself to supporting integration and stabilizing the housing mix.

Since there was an influx of blacks into Ludlow and an outflow of whites, the community association took measures to bring more whites into the area. They sponsored whites-only open houses and raised money to support mortgages for white buyers. Some of this was controversial, but both the black and white members of the Ludlow Community Association were willing to fight hard to keep the neighborhood mixed and promote racial harmony. They responded to legal challenges, they held community events and fundraisers, and they defied the norm of white flight. The Ludlow association was successful in creating a purposefully integrated neighborhood. As far as I could tell it was the only effort of its kind in the country.

When Jay and I found out about Ludlow we wanted to be part of it. An integrated neighborhood with first-rate schools was precisely what we were looking for. After searching for a while we found a house we liked on Albion Road, bought stock in the association, bought the house, and moved in. It was an exciting moment in our lives. Till then we had been living with Mom; now, finally, we had a home of our own.

A year later Jay and I had a fourth child, Lori, born September 16, 1962. I say *we* had a fourth child, because as far as Jay was concerned, Shelley, Angela, and Chuck were her children as sure as if she had given birth to them herself. Lori was a highly anticipated child. Not only were Jay and I eagerly looking forward to her birth, but Shelley, Angie, and Chuckie were excited about it as well. Even though the three of them had been born in a former marriage, they had embraced Jay as their own just as she had embraced them. So this new child was not a half this or that or a step this or that; she was simply their new baby sister. Lori was received with a lot of love and attention and care by all of us. She was a beautiful baby. We doted on her.

Unfortunately, the happy race relations that characterized Ludlow were not by a very long stretch mirrored elsewhere. The country as a whole was in the throes of racial violence, that is, violence of whites against blacks. Martin Luther King Jr. was emerging as a civil rights leader of historic stature, and while he and his organization, the Southern Christian Leadership Conference, were committed to nonviolence, his marches and actions precipitated outpourings of hatred and brutality by white mobs.

I was, of course, watching everything that was happening in the South, and I got to know or at least meet many of the national civil rights figures when they came to Cleveland: Bayard Rustin, Andy Young, Roy Wilkins, Jesse Jackson, Hosea Williams, A. Phillip Randolph, even Dr. King himself. I worked with Bob Carter, Thurgood Marshall's second at the NAACP Legal Defense Fund. I knew Medgar Evers, who spoke in Cleveland not long before he was murdered. I attended all the big meetings and rallies the NAACP had at the churches. I was close friends with the nationally prominent rabbi Arthur Lelyveld who was on our own NAACP board. He had gone to Mississippi to help register black voters, and in Hattiesburg he was beaten mercilessly with a tire iron by thugs opposed to voting rights for black people.

Cleveland was not the South, but in Cleveland as in other northern cities, the lack of opportunity, poor schools, poor housing, poor social services, the lack of health care, and exploitation by landlords and other businesses all went into a climate of distrust and alienation. In Cleveland anger in the black community had been simmering for years, stirred up regularly by the brutality of Cleveland's almost all-white police force and what was regarded as a deeply prejudiced judicial system.

The first police brutality case I took on as head of the NAACP's Legal Redress Committee was the killing of Jeffrey Perkins, an unarmed black man, by a motorcycle policeman named Bobby Dunn. When the case came to me I immediately got some of our other redress committee lawyers involved and we undertook our own investigation. Dunn had pulled Perkins over, and as he was approaching the car he had shot Perkins. Dunn claimed he saw Perkins reaching over to the glove compartment and was afraid he had a gun there. He had shot Perkins, he said, in self-defense. No gun had been found, and when Perkins's body was removed from the car, his hands had been gripping the steering wheel so tightly they had to be pried loose—this according to the police report. He had, clearly, not been reaching for the glove compartment. Beyond that, the autopsy report stated that Perkins had been shot through the left eye, evidence that he had been looking at Dunn when he was killed.

Instead of allowing the case to rest with an internal investigation by the police department, I put pressure on the police prosecutor, Bernard Conway, to have it turned over to the grand jury. We held community meetings at the churches and got the black ministers involved. That helped get people out and talking about what was going on, which rallied support for our demand that action be taken. As sentiment grew, the newspapers and other media turned their spotlights on the case, which increased the pressure.

To the surprise of many, Police Prosecutor Conway did have the case bound over to the grand jury. He "deferred," as he put it, to the grand jury's judgment. During the grand jury proceedings the county prosecutor, John T. Corrigan, allowed Dunn to testify on his own behalf, an unheard-of violation of the code governing grand jury procedures, which specifically prohibited accused individuals from appearing. In the event, the grand jury issued a "no bill," that is, they refused to indict Dunn. We pressed the mayor, Anthony Celebrezze, to open a special investigation, but we had no success there, either.

A month or so later A. Phillip Randolph, president of the Pullman Porter's Union, came to Cleveland to speak at a mass protest against the city's double standard of law enforcement. Meanwhile, Patrolman Dunn continued on with the police force. He had never even been suspended during the investigation. Nothing was done about him, and I was left with no recourse.

A year and a half after the Perkins shooting, another police killing roiled the community. Albert Rugley had just arrived at a party at his cousin's apartment when two plainclothes detectives appeared at the door, came in, and shot him. There were a number of witnesses present at the scene, only a few feet away. We interviewed each of them, and they all told the same story. There had been no fight, no scuffle—one of the detectives had simply drawn his gun and fired.

The detectives maintained that they had thought Rugley was a robbery suspect they were pursuing, and when they confronted him in the apartment he had hit one of them in the eye with the butt of a knife. The one who shot Rugley did have a bruised eye. The witnesses told us that after the shooting the two police had gone back into the hallway, where one of them most likely had punched the other in an effort to justify the shooter's claim that he was simply defending himself. We knew the story was bogus. We knew the knife story was bogus, too. The Cleveland police were in the habit of carrying what were called "drop knives." In police shootings of blacks, knives regularly appeared on or near the black person, planted there by the cops. One way or another knives were always in the picture. This fit the description perfectly.

Another element of the usual police modus operandi was that after something like this happened, they would go out and try to find past criminal behavior to create the impression that the victim had been a bad guy, capable of doing whatever they said he had done—to "dirty them up," we used to say. They desperately tried to find something on Rugley, but he turned out to be completely clean. Married, a good family man, gainfully employed for years. And now dead.

When the police prosecutor ruled the shooting a "justifiable homicide," we went to County Prosecutor John T. Corrigan demanding that he turn the case over to the grand jury. "I will not rest," I told the papers, "until I am satisfied that justice triumphs in this case." Corrigan did turn it over to the grand jury, which met and decided not to indict the detective who had killed Rugley. Justice was not only not satisfied; justice was, in my opinion, outraged. But again, as in the Dunn case, I had no recourse.

Nor did I have recourse in other cases. Police abuse of blacks was commonplace then. The *Call and Post* was filled with stories of police beatings, police breaking into people's homes and terrorizing them, police assaulting blacks demonstrating on orderly picket lines. When these incidents occurred I would take a team of lawyers with me to County Prosecutor Corrigan's office and demand indictments. But no matter how blatant the cases, Corrigan and the grand jury would never indict. It was a continual frustration.

In 1961, the year of the Rugley shooting, the U.S. Civil Rights Commission issued a special report on police brutality. In it, Cleveland was indicted along with other northern cities. Some of that brutality I witnessed firsthand in yet another situation that added to black people's litany of injustice in the city.

~~✑

By 1961 a long-festering crisis in Cleveland's school system was coming to a head. For a decade the city's black population had been growing steadily, due largely to what was called the Second Great Migration of blacks from the South. One consequence was that between the early 1950s and early 1960s Cleveland's minority school population increased dramatically. The city's already congested black neighborhoods became even more congested, and overcrowding in neighborhood schools reached unsupportable levels. The school board's response was to institute half-day classes in the worst affected black elementary schools. Half the school kids attended morning sessions and half attended afternoon sessions, a so-called relay system that played havoc with the children's education. At the same time, white elementary schools were often underutilized, with many empty classrooms.

In its 1954 *Brown* decision the Supreme Court had ruled that separate but equal was impermissible. Cleveland's schools were de facto segregated because of neighborhood residential patterns and they were starkly unequal. It's likely the Brown decision may have said more to black people than to white. For whites it meant the court had struck down de jure segregation in the South. But when the black community heard that separate but equal was unequal and illegal, it meant that the principle applied to children everywhere in the country, not just in the South with its Jim Crow laws. That had personal significance for the parents whose children were suffering under the relay program, and they began to protest. There was plenty of room in white schools. They demanded that black children be integrated into those schools.

After protracted negotiations and months of picketing by the relay parents, the school board finally agreed to bus the children to those underpopulated white schools. But instead of integrating them into the normal school routines, the black kids were kept isolated in special classrooms without access to school lunchrooms, regular recess periods, or after-school programs. They were simply bused in with their own teachers, taught in their own classrooms, then bused out.

As this treatment became known, anger at the school board ramped up. The NAACP along with CORE (Congress of Racial Equality), the Urban League, and other civil rights groups decided that a common front was needed to address the schooling and other issues, and the groups formed an umbrella, the United Freedom Movement. As the lead NAACP attorney, I was asked to provide legal representation, so I became counsel for the UFM as well.

As the school board delayed any action, making agreements, then breaking them, then restarting negotiations, the UFM started demanding system-wide integration as the only way to resolve the unconscionable disparities that existed throughout the segregated school system. Picketing had been under way on and off for a long time, at school sites and especially in front of the board of education building itself. I was one of the marchers there, along with other UFM leaders, and at one point we decided to raise the level of protest by sitting in inside the building itself as well as marching on the sidewalk. Many of the marchers went in. I didn't. I was sure that people would be arrested and that I would have to be available to get them out of jail.

That day UFM members were joined by young people who came into Cleveland from colleges all around Ohio, white as well as black. At the school department headquarters there was a full house of sit-ins; all three floors were lined with protestors, and when the police ordered them to leave they refused to go. When the protestors stayed put the police began throwing them out, literally, picking people up and throwing them down the stairwells, older people as well as students, women and men. Photographers who had managed to get in were able to take pictures, and the next day newspapers showed police manhandling protestors. It was an ugly scene. Demonstrators, some of them injured, were hauled off to jail and charged with trespassing and in some cases assault and battery on police for trying to protect themselves.

Such a crowd of people were arrested that my Redress Committee colleague Russell Adrine and I spent the better part of the next six months defending them in court where a special judge, Theodore Williams, was assigned to hear the cases. The activists didn't want to plead to anything. Their position was that they hadn't done anything wrong. They were being persecuted and prosecuted for nothing. They had done nothing illegal, they hadn't committed any crimes, and they just weren't going to plead guilty to any misdemeanors or felonies. That was the basis on which Russell and I tried those cases. Eventually we got every one of them acquitted, but it was a long, arduous affair.

Despite the police violence, we didn't bring suit against either any of the individual policemen or the department. When I think about it now, I don't recall that anybody ever discussed it with us. The thought never came up. For people involved in the civil rights movement, being brutalized was more or less a hazard of the profession.

From any objective viewpoint, the demands for fair educational treatment for black students were only reasonable. Yet for a span of years the Cleveland school board did its best to preserve what was in essence an insidious system that ensured that black children would be subjected to segregated, inferior conditions. Demonstrators in some places were victims of mob attacks. Police violence at the school board sit-in was shocking even to seasoned demonstrators.

Confrontations didn't always turn out that way, though. While the school conflict was revving up, I was walking the picket line in front of Cleveland Trust, one of America's biggest banks at the time. Cleveland Trust had never hired a single black teller, although many thousands of African Americans used the bank. Our position was that since black people used the bank, they should be hired to work there as well.

George Gund was Cleveland Trust's CEO and chairman, a man of great wealth and power. When we demanded a meeting with him we were told he was away, so we continued demonstrating. When he got back he saw the pickets in front of his bank.

"What's the problem?" he asked.

"They want to meet with you," he was told.

"So set it up," he said.

When our NAACP leadership group walked into his office, Gund turned to his people and said, "What do they want?"

"They want jobs," somebody told him.

"Well," Gund said, "hire them."

And that was that. Cleveland Trust hired black tellers throughout their many branches, and some years later the bank appointed Bertram Gardner as its first African American vice president.

These things could happen in an atmosphere of reason, years of discrimination cancelled, just like that. But there was precious little reason at work in the school crisis, which only deepened. Before long it turned deadly.

By early 1964, the time of the school board building picketing, the United Freedom Movement was pressing for citywide integration of Cleveland's schools. Over the five or six years of protests against overcrowding, half-day sessions, segregated relay students, and subpar education generally, the realization had struck home among African American parents that the only way to ensure equal education for their children was to bring black students together with white students throughout the system.

As calls for integration grew louder, the school board responded with a last-ditch plan to maintain the pattern of segregated schools. They began building several additional elementary schools in black neighborhoods—the intention being that these new facilities would alleviate crowding and allow the return of the children who were being bused to empty white classrooms back to their own 100 percent black schools.

When negotiations to roll back these plans proved fruitless, the UFM decided to picket the construction sites, one of which was in the Lakeview neighborhood in northeast Cleveland. On April 6, 1964, a hundred or so demonstrators gathered there to protest. As power shovels and bulldozers got to work excavating the foundation, one of the demonstrators broke out of the picket line and jumped in front of a dump tuck. As he was being dragged away by police, a dozen other protestors broke ranks and lay down in the path of construction vehicles.

One of these protestors was Bruce Klunder, a young, white Presbyterian minister working for the Christian Union at Western Reserve University. Klunder was an activist who had participated in restaurant sit-ins in the South. In Cleveland he had joined CORE and was one of the leaders in the UFM's opposition to the construction of these new "ghetto schools." As a group of protestors threw themselves in front of a bulldozer, Klunder lay down in a ditch behind it. The bulldozer operator stopped to avoid the people lying down in front of him and slowly backed up, right over Klunder's prone body. Klunder was killed instantly.

That night a memorial service for Klunder at Cory Methodist Church drew more than two thousand people. At the service CORE's president, Ruth Turner, called for a school boycott and the start of economic boycott of major white-owned businesses. A day was set for students to stay out of school and instead attend so-called freedom schools that would be set up in churches and community buildings.

Freedom school day took place two weeks after Klunder's death. Almost all of Cleveland's black students stayed out of their own schools and attended more than eighty freedom school sites, where the UFM had organized volunteer teachers and curriculum materials that centered on African American history and culture, subjects I had never been exposed to when I was a public school student and now, more than two decades later, were still nowhere to be found in the curriculum.

Ruth Turner (later Ruth Turner Perot) was a firebrand. A beautiful, young Oberlin graduate, her intelligence, her personality, her passion, and especially her militance made her a magnet for attention. Ruth was tough. She knew Cleveland's system from the inside—she had taught in high school. She didn't cut deals. She was a particularly painful thorn in the side of the school board.

Ruth was one of the protestors at the Lakeview construction site, and she was one of the UFM representatives who locked horns with Mayor Ralph Locher during the crisis. At one point she and a group of ministers went to Mayor Locher's office and were summarily shown out, which infuriated the black community. On that occasion Ruth had refused to leave and was arrested for trespassing. Along with the other cases I was handling I became Ruth's lawyer too and together with Russ Adrine managed to get her acquitted despite the city's determined effort to make life as hard as possible for her.

While Russell Adrine and I were defending the dozens and dozens of arrested protestors, I received a call from Bob Carter, the national NAACP's general counsel. For years Carter had been Thurgood Marshall's second-in-command at the Legal Defense Fund. He had never received the same kind of public attention as Marshall, but he had argued many of the southern antisegregation suits and was Marshall's chief deputy during the *Brown v. Board of Education* case at the Supreme Court. Carter was the architect of much of the Legal Defense Fund's strategy and was highly regarded for his intellectual weight as well as his courtroom skills. Among Marshall's inner circle he may have been the most radical.

On the telephone Carter told me he'd like to come to Cleveland to talk about bringing suit against the school board. The Legal Defense Fund had been following events here and thought the time had come to challenge the de facto segregation of schools in the North. Cleveland, he said, seemed the right place to start.

Carter came, and we decided to go ahead with a court challenge. We knew this would be a difficult case. It was one thing to strike down laws that mandated segregation in ways fundamentally violative of the Constitution's guarantee of equal protection. It was quite another to prove that a school board's actions were based on an *intent* to unconstitutionally enforce segregation. It was clear to us that this was exactly the case in Cleveland and that de facto segregation, with all its harmful concomitants, was just as pernicious as de jure segregation and should be considered equally illegitimate.

To pursue the case I put together a team of outstanding white and black attorneys, including Jack Day, Russell Adrine, and other members of the Legal Redress Committee. Together with Carter we drafted pleadings and filed suit on behalf of Charles and Daisy Craggett, parents of one of the elementary students who was being bused to a white school but would be returned to a segregated school in the event the new school construction went ahead. Daisy Craggett, one of the Relay Student Association parents, was, incidentally, the sister of George and Caldwell Gaffney, my neighbors across the street who had gotten me my first newspaper delivery job when I was twelve. George Gaffney had become an artist and Caldwell had gone on to become a renowned surgeon in Saint Louis. Daisy and her husband, Charles, were living in the Hough neighborhood, where Daisy was one of the community's best-known activists.

With Carter as lead we asked the court for an injunction to stop the new school construction, arguing that the proposed schools were part of the school department's strategy to perpetuate segregation by containing blacks and whites in racially separated schools according to neighborhood population patterns.

We argued the case in district court before Judge Girard Kalbfleisch. I didn't know Judge Kalbfleisch. I had never appeared before him and wasn't aware of any decisions he had been involved in concerning racial matters. We submitted briefs and in court Carter stood up to present our case. I was sitting at our table as second when Bob began his presentation, and I was shocked at Judge Kalbfleisch's open hostility and disrespect. Bob Carter had appeared in courts all over America. He had argued various times before the Supreme Court, winning all but one of his cases there. Later in his career he was appointed to a federal judgeship by Richard Nixon. He was a learned, distinguished attorney, and Kalbfleisch was treating him and our case in what I considered a blatantly racist manner, dismissive of both Carter personally and the arguments we had crafted.

Carter and Thurgood Marshall had argued in the Deep South in front of hard-core racist judges. I wondered if Judge Kalbfleisch's hostility was any different from what they had experienced there. I was stunned by it. Kalbfleisch treated Carter as if this were some southern town and Carter some inferior being who dared to stand up and try a lawsuit in his court. It was the most appalling racist performance I had ever seen in any courtroom since I had been a lawyer, and when the defense asked for dismissal Kalbfleisch threw our case out of court.

Craggett v. School Board was the first of the cases against northern school systems. Another ten years passed before an Ohio federal court ruled that the Cleveland schools were in fact guilty of consciously perpetrating segregated schooling in the city and had been guilty of it for many years, just as we had argued in our own attempt to prevent its perpetuation.

For the time being, that was the end of the school desegregation conflict. But it was hardly the end of frustration, resentment, and despair in Cleveland's black community. For leaders like Ruth Turner and Daisy Craggett, as for other more ordinary citizens, living conditions in the ghetto were less and less tolerable. The lack of jobs and health care, the absence of essential social services, the ongoing victimization by police, the general perception of black disenfranchisement and white entitlement fed a growing undercurrent of anger. On July 18, 1966, the anger boiled over.

I'm not sure anyone knows exactly what triggered it. What I heard was that in the bar at Seventy-Ninth and Hough, a white bar in the very center of Cleveland's almost all-black Hough neighborhood, an African American individual had walked in and asked for a glass of water, which was refused. Some accounts said that the bar then posted a sign, "No Water for Niggers." Whatever the proximate cause, a confrontation started between the bar people and a small crowd of locals. The police were called, the conflict escalated, and in short order a full-blown riot was spreading through the area.

That evening Carl came by, urgency written on his face. We were still practicing law together, but his legal work was by then a minor part of his professional life. Four years earlier Carl had been elected to the Ohio House of Representatives, the first black Democrat ever to serve in the state legislature. He had even run for mayor of Cleveland the previous year and had just missed getting elected.

"Lou," he said, "I want you to ride with me. We've got to go over to Hough and see what's going on there."

When we got to Hough it was early evening. Fires were raging, flames leaping out of storefronts and billowing up into the darkening sky. Firemen were doing their best to fight them, but there were too many pockets of fire for them to handle. Police cars were everywhere, lights flashing and sirens wailing. As we got out of our car we heard shots ringing out above the police sirens and the crackle of flames. The shooting seemed to be coming from all around. People were in the streets, running and shouting. We were in the middle of bedlam.

Many people knew Carl; he was their legislator. Some knew me as well. As we started walking people came up to talk to us, sometimes one at a time, sometime in little knots. They wanted to tell us what was happening to them. They needed somebody to hear them. They talked about police brutality, the most recent incidents that were making the rounds: police bursting into the wrong homes, rousting people out of bed, how the police had forced one sleeping couple to parade around in front of them naked. They told us about how white owners treated them in the local stores, about rotten meat and moldy vegetables, about how they couldn't find jobs and couldn't feed their families. An endless litany was coming at us as we walked all the way through Hough up to 105th, burning and shooting and looting raging all around us.

The next day the National Guard arrived. Lines of jeeps and military trucks, half tracks with guns mounted. For several days and nights the riots continued. Four people were killed, others wounded. Many hundreds were arrested. Homes and businesses had sustained millions of dollars' worth of damage.

I thought that something had to be done. People had to have some avenue to express themselves, to tell their own stories of Hough, its problems, of what had happened to them personally. Stanley Tolliver, a longtime civil rights and criminal defense lawyer, was CORE's attorney. Stanley called himself a "ghetto lawyer." He was a fearless person; the previous year he had gone down to Mississippi to take on cases there in very dangerous circumstances. Stanley and I talked about the situation and decided we would hold hearings to let people describe what had happened.

We did that for three nights at the Liberty Baptist Church on Euclid Avenue. One after another, people testified about things they had seen. They described what living conditions in Hough were like and what they had experienced in their lives. Already the newspapers were reporting that the riots had been precipitated by agitators, communists who had infiltrated from the outside to foment violence. But at Liberty Baptist we heard nothing about outside agitators, only stories of deprivation, hard lives, police brutality, neglect, rotten food, exorbitant prices, and callousness and hostility from the city and its agencies.

Not long after our hearings, Cleveland's City Club invited me to speak. The City Club was and still is one of the great forums of free speech, famous as a place where speakers of every persuasion from all over the world came to talk about significant regional, national, and international issues, the speeches followed by no-holds-barred question and answer sessions.

By then the pain of what had happened in Hough was exacerbated by a formal report by a county grand jury. The grand jury was chaired by Louis Seltzer, the owner of the *Cleveland Press,* the primary newspaper that had been writing about the supposed role of outside agitators in precipitating the riots. The grand jury report concluded similarly that communist infiltrators had exploited the despair in the neighborhood and had instigated and organized the violence. The report gave short shrift to the poverty, police brutality, lack of jobs, lack of housing, lack of health care, all the elements that in reality had fed the anger that exploded so catastrophically. No, the riots were caused by infiltrators from the outside. FBI director J. Edgar Hoover was just then claiming that Martin Luther King Jr. was himself a victim of communist influence, the underlying idea being that a black man, evidently, was not capable of thinking for himself. He had to have a white man tell him what to do. In our case it was the white communist infiltrators, according to the report, who were telling people to go out and riot.

The Hough community did not need an additional disaster heaped upon them by this disservice of a grand jury report, I told the City Club audience. We didn't need the charge that Cleveland's blacks had to have communists to tell them it was time to riot, people who had reached the depths of despair without needing any outsiders to tell them that.

I talked about the conditions, the explosiveness that had built up; I tried to do it in measured, even-tempered language, even though I wasn't feeling measured or even-tempered. CORE spokesman Baxter Hill, who followed me to the podium, was less restrained. "By your failure to act," he told the City Club's mostly upscale audience, "you are equally responsible. The problems are still unanswered! The bricks and bottles have stopped being thrown, but the riot is still going on."

Baxter Hill was dead right about that.

CHAPTER 6

Two Brothers

Mayor and Congressman

THE ONE angry argument Carl and I ever had took place some time after we started our law firm, Stokes and Stokes. At the time Carl had also been appointed as a municipal court prosecutor, which meant that first of all he was only working part time for Stokes and Stokes and second, because of his prosecutor's job he was only able to handle civil cases. On top of that, he was using the office for meeting after meeting with people coming in to work on political races for city council and other positions and using our secretary for the typing and clerical work that went along with those things.

Carl was paying his half of the office expenses, but I was carrying the firm. You could hardly even say that Carl was practicing law. Eventually I confronted him about it. "We're in a law practice here," I told him, "but you're not really doing law business. You're just doing political work."

"Well, I don't have any legal business," he said. "But I'm also paying half the rent up here. So I can use my office for whatever I want to use it for. I'm paying for it, so I can use it."

I thought about it. He was right. He was paying half the rent. Of course he could do what he wanted. But at the same time I was disappointed. I thought we would be building a practice together. The two of us, Stokes and Stokes.

Years later I told him, "I saw us as having the best black law firm any-where in the country. That was my dream."

"Lou," he said, "the problem was that you never shared that dream with me."

I came to understand that politics was Carl's life. My dream was the law, but Carl was bound and determined to serve in public office. The best thing for me to do, as his brother, was to understand that while I loved being in the courtroom trying cases, that was not his strength, not his own love. Carl was a good lawyer; he knew how to try a case. But he didn't love the law. His heart and life were in politics. I realized that if we were going to be compatible, I had to let him follow his path, just as I was following mine.

Carl had begun pursuing his political bent early on, picking up his first lessons from perhaps the most remarkable black civil rights leader in Ohio history, John O. Holly.

John O. Holly came to Cleveland from Tuscaloosa, Alabama, via Roanoke, Virginia, and Detroit. He had worked in the coal mines as a teenager and as a truck driver, porter, and factory hand later on. But both black and white Cleveland got to know who he really was in the mid-1930s when he established the Future Outlook League, an organization that fought for black betterment in ways that preceded Martin Luther King's efforts by twenty years.

Holly was a fiery little man, no more than five foot five or six. But he was an explosive, powerful speaker, a dynamic orator able to sway crowds and move people to action. Holly spoke out for what he believed in, and what he most believed in was opening opportunities for black people.

In the 1930s, when Holly started the Future Outlook League, whites owned almost all the stores in Cleveland's black neighborhoods. Most of these were small businesses, many of them mom-and-pop operations. But the people who owned the stores didn't live in the black community, and they only employed members of their families or other white employees. None of them would hire blacks.

Black residents were dependent on these stores, but Holly's theory was—You should not be spending your money in places where you can't work. He started boycotts of these stores, including the big multistall market at Fifty-Fifth and Woodlyn, putting together picket lines manned by people carrying signs that said "Don't Buy Where You Can't Work." And he got arrested for it, not once but many times. Then, when he was released he'd go right out there again.

Eventually he got the stores integrated. You began to see black faces behind the counters. Then he moved against bigger targets. Cleveland at that time had no black bus drivers in the entire public transportation system.

Holly boycotted the buses and was jailed for that, but in time they opened up and began hiring black drivers. I was a kid then, but I remember it well.

Then there was the Ohio Bell Telephone Company. Bell had many women switchboard operators, but none of them were black. Holly picketed the phone company, and he broke them down. First they hired two or three black women, then more. The first was Artha Woods, who later became a Cleveland city councilwoman. At Ohio Bell she retired many years later as the company's public relations manager. An entrepreneurial person, Artha also owned a millinery shop, making couture dresses and hats. With so few black models available, she started her own pioneering modeling school. My wife Jay trained there.

After opening up the Cleveland Transit System and Ohio Bell, John Holly turned his attention to the May Company department stores and made them hire black women elevator operators. Long before there was a Martin Luther King Jr., here was this little dark-skinned African American man in Cleveland who was breaking down all these barriers. It's not possible to say how many people found employment because of John O. Holly, but it was a large number. Even more significantly, his efforts permanently opened what was in so many areas a closed employment scene for Cleveland's black community.

Holly's Future Outlook League wielded power. Everyone who got a job through the League joined as a dues-paying member. Holly set up a board of directors consisting of community people, women as well as men, so there was a general feeling of belonging. He had political ambitions, too. At one point he ran for city council, then in 1954 he attempted to gain the Democratic nomination for the House of Representatives. Holly was probably the first black to even think about running for Congress. He lost, but he ran. And in doing so he created political waves.

In 1947 Holly was organizing around the state for Frank Lausche's third run for governor. Lausche, a well-liked Democrat, had served one term then lost to Republican Thomas Herbert. In 1947 he was running again. Just back from his two years of college in West Virginia, Carl got a job driving Holly around on his visits to Ohio's various black Democratic constituencies. Carl would drive Holly from city to city and help him with whatever tasks had to be done for his meetings. Carl listened as Holly talked to him about how things were done and watched him in action during his meetings. He learned how Holly set up local organizations, whom he went to for support, and why, and what kinds of people he stayed away from. Carl absorbed lessons in how to generate grassroots support and how to leverage minority backing in a white majority race, lessons that stayed with him when he began running for office himself.

Carl's first political run came in 1960 when he very nearly won the Democratic district primary for state representative. Two years later he did become the nominee and went on to win in the general election, becoming the first black Democrat to ever hold a seat in the Ohio legislature. Then in 1965 he ran for mayor.

Carl's campaign for mayor was groundbreaking. For years there had been blacks on the city council, but no African American had ever had any kind of chance to be mayor. In those days even the thought of it seemed outlandish. Cleveland was a white majority city, with powerful ethnic groups that had for many years controlled the political machinery and harbored deep-seated antiblack prejudices. But Carl wasn't afraid to court their votes, and he was a smart, articulate, energetic person with a firm grasp of the issues. For many whites he was a revelation. As he put it, "they may have disliked Negroes, but they didn't dislike Carl Stokes."

It also happened that Martin Luther King Jr. came to Cleveland that year on a voter registration drive. King brought his lieutenants with him—Andy Young, Jesse Jackson, Walter Fauntroy, and others. They moved through the black neighborhoods on a long platform truck that pulled up on the corner of 105th and Carnegie, 105th and Superior, all through the community, King standing on the back of the platform giving speeches and exhorting the crowds to register and vote.

King's drive was separate and apart from Carl's campaign; there was no coordination between them. But black people registered as they never had before, and we all knew who those newly registered voters were going to help.

Carl ran that year as an independent. His opponent was the incumbent mayor, Ralph Locher, whose tenure had seen a dramatic worsening of black/white relations. In the event, Carl lost to Locher by two thousand votes. But that demonstrated for us that he was capable of winning. Despite King's efforts, black people weren't used to an African American running for mayor. To many the idea seemed strange, and they shied away from getting involved. But given the fact that Carl so nearly won, everyone agreed that if he ran for mayor again he'd have an excellent chance of getting elected.

Carl was thinking about that, but he had other aspirations, too. He had established a strong base in the largely black Twenty-First Congressional District. His run for mayor had given him significant name recognition throughout the city. Carl was thinking about the next mayor's race, but the congressional seat was even more attractive to him. The Twenty-First District had never elected a black; the traditional black political psychology had mandated against it. But now, with the civil rights struggle uniting people and the growing sense that blacks deserved not only equal rights but also political power, the stars were aligning differently. The Twenty-First District congressional seat might be well within reach for a black candidate—that is, within Carl's reach. There was only one problem.

In 1964 the Supreme Court had decided that Ohio's congressional districts needed to be redrawn. The redistricting was in the hands of the Ohio legislature, which in essence meant that it was in the hands of the Republican and Democratic Party leaders. And when it became known that Carl had his eye on the seat, they took action to thwart him by gerrymandering the district. When the new districts were promulgated, the former black majority Twenty-First had been carved up so that the district's voters were distributed throughout the county, thoroughly diluting black voting power. With the black vote subsumed within white districts, neither Carl nor any other black candidate would have the base necessary to win a campaign.

Carl was more than upset about this, for good reason, and he led a spirited fight in the legislature to block the new districting. When he lost and the redrawn plans became law, he came to the Cleveland NAACP and asked if we could file a suit on his behalf. The NAACP then turned Carl's case over to me and the Legal Redress Committee.

When we investigated the facts, we determined that in their desire to stop Carl running for Congress from a black base, the legislature had indeed redrawn the district in an illegal manner. In our calculations, had the district been configured along "one man, one vote" contiguous lines as was required by law, a constitutionally redrawn district would have come out 65 percent black. Consequently, we filed suit before the federal district court, which appointed a three-judge panel to hear the case: *Lucas v. Rhodes*. Charles Lucas, our plaintiff, was the NAACP's former president, and Rhodes, of course, the governor. One of the panel judges was Anthony Celebrezze, who had been Cleveland's mayor, then HEW secretary under Presidents Kennedy and Johnson. The second was district judge James Connell. Interestingly, the third was Girard Kalbfleisch, the judge who had thrown out our suit against Cleveland's segregated schools.

Harry Lehman was instrumental in putting this case together. Harry was a leading Cleveland trial attorney, a member of our Legal Redress Committee and later a state legislator. He wrote the trial briefs and took the lead in arguing the case. We thought we had a good chance to win and would have won, had it not been for a truly bizarre occurrence. After the three judges had come to their decision but before they issued it, Jim Naughton, the chief political writer for the *Cleveland Plain Dealer*, was told (possibly off the record) by one of the justices' clerks that the decision was two to one in our favor. The panel had decided to strike down the legislature's redistricting. The Twenty-First would remain intact, which meant that Carl would be able to run for Congress with assurance.

The whole political and legal community was anxiously awaiting this decision, and the next day Naughton published an article, "Court to Upset Districting," announcing what the panel had decided. Needless to say, the disclosure outraged the three judges, and after conferring again Judge Kalbfleisch decided to change his vote. Instead of winning the case two to one, we had now lost by the same vote.

We filed the original suit in May 1965. The three-judge panel issued its ruling two years later, on May 10, 1967. It had taken them that long. In his heart, Carl wanted to run for that congressional seat in the 1968 election, but on the other hand the deadline for filing for the 1967 mayoral election was coming up fast. When he and I had lunch with Harry Lehman a few days after the ruling came down, Carl had two questions. Because the case had been heard in front of a federal panel, we would be able to appeal directly to the Supreme Court. If we did that, what did Harry think about our chances of winning there? When he said he thought they were excellent, we asked what kind of time frame he thought might be likely. Twelve to eighteen months, he said.

Harry was mistaken about that. It took the Supreme Court less than eight months to render a per curiam verdict reversing the three-judge panel, declaring the new district boundaries null and void and requiring a constitutionally valid redrawing of the lines. That happened at the beginning of January 1968. Of course Carl hadn't waited for that. He had thrown his hat into the mayor's race, and this time he had won. Not by much, but he had won.

Carl and I were still technically practicing law together when he was in the state legislature. Our original firm, Stokes and Stokes, had become Minor, Stokes and Stokes when Norman Minor asked us to join him. Then in 1966 Carl and I came together with a group of other black attorneys and formed Stokes, Stokes, Character, Terry, Perry, Whitehead, Young and Davidson. We moved into downtown offices, at 75 Public Square, the center of Cleveland's legal and business district, an area where a dozen years earlier no black lawyer could have dreamed of renting space. Each of the lawyers we brought with us into our new firm was a top specialist in one field or another. I saw this as the beginning, not of one of the top black law firms in Cleveland, but of one of the best law firms in the country, period. Carl was a partner but in fact did little legal work. I had adjusted to that long ago. I was just happy to have him with me.

There had never been any sibling rivalry between Carl and me; on the contrary, we had grown up as closest companions and allies. Then, although we both became lawyers, our paths had diverged, so we were not building our names in the same arena. He was going in a direction I had no interest in going myself. As a result, I was happy to help him in every way I could. So that's what I did. In his campaigns, if he needed me to go somewhere to speak on his behalf, I did. If he had too many meetings, I would go to some for him. There were a couple of occasions when he asked me to get involved in other people's campaigns where that would be helpful to him; John Glenn's first campaign for the Senate was one of those, and his second campaign also. There were others as well. I helped motivate supporters, I gave a speech here and there, whatever Carl thought might be beneficial.

I played that kind of minor role in Carl's own campaigns, in addition to providing whatever moral support I could. I was, simply, proud of Carl. He had the intelligence, the drive, and the charisma to go far in politics. I saw that, but I was hardly alone. Carl was a dynamic political presence. People were keeping their eyes on him.

Carl had run for mayor in 1965 almost by accident. His campaign had started with a Draft Carl Stokes movement that organized a petition drive to get him on the ballot as an independent. By 1967 he was a far more seasoned politician. He knew how to put together a political organization, and he strategized carefully with both white and black advisers on how to maximize the black vote and make inroads on the white. In the Democratic primary he trounced his former opponent, Ralph Locher.

In the general election Carl faced a far more formidable adversary, Seth Taft, scion of one of the country's most prominent political families, nephew of "Mr. Republican" Senator Robert Taft and grandson of President and Supreme Court Chief Justice William Howard Taft. For every observer, personally involved or not, it was an interesting race. The grandson of a president, the epitome of the WASP establishment, versus the great-grandson of a slave and graduate of Cleveland's housing projects and street corners.

In 1967 Martin Luther King Jr. came back to Cleveland and launched the same kind of voter registration drive he had done two years earlier. Jesse Jackson also came and got involved in Carl's campaign. King's presence especially was a double-edged sword, energizing the black community but also providing ammunition to the other side, aggravating white hostility and anxieties. During the primary, Democratic Party chairman Albert Porter had played on white fears. "Will Carl Stokes' election mean that Martin Luther King will be mayor?" he had asked. Seth Taft himself was above such things, but the fears were real and Carl knew that King's presence was going to exacerbate them.

Around ten o'clock the night before the vote, I stopped by Carl's house just to see how he was holding up. He was in the kitchen.

"I just came by to check on you, see how you're doing," I said. "See if there's anything else you think I might help you with."

"Lou, there's nothing else we can do. I've gone everywhere and done everything you can do in an election. Now it's up to the people."

On election night I was in the offices of Carl's campaign headquarters in the Rockefeller Building with Carl and his circle of people. Dr. King and Reverend Ralph Abernathy had joined us there as we watched the vote count come in. All the newspapers and pundits had said the race was going to be neck and neck, but as the night went on Taft took a lead that looked like it might be insurmountable. The last wave of votes, though, would be coming in from the black wards. The tension was almost unbearable. Then, a little before three o'clock in the morning, the official tally was announced. Carl had won by 1,700 votes.

That moment delirium struck. What had happened was historic; we all knew it. We felt it. Down outside the building the streets were suddenly thronged with people literally dancing for joy. We could hear the shouting for Carl to come down. People were overcome with happiness, laughing, some of them crying. Everyone wanted to see him.

Carl told me that he, his campaign manager—Dr. Ken Clement—and the others were going to go down. But would I please stay here in the offices with Dr. King? Which meant that Dr. King was not going to be with him on the podium when he gave his victory speech. I was sure they had decided that together. This was an immense victory for black people. Nothing like it had ever happened before in American history. But Carl wanted the symbolism to be clear; this mayor's race was not a civil rights struggle, it was the campaign of someone who deserved the office because of his qualifications. Carl was the new mayor of all of Cleveland's people, not just the city's black citizens. So he went down to give his speech, and I sat upstairs with Dr. King.

While Carl and his entourage went off to face the delirious crowds, Dr. King and I sat together, talking about what Carl's victory meant to the country and how proud he was to see Carl achieve this, what it meant to have this kind of political progress as we marched forward for full equality. He said that along with political equality we had to do what every other ethnic group that has acquired parity in this society had done: we had to achieve economic equality. "No ethnic group," he said, "has been able to achieve parity here without both political and economic equality."

I did go downstairs a little later. Superior Avenue was still crowded with people celebrating. Somebody ran up to me, a man I knew from the neighborhood.

"Lou! Lou! Do you know what this means to me!"

"Tell me, what does it mean?"

"It means that for the first time in my life I can tell my son he can be anybody he wants to be."

Carl's victory wasn't just national news, it was international news. His picture was on the covers of *Time, Newsweek,* and a dozen other American and foreign publications. America had elected its first black mayor of a major city. It was a stunning event. The civil rights movement had been burning for more than a decade, bringing with it terrible tragedies as well as historic victories. Carl's election was a huge triumph; it seemed like a sign, maybe a turning point. Cleveland had been the scene of such angry racial conflict, and if Cleveland could achieve this who knew what the future might hold in store? Carl was being seen as a pioneer of black political progress. Serious people were already starting to talk about the possibility of running Carl as the vice presidential candidate.

I felt immense pride in Carl, that he was the mayor, and that he was my brother. But meanwhile I was back at Stokes, Stokes, Character, Terry, Perry, Young and Davidson hoping to continue building my own dream. But I was facing headwinds. Carl Character, an outstanding trial attorney who was heading up our civil litigation department, was appointed to a judgeship in the Court of Common Pleas. James Terry, an expert in transportation law, became the transportation commissioner for Saint Louis, Missouri. Samuel Perry was elected the mayor of Woodmere, a little town just outside Cleveland. We were losing people right and left. And now Carl was gone as well.

I began to sense that Carl's election was going to create changes in my
life, too, whether I wanted it or not. Once Carl became mayor people started
trying to get to me since they couldn't get to him directly, the idea being that
if they got to me, whatever their problem or request was would also get to
him. One morning I was in my office preparing for a murder case, when a
lady called. I answered the phone, and she asked for Carl Stokes. I explained
that he had now been elected mayor, so he was no longer a member of the
firm.

"I'm his brother. Is there anything I can do for you?"

"Well, these people out here have shut off my gas."

"They shut off your gas?"

"Yes."

"Madam, let me ask you a question. Have you paid your gas bill?"

"That ain't got nothin' to do with it. Mr. Stokes isn't going to let them cut
off my gas!"

That was how he was perceived. Notwithstanding whether or not she had
paid her bill, Carl Stokes was not going to let anybody cut off her gas, and I
was supposed to get him the message.

Two months after the mayoral election the Supreme Court issued its
verdict in *Lucas v. Rhodes,* mandating the integrity of the Twenty-First
District. I called Carl and told him we had just been advised that the case
was remanded and the district court was instructed to redraw along constitutional and contiguous lines. "This means you can go to Congress," I told
him.

"Go to Congress?" he said. "I'm mayor of Cleveland!"

I began laughing. Suddenly Carl no longer had any interest in going to
Congress. He was the mayor, blazing a trail in America's political life.

When word got out that even though we had won his case Carl was no
longer interested, it seemed that almost every politician in town decided that
this was his time to go to Congress. Most of them knew that I had absolutely no interest in a political career, so they didn't think I would run. And
even if I did run, they were veteran politicians. I was no politician at all, so
they wouldn't have to worry about any candidacy on my part.

They weren't wrong. I was perfectly content with practicing the law. I
was in some judge's courtroom every day trying a case. As far as I was concerned, that was the way I wanted to spend the rest of my life. I intended
to pursue my career and rebuild the firm, a big challenge now that we had
lost so many people. So that was where I stood, watching the scramble and

the emerging strong men: George Forbes, Leo Jackson, and George White, each of them an experienced, elected black official with high visibility in the community.

Those of us on the executive board of the Cleveland NAACP branch were in the habit of getting together for breakfast on Sunday mornings to talk about problems in the community. As the district's political situation was heating up, our discussion one morning centered around the different individuals who were announcing they were going to run.

As the discussion continued someone said, "Well, none of them had anything to do with the suit that created the district. You did, Lou. You ought to consider running yourself."

"No," I said, "I'm not really interested."

"Well, it should be either you or Dr. Clement."

Dr. Kenneth Clement was a renowned black physician who was highly respected in both the black and white communities, a professor of surgery at Case Western Reserve Medical School and very active in black community issues. He had been Carl's campaign manager. He was sitting in at breakfast with us.

The discussion continued about either me or Dr. Clement—Kenny to all of us—running.

I said, "Well, I'd certainly yield to Kenny. Kenny, if this is something you want to do, I don't have any problem with it. I'll step aside."

Someone finally said, "We need to go see Carl, let him help us decide whether Kenny or Lou should run."

Clement and Carl were very close, although they had a falling out later. Clement had run Carl's two mayoral campaigns. So even though he was a distinguished surgeon, politics was in his blood.

My own political relationship with Carl, as I've explained, was fairly simple. I occasionally appeared for him at some meeting or other if he was unable to make it, the theory being that if Carl couldn't be there, people's disappointment would be assuaged if at least his brother came. That was basically it.

But as we headed over to Carl's house I was thinking hard about this turn of events. I didn't have any political ambitions; I never had had any. On the other hand, whoever was elected here was going to be the first black Ohioan ever to serve in Congress. Carl's election was historic; this was going to be historic, too. It began to dawn on me that as much as I loved the law, this would be a higher calling to reach for. I didn't know exactly how many blacks were serving in Congress, maybe four or five—anyway, a very small handful.

What a challenge it would be to join them, and what an opportunity. All of a sudden I found myself completely caught up in the moment. And I started thinking about what it might mean for Shelley and Angie and Chuck and Lori to be the children of a U.S. congressman. Maybe this is something I would want to do after all. I started thinking, Why not?

So we left the restaurant and went directly to Carl's house where we presented him with the situation. The NAACP felt that either I should run, since I was directly responsible for the lawsuit that created the district, or that Kenny should.

Carl thought about it a moment, then asked Kenny to go into the kitchen with him. The two of them stayed in there for almost an hour while the rest of us sat in the living room chatting.

When they finally came out, Carl said, "Lou is our candidate."

"Well," I said, "I've got to go home and talk to Jay and the family about it. This whole thing just started at breakfast this morning."

"Of course you've got to talk to Jay," said Carl. "But assuming everything goes okay, we have to get Arnold Pinkney to run your campaign."

Arnold was part of our group; he was sitting right there with us. I turned to him.

"Arnold, what about it?"

Arnold Pinkney had an acute political mind, actually an acute mind period. After college he had become a highly successful insurance agent for Prudential, in fact Prudential's first African American agent. After that he opened his own agency, Pinkney Perry Insurance, which became the city's largest African American insurance company. We all bought our insurance from him. But like Ken Clement, Arnold also had politics in his blood. He had worked for Carl on both his campaigns. He had managed successful campaigns for two Cleveland judges. Later in his career he would go on to become Hubert Humphrey's deputy campaign manager. In 1984 he managed Jesse Jackson's presidential run. Jesse won primaries in several southern states; Arnold was the mastermind behind that. He was an absolutely first-rate strategist.

"Lou," Arnold said, "I have to discuss it with Betty [his wife]. I've promised her I wasn't going to take any more campaigns. She's up in Michigan with her family now, but I have to talk with her."

I went to leave; I was eager to sit down with Jay about all this. But before I did Carl said, "Lou, with George Forbes and Leo and George White running, we've got to get W. O. Walker to support you. You've got to get to W. O. right away."

W. O. Walker was the owner and editor-in-chief of the *Call and Post*. If there was a kingmaker in Cleveland's black community, W. O. Walker was it. But first I had to discuss it with Jay and the children.

It was still Sunday morning, so everyone was at home. We all sat in the living room and talked it over, that is, Jay and I talked it over while the children sat and listened. Jay said, "Honey, you know I support whatever you want to do. If this is what you want to do, I support you in it. You let me alone to take care of the kids. You know how I feel about speaking in public and those kinds of things. But if you really need me, I'll be there."

With that I went to see W. O. Walker.

W. O. Walker, known in the community simply as W. O., was at home. We sat together as I described the discussions that had taken place about Ken Clement and myself, and what Carl's decision was. I told him that Carl had suggested I see him right away.

W. O. gave it some thought. "I'll support you," he said. "But we also have to have somebody on the Republican side who can take care of this community in the event something untoward happens to you. I have to have a Republican to support if you go down for some reason. That person would be Charlie Lucas."

"Great," I said. "Charlie would be an excellent candidate to have on the other side."

I wasn't kidding. Charlie Lucas would have served the community well. He had been NAACP president earlier on. He had been a school principal and a member of the state board of education. He was a leader in the fight for fair housing. Charlie was one of the best speakers I'd ever heard—articulate, knowledgeable, always well prepared. A man of great dignity, highly respected. Like me, he had never run for office, but he had the kind of stature where he could run and be accepted. Charlie had been our plaintiff in *Lucas v. Rhodes*. And now, according to W. O. anyway, he was going to serve as my opponent in the congressional race—assuming, of course, that I could get through the primary.

Shortly after W. O. pledged his support, Arnold Pinkney got back to me. He told me that his wife, Betty, had said, "Arnold, I did tell you not to do any more campaigns, but if this is for Lou Stokes, you've got to do it." With that, Arnold came on board as my campaign manager.

Not long after the Supreme Court ruling came down, the legislature revamped the district boundaries and we launched into the primary campaign—myself, George Forbes, George White, Leo Jackson, and ten others. Of the other three leaders it was generally thought that Leo Jackson was the strongest and would be my nemesis, but the two Georges also had their own constituencies and they too were going to be hard campaigners.

Right after I announced, George Forbes called and asked if I'd have breakfast with him. George was at that time a councilman and very close to Carl at City Hall (he later became council president). Whatever political business Carl needed done in council, he'd go to George, a wily politician who knew all the ins and outs of city government. The two of them worked hand in glove.

When George asked me for breakfast I said, "Sure." Over our bacon and eggs George looked at me. "Lou," he said, "you've never run for public office, have you?"

"No, I haven't, George."

"Lou, I want to tell you something. There is no possible way for you to win."

I didn't know what to say. George was a formidable opponent, a veteran politician, telling me I couldn't win. I didn't say anything.

I went to Carl afterward. I was a novice at this. Maybe I *was* in over my head. Maybe this was just pie in the sky.

"Listen," I said. "I had breakfast with George Forbes. George says I can't win."

"Lou, George is a politician. He said that to make you *think* you can't win. You can't listen to George Forbes!"

One of my aides was Sam Tidmore, a former star linebacker for the Cleveland Browns. Sam was a fun guy. He loved being in the campaign, being a part of things. In campaigns you go to ward meetings, you make your pitch at these places.

On one particular night Arnold Pinkney said, "We're going to George Forbes's ward meeting."

"We're going where?" I was a little startled. "You want us to go to George Forbes's ward meeting?"

George was the head of the Democratic Club in his ward. "We're going to George's meeting?"

Tidmore was all for it. If there was any kind of confrontation in store, he was for it.

George Forbes's brother Zeke met Arnold, Sam, and me at the door. He looked at us, nonplussed. "What do you guys want?"

Arnold said, "We want Lou to speak."

"Man," said Zeke, "this is *George's* ward meeting."

"Well," said Arnold, "we're a candidate. We want to speak."

Zeke shook his head, took a moment. "Let me talk to George. I'll come back."

We stood at the door while Zeke went down front to talk to George. I was thinking, Carl and George are working together every day. Carl's supporting me, and George is my opponent. What in the world is going to happen here?

Zeke came back. "Okay," he said, "you can speak."

I gave a little speech, making complimentary remarks about George, of course. Then I headed to the door where Arnold and Tidmore were waiting. Zeke showed us out, still shaking his head. "You guys have a lot of nerve," he said. "A *lot* of nerve."

To outsiders it might have seemed a little odd. George was probably Carl's closest political associate. Yet Carl was supporting me. You'd think that might have strained their relationship. But they were two astute politicians. They understood. This was politics. It didn't faze them. They just kept doing business as usual. After I won, George and I stayed good friends and allies as well. He was the first to congratulate me on the victory stand.

Leo Jackson, though, was a rough type of politician. At one point he challenged me about some case or other that I had represented. I was a defense lawyer; I had defended some highly questionable people. When Leo attacked me on that I told the audience, "I'm proud of that fact. I'm a criminal defense lawyer. I represent a lot of people charged with crimes. I'm the kind of lawyer who protects the Constitution of the United States. I protect civil rights. I do it through people who are not quite like you and me, people who get involved with the law. But that's how I protect *your* rights, by protecting *their* rights." People always accepted that.

But Leo was tough. He was in city council, very vociferous. He attracted a lot of attention by taking controversial stands on things. Like George Forbes, his fellow councilman, he was a character, but Leo was quite the fiery character.

I was in a good position, though, versus both Leo and George, and George White as well. I was well known among the middle class and professionals, the lawyers and doctors, the teachers and business people. I also had a solid reputation with the grassroots, the radicals and activists along with the more moderate people. I had walked picket lines. I had represented CORE's feisty, outspoken president Ruth Turner and Hough's stand-up community leader, Daisy Craggett. Only a year or so earlier I had also won a case for the black militant Harllel Jones.

Harllel was a controversial figure, a black nationalist, one of the founders of the Jomo Kenyatta Freedom House, a youth center that taught black pride, sold African-themed clothing, sponsored a drill team, and generally made white people nervous. The Cleveland police feared and hated Harllel, and he didn't have any love for them, either. Some years later they accused and convicted him of murder on the basis of false evidence. He served time for that in Lucasville Penitentiary before a judge released him when it was brought to his attention that Jones had been framed.

Harllel was an interesting mix, a natural leader, a hard, defiant individual, but at the same time mild and thoughtful, a reasonable person to deal with. Carl and I recognized him for what he was, a leader of a segment in the black community. We both had good relationships with him.

Harllel and his JKF House colleague, Lewis Robinson, had been accused by the police of being instigators of the Hough riots, along with the outside "communist infiltrators." The fact was that during the riots Harllel had worked to calm the angry young people who were doing most of the damage. After the riots the police tried to frame him on a malicious vandalism charge. Somebody (or somebodies) had splashed black paint on statuary and plaques at the Cleveland Cultural Gardens, a collection of gardens each honoring the city's various ethnic communities: Poles, Italians, Slovenes, Finns, Germans, and others, maybe seventeen or eighteen in all at that time—though no African American garden. Harllel and four others were arrested. I defended Harllel and won the case on a hung jury (three others were also acquitted).

The case received heated publicity because of its racial nature. When the verdict was announced the *Call and Post* ran a big front-page picture of Harllel, me, and some of the other defense attorneys, including our Redress Committee's Harold Weinstein, who had been my co-counsel. Harllel said in an interview that the trial's outcome had given him faith in the American judicial system like nothing else had in all his experience.

Harllel was charged with this crime not long after the riots. The jury finally returned its verdict in late January 1968, just as the Democratic primary was kicking off. The publicity it generated further strengthened my standing with the more alienated element in the community.

Still, I was a novice. I had no experience. When they speak of "running scared," I was running scared. We were doing everything to win, but I had no feel for what the outcome might be. Everywhere I looked it seemed that Leo Jackson or one of the others had some kind of big sign. I had one billboard, that was it, and somebody gave us that. It was on the side of the building where my campaign office was. My opponents were everywhere, all over the district, and all those signs seemed to be saying something. I felt threatened. I thought, how much support do those guys have? It looked like they had much more than I did.

I complained to Carl that Leo Jackson and the others had all those signs. We needed more signs.

"Take it easy, Lou," Carl said. "Signs don't vote. People vote."

Of course, it was very helpful to me that my brother was mayor and had generated all the national and international attention he had. And Carl put his political organization behind my campaign. They got literature to the right homes, they had access to ward leaders, precinct captains, political workers who would get people out of their houses, take them to the polls, tell them whom to vote for. Carl's machine could do all that kind of stuff, in addition to the people Carl Pinkney brought into my campaign.

We took the campaign to the streets. We were running a grassroots effort, going to every precinct meeting, greeting voters on the sidewalks, going from door to door. At that time television wasn't utilized as it is today. We knew that this campaign would come down to people who had actually met me or shaken hands with me, who would in some fashion be able to identify with me.

My children participated; they walked with me, asking people to vote for their father. I'd knock on a door and they'd be trailing behind me. Or somebody on the staff would knock and say, "These are Louis Stokes's children. They want to ask you something." Then they'd say, "We'd like you to vote for our father."

Lori was only five or six, but she was out there with the others. She was an adorable child. It was hard to resist a plea like that.

I spoke in churches. We organized my appearance in five or six churches every Sunday morning all across town. There's an art to that. You need somebody who can ascertain what time the minister is going to entertain your being there, then coordinating so you can show up at that specific time so as not to interfere with his service. The minister will present you and let you talk to his congregation. In many cases candidates are endorsed by the ministers. It's an advantage black candidates have over white candidates. White candidates don't usually have that in white churches. But the black church has always been helpful to candidates they want to give some special attention to.

That had happened most significantly in Carl's 1967 election run, which was so momentous to the community. The ministers endorsed him. They gave him strength. On Election Day more than a few of them went to the polls and stood outside so their congregation members would see them and be reminded of whom to vote for. Of course, Carl's campaign then was like a crusade. W. O. Walker had run an editorial on the front page with the headline: "Any Negro Who Does Not Vote for Carl Stokes Is a Traitor to His Race." Now, a year later, I was running and the ministers gave me powerful support as well.

Backing from the ministers gave me a huge lift. So did W. O.'s endorsement. Another thing that separated me from the others was that I came out against the Vietnam War. That was a real departure, a little tough for Carl because he was at that time trying to work with President Johnson. But we issued briefing papers and press releases. I addressed Vietnam in my speeches. It was very difficult for people in the Twenty-First District to understand why black boys were dying in a country 12,000 miles away that seemed to have little to do with us. The domino theory was being advanced as the rationale for our being there—a false theory, I strongly believed. I was very opposed to our involvement and I said loudly and clearly that we ought not be there. That got me attention. It also got me a couple of calls from Carl. But I told him this was what I had to do.

On the night of April 4 I was on my way to a ward meeting in Garfield Heights, a predominantly white part of the district with my driver, Art Nokes. As we were driving Art had the radio on and an announcement came across that Dr. King had just been shot. We pulled the car over and we listened to the broadcast, stunned. I said, "Art, I can't attend any meetings tonight." He found a phone and called the ward people telling them I couldn't be there, then he took me on home.

The King family invited Carl to attend the funeral in Atlanta. Arnold felt it would be important if I too went. I did go down there; I was in Ebenezer Baptist for the funeral. It was so moving to hear the honor paid to King by the speakers, Ralph Abernathy and others. Mahalia Jackson sang "Take My Hand, Precious Lord." Arnold said, "Lou, you know how much it would mean to the people in our district if you gave them a copy of the program of Dr. King's obsequies."

So we did that. We had a mass reprinting of the program. That Sunday morning when we got back from the funeral we passed it out at the black churches. People loved having those programs.

Following the funeral we had a march in Cleveland, Carl leading. The following day the city sponsored a memorial prayer service for Dr. King at the Old Stone Church, a beautiful church that sits at the corner of Ontario and Superior Avenues. Carl spoke at the service. There's a famous photograph of him sitting on the dais with tears rolling down his face. Then he took leaders of the community walking the streets in Hough and other neighborhoods, keeping people calm. We had no rioting in Cleveland.

After the assassination Leo, George White, George Forbes, and I made some appearances together. A little later I went to visit the Poor People's Campaign encampment in Washington that Dr. King had been in the middle of organizing when he was killed. The other organizers had decided to go ahead with it to honor his memory.

I had gone into the primary race feeling tentative and unsure. But when Election Day came and the votes were counted, I had beaten Leo Jackson two to one, with George Forbes and George White coming in well behind Leo. I took every ward and every precinct.

I think we all felt that the primary was tantamount to being elected to Congress. We had to go through the general election campaign, but this being a Democratic district the sense was that I should be able to win. But regardless, this wasn't something I was about to take for granted, so I continued campaigning hard, this time against the Republican candidate, Charlie Lucas.

Charlie and I appeared together a number of times, but it was a civil contest. The fact was that we had nothing but respect and regard for each other. We had worked so much together in the community that neither of us would ever think of speaking disparagingly about the other.

We did debate issues, though. I hammered on my opposition to the Vietnam War. I said we needed to declare victory and bring our boys home. We were in a losing war; they were defeating us. It was embarrassing.

I struck out at Republican presidential candidate Richard Nixon's policies, maintaining that he and his allies would do little of benefit for blacks. I talked about what needed to be done in our district, a poor district with high rates of crime and high numbers of elderly, a district where, notwithstanding the fact that we had many hospitals, a large number of people were without adequate health care. As a result, they were going to the emergency rooms for medical treatment, which meant they were not receiving primary and preventive care, bad for their health and costly for the system. I talked about how badly the district needed more affordable housing, and more housing for the poor. I talked about the need for jobs, and how to create jobs. I said we needed to beef up federal initiatives such as Head Start and programs for special education. I said that I would be the best person to send to Congress to work on these issues that so vitally affected our district.

On the night of November 4 I watched the votes come in from a hotel room Arnold had rented. The first thing the election board counts are the absentee ballots. Those give you some indication of how the rest of the vote is going to go. They're an indicator. Then at intervals the board will release results up to that point. They will announce, "150 precincts counted. The vote is Stokes 12,090, Lucas, 7,500" or whatever the numbers are. Then you wait for the next batch to be released. We had somebody at the election board who called the results in to our people the moment they were announced. Fairly early in the counting, when we were sure I was going to be elected, I made my way from the hotel to our campaign headquarters.

The place was packed. When we came in the crowd was so happy to see us. They took us up to the stage. Carl was there. He spoke. I spoke. I introduced Jay and the children. It was one of the most jubilant nights of my life, and probably the second most jubilant for Carl. It was a historic night. A lot of media was there, a lot of speculating about what it would mean to have a black congressman from the state.

I was heading for an unknown adventure. I was going to be one of 435 representatives in the U.S. Congress, the greatest legislative body in the world. The political arena would be new to me. But I didn't have any qualms that I'd be able to take my place there. I was ready to go to Washington—and go to work.

There was such an overflow of jubilation in the community that hundreds of people wanted to come with me to Washington. And they did. Busloads of people left Cleveland and came to see me take the oath of office. We had difficulty getting enough gallery tickets, even though many representatives who had been reelected and didn't have people coming in were kind enough to give our office additional tickets. But even then we couldn't get anywhere near everyone in.

On January 3, 1969, Speaker John McCormack gaveled the House of Representatives to order and instructed the newly elected representatives to rise and take the oath of office. We stood. A hush came over the room. Speaker McCormack intoned the words: "I do solemnly swear that I will support and defend the Constitution. . . . I will faithfully discharge the duties of the office on which I am about to enter."

I raised my right hand and as I took the oath I looked back at the packed gallery. Sitting in a section reserved for the family of the president on special occasions were my mother, Carl, Jay, and our older children, Shelley, Angie, and Chuck. Lori, our youngest, was in my arms as I took the oath.

I fixed on my mother's face for a moment. She seemed to be glowing with pride. She had started her life as a Georgia sharecropper and here she was at age seventy-three with one son Cleveland's first black mayor and the other Ohio's first black congressman. What that must have meant to her. I was struck by how beautiful she was, despite the hard life she had lived, from the cotton fields to the projects, scrubbing other people's floors, doing their laundry, caring for their children—and now to Washington, D.C. What a journey. Only in America.

I turned back to face Speaker McCormack, my right hand still raised along with the hands of the other 434 new members. Lori, nestled on my shoulder, had raised her own hand and was taking the oath along with us. Carl's victory had been such an unforgettable moment. My victory also. But Lori with her hand raised was a picture beyond any price.

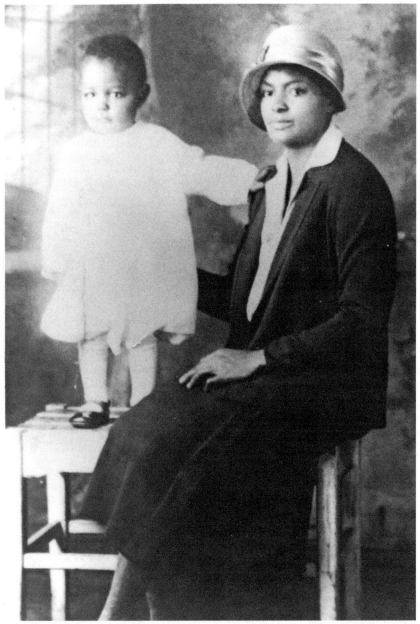

1. An eternal loving and trusting bond, the future Mr. Chairman and his mother, Louise. (Linton Freeman/Louis Stokes Collection)

2. Charlie, Louise, and
newborn Louis nicknamed
"Billy" in 1925. (Western
Reserve Historical Society/
Louis Stokes Collection)

3. "Billy" (3 years old) on the steps of
the "rickety old house" on East 69th
in 1928. (Louise Stokes Collection)

4. "Brother" and "Billy" with cousin Claudia in 1930—"poor as poor and we knew it." (Linton Freeman/Louis Stokes Collection)

5. Louise with Louis (11 years old) and Carl (9 years old)—her children were her "hope in life." (Louise Stokes Collection)

6. Grandma Fannie in 1940—"sweet but strict." (Louis Stokes Collection)

7. Poughsley Stone "Uncle Doc." (Louis Stokes Collection)

8. A break from his ten-block route, Louis (left) with entrepreneurial Caldwell Gaffney hiding a hole in his shirt. (Western Reserve Historical Society/Louis Stokes Collection)

9. Carl, Louise, and Louis in front of the Outhwaite House Project. (Linton Freeman/Louis Stokes Collection)

10. Louis proudly wearing his uniform in a segregated Army in 1943. (Louis Stokes Collection)

11. Cleveland Marshall Law School graduate—a dream that started at 12 years old and was realized in June 1953. (Louis Stokes Collection)

12. On August 21, 1960, Louis and Jay married at East Mt. Zion: "I was surprised she said yes." (Louis and Jay Stokes Collection)

With highest esteem
to my partner
Louis Stokes —
Norman S. Minor
'63

13. Cherished message from mentor and law partner Norman Minor in 1963.
(Louis Stokes Collection)

LOUIS STOKES
FOR CONGRESS — 21st DISTRICT

for better schools

Lou was there to argue de facto desegregation in the Federal Court!

for better representation

Lou was there before the United States Supreme Court to WIN the New 21st District.

for civil rights

Lou was there to spell out the truth about the Hough riots to the U.S. Commission on Civil Rights . . .

for individual rights

Lou was there before the United States Supreme Court to defend the right of privacy of citizens stopped and frisked on the street . . .

for youth opportunity

1968 District Chairman, Cedar YMCA Membership Drive . . .

for you

Public Service, whether given as a private citizen or an elected official is an expression of concern for one's fellow man. It is a commitment I made many years ago . . . and I have never regretted the decision to be involved in the problems of my community and those of my fellow man, in spite of his station in life. It is with great humility and belief in human dignity that I ask you, during this crucial period in our history, for the vote to change my position from that of a privately involved citizen to that of a totally involved Congressman.

LOUIS STOKES

[signature]

now...
**make
your
action
count!!**

VOTE
TUESDAY
MAY 7th

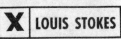

X | LOUIS STOKES

DEMOCRAT

14. Always grassroots, a campaign flyer with family and accomplishments. (Louis Stokes Collection)

15. Campaigning in style. (Western Reserve Historical Society/Louis Stokes Collection)

16. On the cusp of election, Louis Stokes and and his wife Jay attend President Lyndon B. Johnson's state dinner on June 4, 1968. (Louis Stokes Collection)

17. Victorious election night in 1968—Stokes never lost an election. (Louis Stokes Collection)

THE WHITE HOUSE

WASHINGTON

November 9, 1968

Dear Mr. Stokes:

Please accept my heartiest congratulations
on your recent election to Congress. I am
sure that the leadership team of Stokes and
Stokes will fully justify the faith that the
people of Ohio have shown in you and your
remarkable brother.

I look forward to meeting you in Washington.

Sincerely,

Honorable Louis A. Stokes
3130 Albion Road
Cleveland, Ohio 44120

18. Congratulatory letter from President Johnson to Stokes dated November 9, 1968.
(Louis Stokes Collection)

19. The gentleman from Ohio goes to Washington. (Louis Stokes Collection)

20. Stokes and Speaker Tip O'Neill: "Louie, my pal . . . ." (Louis Stokes Collection)

21. Charlie Vanik and Stokes at a meeting in Oberlin for a hearing on the Northeast Ohio Correctional Center in 1973. (Western Reserve Historical Society/Louis Stokes Collection)

22. Early days of the Congressional Black Caucus. Back row (left to right): Rangel, Clay, Collins, Metcalfe, and Mitchell. Front row (left to right): Stokes, Chisholm, Diggs, and Conyers. (Louis Stokes Collection)

23. Chicago press conference on the killing of Black Panther Fred Hampton. Left to right: unknown, Stokes, Congressman Adam Clayton Powell, Congressman Charles Diggs, Congressman John Conyers, and Congressman Bill Clay. (Louis Stokes Collection)

24. Stokes at the Assassination Committee Public Hearing, 1976–78. (Louis Stokes Collection)

25. An unprecedented sit-down with Cuban president Fidel Castro on April 3, 1978: "I got to the point." (Louis Stokes Collection)

26. Stokes speaking at a Cleveland Clergy Luncheon in 1978. Left to right at dais: George Forbes, Arnold Pinkney, and W. O. Walker. (Alfred Associates/Louis Stokes Collection)

27. Stokes cherished his long friendship with Senator Ted Kennedy: "my counterpart in the Senate." (Louis Stokes Collection)

28. Stokes with Dr. Louis Sullivan: "A close ally and dear friend . . . Dr. Louis Sullivan and I collaborated in unprecedented ways." (Louis Stokes Collection)

29. Interrogating Col. Ollie North in 1987: "The good, the bad, and the ugly." (Louis Stokes Collection)

30. Stokes next to Chairman Natcher on the Appropriations Committee in 1992: "The epitome of a congressman." (Louis Stokes Collection)

31. Congressman Jerry Lewis and Stokes had a "warm relationship": "we ironed out our differences." (Louis Stokes Collection)

32. Stokes with 21st District Congressional Caucus executive director Anna Chatman—"church lady with an iron fist in a velvet glove." (Janet Century/Century Photography)

33. Stokes honored for work on behalf of Soviet Jewry and work in Congress to liberate Refuseniks, January 29, 1992. (Louis Stokes Collection)

34. Chairing the Ethics Committee allowed Stokes to use his skills as a criminal law attorney. (Louis Stokes Collection)

35. Chairing the Health Braintrust hearing with Hillary Clinton participating. (Louis Stokes collection)

36. Stokes's family. Back row (left to right): Chuck, Angie, and Lori. Front row (left to right): Louis, Jay, and Shelley. Stokes once said, "I have a wonderful family . . . I never told my children what to be, just be happy doing it." (Louis Stokes Collection)

37. The power broker: Stokes looking out at his constituents at Labor Day Picnic. (Chuck Stokes)

38. Stokes with his tailor: "I liked dressing sharp. Izzy taught me cloth." (Alfred Associates/Louis Stokes Collection)

39. Stokes overwhelmed looking at "his" building on the NIH campus—an affirmation of thirty years of hard work in Congress. (National Institutes of Health)

40. Stokes always cherished the words from President Obama before his election: "I'm here because of you and your brother." (Official White House Photo by Pete Souza)

CHAPTER 7

Black Political Power

SIXTY-EIGHT YEARS before I was sworn in, an earlier black representative had made a speech on the House floor.

> This, Mr. Chairman, is perhaps the Negroes' temporary farewell to the American Congress. But let me say, Phoenix-like we will rise up some day and come again. These parting words are on behalf of an outraged, heartbroken, bruised, and bleeding people. (Cong. Rec. 56th Cong. 2nd session, 29 Jan. 1901)

That was George Henry White of North Carolina addressing the House of Representatives on January 29, 1901. It was his farewell speech. White was the last of the post–Civil War blacks elected to the U.S. Congress, the lone survivor, and now he was departing. North Carolina, along with other Southern states, had passed laws choking off black voting rights. Side by side with decades of terror and intimidation, white supremacist state and local governments had effectively disenfranchised black citizens; White's base of support had all but disappeared. "The political part of it is a mere subterfuge, a means for the general degradation of the Negro," White told a reporter. "I cannot live in North Carolina and be a man and be treated like a man."

Before White, twenty-one blacks had served in Reconstruction-era congresses: nineteen in the House, two in the Senate. The first was Hiram Revels, a free black elected from Mississippi. Revels was an educator who had himself learned to read in an underground school. An ordained A.M.E. minister, during the Civil War he had helped raise two black fighting regiments and had served as a Union army chaplain. Congress's second black was Joseph H. Rainey of South Carolina, who during the Civil War had escaped with his wife and children to Bermuda. Returning to Charleston after the war, Rainey became a well-known figure in the business community and in 1870 was elected to Congress. He helped pass the 1875 Civil Rights Act, which prohibited racial discrimination in public accommodations. The act was ruled unconstitutional by the Supreme Court in 1883, but a number of its provisions served as models for the landmark 1964 Civil Rights Act. Jefferson Franklin Long of Georgia was Congress's third African American. Born and raised a slave, Long had taught himself to read, and after the war he joined the Macon Union League where he was recognized for the power of his oratory. After giving a series of speeches to blacks in Georgia's special election for the Forty-First Congress, he led a mass march to the polls. On the way they were attacked by armed whites who tried to kill him. Long escaped. Others weren't so lucky. Even though many blacks fled without voting, he was still elected.

Most African American congressmen during the post–Civil War period were former slaves, but each was driven by the need for education. They did remarkable things with their lives, these men who had lived for years in bondage. Among them were farmers, preachers, lawyers, barbers, soldiers, sailors, newspaper editors, businessmen, teachers. One, Robert Smalls, was a renowned hero of the Union navy. Some became professors, three were university presidents. But by 1901, thirty-six years after the war, they were all gone. The Ku Klux Klan, the Red Shirts, the White Brotherhood, and other violent vigilante groups had terrorized their constituencies. Anti–black voting laws had slammed the door on African American congressional representation.

For twenty-seven years black America had no African American representation at all in the U.S. Congress. Then, in 1928 Oscar de Priest was elected from Chicago's South Side, home to a large population of blacks who were part of the wave of migration from the South that included my own parents. Over the next forty years seven other African Americans were elected to the House and one, Edward Brooke, to the Senate. Until the 1940s there was one African American at a time in the House; the Senate had none. When Adam Clayton Powell was elected from Harlem in 1945, he joined William Dawson of Illinois, and then the House had two. Sparse is not an adequate term to describe black national representation—all of it from the North. From the South there were none.

When I entered Congress in 1969, seven other African Americans were serving: Dawson, Powell, Charles Diggs and John Conyers from Michigan, Gus Hawkins from California, and Robert Nix from Pennsylvania in the House, and Ed Brooke in the Senate. Brooke was the first black senator since Blanche Bruce left office in 1881. Two other African Americans came in with me: William Lacy Clay from Saint Louis and Shirley Chisholm from Brooklyn. That brought us up to nine in the House. George White's prediction that phoenix-like we would rise again had come true. Nine was a historic number. Nine black members had never before served together in the U.S. House of Representatives.

African Americans around the country were aware of the forlorn history of black representation. But in 1969 there was a sense that something different was happening. The civil rights movement, the death of Dr. Martin Luther King, and the big city riots had shifted people's mindsets. The stage had been set for an assertive emergence of black political power. Bill Clay, Shirley Chisholm, and I recognized that we couldn't just come to Congress and serve the same way white representatives could. We weren't there simply to serve our districts. We were part of a historic cohort. We had an obligation to reach out and represent black people wherever they were, most of whom, especially in the South, had not a single black representative of their own.

Shirley Chisholm I knew by reputation. She was a schoolteacher from Bedford Stuyvesant in Brooklyn, a civil rights activist. She spoke Spanish fluently. She was bright, articulate, tough, and very militant. Shirley Chisholm stood her ground. She spoke out against the relegation of women as well as blacks, protesting against males who thought women had no place. Shirley wanted to serve on the Education and Labor Committee, but her outspokenness didn't go over well in the staid white Congress and she was placed on the Agriculture Committee instead, a kind of insulting joke. She said that just because a tree grows in Brooklyn didn't mean she knew anything about agriculture, and she went down to the House floor to protest. They put her on the Veterans Committee instead—not her first choice, either, but at least more in keeping with her constituency. "I've got a lot more veterans in my district than trees," she said.

Bill Clay and I clicked from the first day we met. He reminded me a lot of Carl: gregarious, astute, and blessed with a highly developed sense for how to do politics. I found myself picking up lessons from him almost from the start. Bill was another militant. He had spent 112 days in jail back in Saint Louis for contempt of court during the long struggle for civil rights there. He was strong in defense of black people. He advocated for them. He didn't play about those things, and he was not a man who minced words. One day, as Charlie Diggs and I were having lunch in the House dining room, we noticed Georgia's racist governor Lester Maddox—in the House to testify against a voting act bill—distributing ax handles as souvenirs of his visit (Maddox had driven away blacks attempting to be served in his Atlanta restaurant with ax handles). Charlie went up to him and took the ax handles away, then we went upstairs to tell the others. Shortly afterward several of us took to the floor to denounce what had happened. Bill told the House, "This idiot invaded our cafeteria." "It was not only ironic," he said, "but tragic that the lunatic from the state of Georgia was not arrested." Maddox was a despicable character and the ax handle stunt was bizarre. But Bill didn't suffer fools in the more ordinary course of affairs, either. He'd knife right through obfuscatory or hypocritical speech. "Why don't we just cut the bullshit," he'd say. And often that would get the discussion on track.

Almost from the moment we arrived, Bill Clay and I began talking about the possibility of putting together a formal organization of black representatives that would enable us to leverage our talents and experience as a coherent and politically forceful body, so that we could press issues of special concern to our communities and to blacks nationwide. Under Charlie Diggs's leadership, black members had already organized an informal group that met on occasion with the House leadership. But what Bill and I had in mind was an independent black power bloc.

Interestingly, at about the same time back in Cleveland, Carl was also considering how to structure and utilize independent black political power. Carl was Cleveland's mayor, but his roots and the base of both his power and mine were the Twenty-First District—65 percent black, almost uniformly poor, and traditionally loyal to the Democratic Party. But Carl's theory was that black people should not be beholden to either political party. They should support Democrats when Democrats were responsive to the community's needs. But when Democrats' actions were detrimental, we should work as hard to defeat them as we would have worked to elect them. We needed an organization that would embody this approach, that would assert its independence and manifest the independent power of Cleveland's black voters.

Shortly after I went to Congress, Carl had Arnold Pinkney start working to set up what would be called the Twenty-First District Caucus. Not everyone was in favor of doing this. The Democratic Party and its machine were the traditional home for Cleveland's black politicians. Many had carved out secure and comfortable niches there. But as mayor, Carl had enormous clout. He could wield power through the black city councilmen. No one was going to deny him on this. The caucus was to include both Republicans and Democrats. As the district's congressional representative, I would lead it; Carl would serve as honorary chairman.

This was a new, visionary type of politics. It revolutionized the old power structure in which blacks were a subservient part of the Democratic machine. Up till then it was an accepted fact that no matter what the Democrats did, blacks would accept it. They might complain, but that would be as far as it went. African Americans were Democrats. They would vote Democratic regardless. Their precincts would work for Democratic candidates. That was the way it had been in Cleveland since the New Deal and that's how it would be forever. The Twenty-First District Caucus was Carl's way of saying, Not any more! We throw down the gauntlet. From this point forward we will not accept you if what you are doing is not in our best interests.

Carl was a brilliant politician. He sensed the currents running through the black community, the struggle for rights giving way to the hunger for empowerment. You couldn't help but see him as *the* political figure nationally who symbolized that historic change. But the local trigger for Carl's foray was the dumb recalcitrance of the Cuyahoga County Democratic Party.

Carl, George Forbes, and Arnold Pinkney had been attempting over a period of time to get the Cuyahoga County Democratic Party to give the black community—which was the base of Democratic support in the county—some form of recognition by way of an executive office in the party. There had never been a black in the party hierarchy, and Carl felt it was time the party acknowledged black loyalty. By this time I was involved with him and the others. We proposed that the party give us a vice presidency. We suggested Dr. Ken Clement. They refused. Then we proposed George Forbes as secretary. They refused. They had no interest. They knew Republicans weren't looking for blacks in their party; Republicans weren't going to offer us anything. Consequently, blacks had nowhere else to go. What were we going to do other than stay and vote for Democrats?

All this came to a head at the Cuyahoga Democratic Party convention of May 1970. Arnold and George were there as well as Carl and myself. We were going to try to negotiate with the leadership for the recognition we were demanding. If they stonewalled, we were ready to pull all the black delegates out of the hall.

As we might have expected, the party leaders didn't budge. So we pulled everyone out, into a hotel meeting room across the street. I don't know that the leadership was prepared for this. It was dramatic, all the black party members standing up and filing out en masse. But surprised or not, all party chairman Joseph Bartunek and the rest of the leadership did was dig in.

With that, we didn't just take everyone out of the meeting; we took everyone out of the party. The Cuyahoga Democratic Party was left with no black ward leaders, no precinct captains, no precinct workers, the party's whole vote-pulling muscle in its most essential district.

That was just the start. We had begun by requesting recognition. Now we began looking at it more comprehensively. We examined all the county offices—the clerk of courts, the treasurer, the sheriff, auditor, and so on, looking at the jobs situation in each. There wasn't a single African American in an elected position in any of these agencies; the whole structure was lily white. And the elected chiefs controlled all the jobs in their agencies, which meant that most employees were white, while any blacks were hired for low-paying mostly menial jobs. So we thought, what are we doing asking for a vice president or a secretary? We need something more than that.

George, Arnold, and I drew up a longer list of demands that we insisted be met before we would bring our people back in. Because no black had ever held an executive-level office, we insisted that a black be appointed either chairman or vice chairman of the party. We demanded that one of the county officers should announce his retirement and let the party appoint a black until the election, and at that time we would elect a black to at least one county office. We insisted that the party appoint an African American to the county election board, which was also all white. I made another demand as well: since blacks were almost 30 percent of the county, I wanted approximately one-third of all county jobs to go to blacks.

As these negotiations dragged on, Bartunek became increasingly hostile. "Bartunek Reads 21st Caucus Out of the Party," a *Plain Dealer* headline trumpeted. "Leaders of the caucus do not want to participate in party affairs except to disrupt them," said Bartunek. "I am going to oppose any effort by Louis Stokes to participate in policymaking decisions of the Democratic party at any level."

"There isn't anything he said that I would give the dignity of a reply to," I told the papers when I heard about it. "He's (Bartunek) got to be kidding," said Carl. "Who endowed him with the right to determine who is or who isn't a Democrat? It's almost laughable." The *Call and Post* editorialized, "No more blind loyalty, no more alliances of convenience . . . no more supine capitulation to the County Democratic bosses who have held the whip hand over Cleveland for more than a half a century and the black vote in its hip pocket."

It wasn't easy for us to turn African American voters around, long accustomed as they were to voting straight Democrat. But in the next race for county commissioner the caucus backed Republican Seth Taft over his Democratic opponent. Taft had been Carl's opponent in his second mayoral race, but he was a decent and competent man, a gentleman of the old school. During his mayoral campaign against Carl he had staunchly refused to play the race card. Afterward Taft, Carl, and I had become good friends. The caucus went all out to support Taft, and we were able to lift him to victory with 49 percent of the black vote over a well-known and well-financed Democrat.

With that race the Twenty-First District Caucus asserted itself as a force to be reckoned with in Cleveland politics. We had the organization to make things happen, and we brought the grassroots people with us. We were making white people respect black political power. Twenty-First District voters loved that. Carl and I had their faith and confidence that we were doing it right and putting an end to the old plantation-style politics.

I kept blacks out of the Cuyahoga Democratic Party for several years, which might have seemed odd to outsiders since I was an elected Democratic congressman. But eventually I arrived at an agreement with the party: blacks in county offices, a percentage of county jobs, a place on the election board. The only demand they would not agree to was that a black should become either chairman or vice chairman. Instead they agreed that we would set up a tripartite form of chairmanship. I would be one of the three co-chairs. The other two would be Hugh Corrigan, a common pleas court judge, and Anthony Garofoli, a former councilman from the predominantly Italian Nineteenth Ward.

In the end, while the co-chairmanship was significant, especially given all we had gone through to get it, the position proved too unwieldy for me to handle effectively. I was in Washington most of the time rather than Cleveland, which meant I wasn't able to participate in the daily running of the party, which in turn meant that I wasn't being included in a lot of the decision making. Even the agreements I had worked out with the party weren't being implemented. Whenever I questioned them about it—the jobs, the places on the county commissions—there was always some excuse. I would remind them, and they would explain, "Lou, we just don't have the jobs." "Lou, we can't get any of these guys to leave office." Before long I concluded that in order for the black community to have a fully participating co-chairman, I needed to get someone to replace me. I approached George Forbes for that and he agreed to come in as my successor.

∽⌒

Carl had served two terms as mayor, but in April 1971 he announced that he wouldn't be running for a third term. With Carl out of office and me in Washington, we also needed a strong hands-on executive director for the Twenty-First District Caucus. After our first director didn't work out, I turned to Arnold Pinkney, who had been working with Carl and me on this from the beginning.

Arnold Pinkney and I, of course, had been strong political allies; we had worked together for years on one thing or another, and he had managed my campaign for Congress. I never anticipated that we would have a falling out, but a grave difference arose over an action he took as executive director that ended our relationship for a good long while.

In 1972 two Democrats were on the ballot who had given Cleveland's black community problems for years. John T. Corrigan was running for county prosecutor again, the same individual who had steadfastly refused to indict any police involved in murdering black people, including in the two notorious cases I had handled as a defense attorney—the killings of Jeffrey Perkins and Albert Rugley. The second person was Albert Porter, the powerful county engineer who had been Democratic Party chief and chief instigator of the 1964 redistricting that carved the black vote up and prevented Carl from running for Congress in 1968—the redistricting that I and our NAACP legal team had challenged and the Supreme Court had overturned.

Corrigan and Porter were outstanding examples of Cleveland's old-time racist politicians. They had both been in public office for many years, and since they were Democrats Cleveland's black Democratic loyalists had always more or less been forced to support them. The two of them were prime examples of exactly the kind of politician the Twenty-First District Caucus had been formed to oppose.

With the election in the offing and a caucus meeting coming up, I talked to Pinkney. Carl had by now left Cleveland to become an anchorman on a New York City news station, so he was no longer the caucus's honorary chairman. But I was still chairman. Calling Pinkney from Washington, I instructed him that the caucus could not under any circumstances endorse either of these candidates, who had never been responsive to our community and in fact had been decidedly detrimental. Having them in office was not in our best interest in any way.

Arnold understood, and that night the caucus met. But for reasons I was not privy to, Arnold changed his mind and had the caucus vote to endorse both Corrigan and Porter. When I learned what had happened I was flabbergasted. If the caucus would endorse people like these, what was the purpose of having it in the first place?

I had to do something about this. Corrigan and Porter were now endorsed; I had no way of turning that around. But I realized I had to remove Arnold as executive director. It was one thing to decide to get rid of Arnold, though; it was another to actually do it. Arnold had been a force in Cleveland's black political world for decades. He was popular, and he had his own circles of allies, including George Forbes. In addition, although the caucus enjoyed enthusiastic support among ordinary black East Siders, many veteran African American politicians had never been thrilled with it. They weren't happy that the caucus had disrupted the way they had always done their business. But Carl had pushed it, and no one had had the strength to stand up to him.

Just attempting to vote Arnold out and a new executive director in would have been a dangerous tactic. As the rift between us became known, some people backed him and some backed me. It wasn't clear who might actually have more support. Fortunately, two of the oldest, wiliest politicians around had stuck with me, Charlie Carr and Jimmie Bell. Both were long-serving city council members. "Lou," Charlie Carr said, "you're right. If you want to run your caucus you have to get rid of Arnold. And here's how you might do it."

I was at that point still learning to be a politician, but Charlie Carr and Jimmie Bell were past masters. They knew every trick in the book. The approach they suggested was to abolish the charter, which stipulated the executive director's position. With no charter there would be no executive director; Arnold would be out.

Everyone in town knew I was angry, that I felt Arnold had hurt the caucus and that the endorsement of Corrigan and Porter was against my wishes.

So practically the whole district was looking forward to that caucus night, knowing that I was going to do something. They were expecting a shoot-out.

We held caucus meetings then in a big hall at Eighty-Ninth and Woodland. Caucus nights might draw a thousand people, especially when I brought in speakers like Bill Clay, Jesse Jackson, and John Conyers. But that night the hall was packed like I had never seen it. Chairing the meeting, I recognized Russ Adrine, the lawyer I had worked with defending school demonstrators all those years ago. "I move," Russ said, "that we abolish the current by-laws and adopt a new more appropriate set." That caught Arnold and George Forbes off guard. They had expected a debate, just not a debate over by-laws. Their hands went up and I gave them a chance to speak their piece. But when it began to seem clear that Russ's motion was going to pass, they walked out—and a lot of others went with them.

After that Arnold worked to pull other elected officials out, and with a good deal of success. My problem was that I had no clout. Carl was gone. He had clout; he could give them jobs, which I couldn't. That meant I had nothing to control them with. So a lot of politicians left the caucus. I was left with the grassroots people and only a few public officials. I was facing the need to rebuild more or less from scratch. Among other things, I needed a new executive director.

One night in Cleveland I was attending a church banquet honoring one of the local ministers. Seated next to me was a lady named Anna Chatman, the widow of a minister who had died some time before. Anna Chatman was a powerful presence in the world of Cleveland's black churches. As we talked she told me about all the church work she did and the various groups she was part of. She and her two daughters, Ruby and Marcy, sang and played piano. She knew all the women involved in the Baptist churches throughout the region. She was quite obviously a dynamo, a natural-born leader.

"Mrs. Chatman," I said, "we need someone like you to come work with us in the caucus."

"Me?" she said. "I don't know anything about politics. I'm a church woman."

"Mrs. Chatman, there's more politics in the church than we have out here on the street. I'd love to talk to you a little more about it."

"Well," she said, "I don't know, I just don't know."

"Why don't you let me call you so we can talk a little more about it?"

I did call her, and she and her daughter Ruby came to see me. I urged her to come on as caucus director. I could see that she would be a tower of strength if we could get her involved. And in the end she did agree. So now we had a new executive director.

When Carl started the caucus he envisioned it as an organization that would weld together the strength of all of the Twenty-First District's political figures, Democrat and Republican. But I understood that if I was going to rebuild the caucus, I was going to have to do it as a grassroots organization, with ordinary citizens who cared about it as a place where they could raise their issues, where their voices could be heard. I considered that these were the real people, the ones who wanted change, who wouldn't be satisfied with the old ways of doing things. And these people were going to be with me no matter what. So that's where I began.

Given the damage, I knew we had to do something dramatic, to show that the caucus was still in business, that the grassroots people were an active voting bloc that couldn't be disregarded. After considering various ideas, we decided to have a big Labor Day parade and march into Luke Easter Park, where we would mount a political program of some kind. We envisioned floats, high school marching bands, fraternal organizations, labor unions, veterans' organizations—whatever groups we could muster from the Twenty-First District. It would be quite an effort to put something like this together, but it would celebrate the district, give people a feeling of togetherness under the auspices of the caucus, and not least important, give us plenty of media attention. A parade would announce in capital letters that we were alive and well and could rally large numbers of people.

It seemed like an excellent idea, but it was also a big risk. What if we didn't have a good, strong following in the park? Charlie Carr, cunning and foxlike as he was, said, "Lou, there are going to be many families in that park enjoying the Labor Day holiday. What you do is you claim everybody in the park."

I needn't have worried. The community responded. A big crowd came and enjoyed themselves. We felt their support for the parade, and for the caucus.

That first Labor Day parade was so successful that we held it again the following year. We embellished it and worked to make it *the* political place to be on Labor Day. In the years following there were occasions where, according to newspaper accounts, we had fifty thousand people. We brought in speakers—Jesse Jackson, Walter Mondale, later on John Kerry. Dick Gregory was often there, entertaining the crowds with his mixture of humor and politics. One year we brought Carl back to speak. The Twenty-First District

Caucus Labor Day Parade was where Jesse Jackson began his campaign for president.

There was a memorable moment that year with Jackson. It was being rumored at the time that he was going to run for president, but he hadn't yet declared. A number of other candidates had announced, though. On TV nearly every day you would see the hopefuls who were declaring their candidacies—Walter Mondale, Gary Hart, George McGovern, and several others, all of them white.

I was in the schoolyard staging area that morning watching the bands and drill teams getting themselves ready when a little boy about twelve years old came up to me. Jackson, our featured speaker, was standing nearby.

"Congressman Stokes?"

"Yes?"

"Is that Jesse Jackson there?"

"Yes, it is."

"Congressman Stokes, I didn't know a black man could run for president."

I thought, of course he doesn't know. How would he? All this kid sees is white males running for president. It's natural that he would think that black people can't run.

I said, "Jesse, come over here. This boy doesn't know that a black man can run for president of the United States."

Jesse took the boy aside and had a nice one-on-one conversation with him. Then we marched down to the park. People had brought out signs, "Run Jesse Run." Later he announced that he was entering the race. Jackson's was the first credible black candidacy. In the Democratic primaries that year he won five states and ran third in the convention to Walter Mondale and Gary Hart. On many occasions later he talked about that little black kid who didn't understand a black man was allowed to run for president in this country. "If you're really serious about running for the presidency," Jesse used to say, "you'll be in Cleveland at that Twenty-First District Caucus picnic on Labor Day."

The Labor Day Parade was a yearly event that soon became a required appearance for Cleveland's candidates and elected officials. But with Anna Chatman as executive director, the caucus itself grew into a unique political organization, unlike anything else in the country. It was different from a congressional office operation, where constituents could go and ask their representative to take action or help on one thing or another. By virtue of the fact that it was independent of Democrats or Republicans, the caucus almost became a form of a political party itself. The caucus was a true grassroots entity, demonstrating for people that they were powerful politically in and of their own right.

Anna Chatman ran the caucus with an iron fist in a velvet glove. She had the caucus meet every single Monday night, regardless of whether it was a holiday or snowing or anything else. That was her way of disciplining the people so that nothing took their minds off the caucus meeting. She taught them that they could be involved in politics as part of their regular lives, that they had a place where they could raise issues, take positions, give voice to their concerns, and be taken seriously. If something happened, some incident of police brutality or some other community problem, they could come to the caucus and be heard, and they could have me or the caucus itself do something about it.

Black people had never had an opportunity like this, to be able to come to a political organization, feel that they could discuss issues, that there was somebody to listen, hear them, and take action on their behalf. They loved it. And Anna Chatman knew how to conduct those meetings. There were some tough street characters who showed up for meetings. She was a church lady, but at the same time she knew how to deal with them in their world. She would let them talk and make all kinds of demands and proposals for action. She'd let them know—"We've got to talk to the congressman. We can't do anything like that until we talk to him." They could object and insist, but she'd tell them, "We have to talk with the congressman, and that *is* what we're going to do." People loved her; they called her "Mama Chatman." But with Mama Chatman you could not get away with anything; no one was going to overawe her no matter how adamant or militant.

Following each meeting she would call me and tell me what people wanted to do. I would decide if there was something I needed to get into or if there was a way that the caucus could provide some kind of remedy. Sometimes we would appoint a committee to look into it. Sometimes we'd refer it to my congressional office. If elections were coming up, we would let the candidates know when they could address the caucus. She made it clear that you didn't just show up because you were a Democrat and expect to be endorsed. We were going to assess you in terms of your responsiveness to the community and its needs. And they came for that endorsement, because they knew that if they didn't have it, people would not vote for them.

There were times when Mama Chatman wouldn't be happy with some action I wanted to take. "Do your really think we ought to do that?"

"Yes, that's what I think."

"Are you *sure* you want to do that?"

Some of those were tough issues. I supported *Roe v. Wade*; I believed that ending a pregnancy or not ending it was a decision between a woman and her doctor. But the black church opposed abortion. On questions like abortion the ministers gave me the leeway to do what I had to do as a congressman. And I knew that they had to do what they had to do as ministers.

"You are going to get me thrown *out* of the churches," Mama Chatman would tell me.

But she was a strong lady, and she could bring the ministers in on whatever we truly needed help on.

As a congressman, I was away in Washington, D.C., through most weeks, and even when I came back on weekends I was handling so many things in the community that I hardly had time to turn around. I needed someone who would take care of the caucus and run it and make sure that we did what I wanted done in terms of Cleveland and Ohio politics. Anna Chatman played that role for almost thirty years, right up until my retirement. She was the irreplaceable person.[1]

While the Twenty-First District Caucus was going through its birth pangs and evolving, in Congress we were also busy figuring out how best to organize and leverage black political power. When Bill Clay, Shirley Chisholm, and I came in we generated a lot of media attention. It was a historic moment, the first time since Reconstruction the House had had so many black representatives. Moreover, after the Voting Rights Act, the Fair Housing Act, the marches and activism, and the death of Martin Luther King, the mood was shifting. Black people, as Fanny Lou Hamer put it, were "sick and tired of being sick and tired." There was a more aggressive spirit abroad, and the three of us were activists. People had expectations of us. We most definitely had expectations for ourselves.

As a result of all the attention, Bill, Shirley, and I found ourselves thrust together. In response to that we started doing things together, holding press conferences and feeling ever more strongly that it was our responsibility to be catalysts, if we could, to bring the whole group of black representatives together in some form where we could more effectively exercise our strength.

---

1. Arnold Pinkney and I eventually did restore our friendship. In 1975 he came to Washington, sat down in my office, and apologized for what he had done. He asked if I would support him in his run for mayor. I agreed to do so, and I worked hard for him. That brought us back together. George Forbes and I also ironed out our differences and became friends and allies again.

At the same time, we were freshmen; we understood we had no real power. If we wanted to get anything accomplished it would have to be through the black members who had seniority. Adam Clayton Powell had been serving for almost a quarter century when we came in, a charismatic, nationally prominent political figure. Several of us went to him about convening us as a formal group.

Powell was by far the most recognized black politician in the country, a legendary figure in the black community. He had been fighting for black civil rights since well before 1945 when his Harlem district first sent him to the Congress. I remembered vividly that when I was serving in the segregated army, he had been pushing hard to allow black units to fight. He had brought fair employment legislation to the floor and bills to outlaw poll taxes and lynching. He had chaired the Education and Labor Committee. Back in his district he had run large programs providing food, housing, and jobs for the poor.

But Powell found himself in trouble with the House Judiciary Committee regarding various alleged violations as well as for his flamboyance and unapologetic in-your-face attitude, and the House had stripped him of his seniority and levied a large fine against him. "Listen," he said, "I'm not going to be around very much. But what I'll do is have Charlie Diggs lead you on this [Diggs himself had been in Congress for almost fifteen years]. You should designate Diggs as chairman."

Even before we got the as-yet-unnamed Congressional Black Caucus formally organized, we began involving ourselves in national black issues. On December 4, 1969, Fred Hampton, leader of Chicago's Black Panthers, was gunned down in his sleep along with another Black Panther by a raiding force of Chicago police. A group of Chicago's black leaders invited us to Chicago where we launched our own investigation. The police claimed there had been a shoot-out at the apartment house where the Panthers were staying. But there had been no shoot-out. Both Hampton and the other Panther had been fast asleep when the police stormed in, guns blazing. Volleys of shots marked the walls in their apartment. "There was no shoot-out," I told the press conference we held. "There was a shoot-in." Interestingly, three of the black leaders who invited us subsequently were elected to Congress themselves: state representative Harold Washington, alderman Ralph Metcalfe, and publisher Gus Savage.

A few months later we went down to Jackson, Mississippi, where two young black men had been shot and killed at Jackson State College. They had been part of a demonstration there against the Vietnam War—this was eleven days after the Kent State killings. Claiming there might have been a sniper on the loose, police had opened fire, killing two students and wounding twelve. No evidence of a sniper was ever found.

We held our own investigation in Jackson and issued a report. We went to military bases to highlight the discrimination still going on twenty-plus years after the armed forces had been integrated. We investigated hospitals in the South that were still refusing to treat black patients. We arranged with the military academies to allow us to nominate black youngsters from the South for appointments, since southern congressmen would not do it themselves. That was a remarkable development—northern congressmen making appointments of young black applicants from southern states. The arrangements here were between ourselves and the academies. It's likely that most southern representatives weren't even aware that this was happening.

The 1970 election brought the number of black representatives up to twelve with the addition of Ron Dellums of California, Ralph Metcalfe of Illinois, and Parren Mitchell of Maryland, then thirteen when Walter Fauntroy was elected as representative for the District of Columbia, technically a "delegate." The black majority District of Columbia had had no African American representation at all for a hundred years. Shortly afterward we passed Bill Clay's proposal to establish a formal organization with officers, by-laws, and procedures. "We have no permanent friends," said Clay, "and no permanent enemies, just permanent interests." Charlie Rangel, who had defeated Adam Clayton Powell in Powell's old Harlem district, proposed the name Congressional Black Caucus, which we adopted. Charlie Diggs had been chairman of our ad hoc group. Now we elected him chairman of our newly established, independent Congressional Black Caucus.

After the first two years Diggs stepped down and I was elected chairman. It seemed to me that two years on we needed to assess what we had been doing and where we ought to be going. I appointed a task force to look at that under the leadership of Ron Dellums, one of the 1971 arrivals.

Dellums was elected to Congress from Berkeley, California, the most militant and vocal antiwar district in the country, with a large proportion of white students and other Berkeley university people. Dellums came from a labor background. His uncle was one of the founders of the Brotherhood of Pullman Porters, his father a longshoreman. Dellums himself had been a social worker and civil rights leader. He came in wanting to play an active role, and he had the kind of philosophical, ideas-oriented mind that seemed to me ideal for defining who we were and what role we should be playing.

The Dellums group came back with a report that said in essence that we could no longer attempt to be all things to all black people. We had to recognize that we were not civil rights leaders, we were legislators elected to legislate in the U.S. Congress. We needed to leave the civil rights leadership to those who were active in that arena. We needed to recognize that we did not have the resources to continue running around the country to respond to the various urgent situations that might develop in one place or another. We had been to Chicago for the Black Panther shootings, to Jackson, to New Orleans, to military bases around the country. We had to recognize that we did not have the personal or financial resources to continue these kinds of activities.

The report recommended that we evaluate how we could most effectively influence legislation in Congress that affected black Americans as well as other minorities and the poor generally. In that vein the task force recommended that we try to expand our presence throughout the House committee system. That way we would be in a position to inject a black perspective on legislation moving through the committees. We had little in the way of seniority yet. But in time that would come, and as it did we would have more and more leverage in the areas most meaningful to us.

CHAPTER 8

~୧

First Years in Congress

WE CONCLUDED that Dellums's group was right and we accepted their report. We needed to apply ourselves to getting the best committee assignments we could. The U.S. Congress runs on seniority, and while most of us had little if any, the fact was that Clay, Chisholm, and I, among others, had been elected from traditionally black constituencies. If we did our jobs well, there was every reason to think that these relatively "safe" districts would keep us in office. If we represented our people as we were determined to do, seniority—that is, legislative power—would come.

That was the long perspective. Meanwhile, as a freshman representative, I was quickly introduced to the way these things were actually handled. The power in Congress resides primarily in three committees. The Appropriations Committee controls all the money—it wields the power of the purse. Whatever kind of legislation passes through Congress, only the Appropriations Committee has the authority to fund it. That is tremendous power. You can pass whatever you want to, but if Appropriations doesn't put the money into your legislation, there's no efficacy to whatever you thought you were going to accomplish. Then there's the Rules Committee, which sets the "rules" for how a bill will be considered on the floor: how long each side will have for debate, what kind of amendments will be allowed or if any will be allowed at all. You may have been working on a bill for three months and find that you have thirty minutes of floor time to present your case. The

Rules Committee determines what is going to happen to that bill, which can be politically explosive. That's power. And finally, the Ways and Means Committee wields the taxing authority. No African American had ever sat on any of those committees.

The Ways and Means Committee had an additional function. It determined which committees members would be assigned to. In this role it reconstituted itself as the Committee on Committees. A newly elected member could express his or her choice, which might or might not be granted. As often as not you, the new member, would find yourself on whatever committee they wanted you on.

For many years prior to Ohio's redistricting, Charlie Vanik had represented what became my district, the Twenty-First. He was well known in the black community and highly respected. He had represented the district well. When the redistricting happened, Vanik gave up the Twenty-First seat and was elected to represent the Twenty-Second District. Vanik had been in the House since 1955; he was the senior member of Ohio's delegation. He was also a senior member of the Ways and Means Committee. It was Charlie Vanik's job to get me my committee assignment.

What I wanted was the Education and Labor Committee. In order to make a difference in the lives of the people I represented, I had to do as much as I could on issues of employment, housing, and education. In terms of social legislation, Education and Labor would give me the best platform. At the same time, a place there would help me enhance Carl's endeavors as Cleveland's mayor.

I explained to Charlie that Labor and Education was my choice. He was a senior person, so I thought my chances were pretty good. Then he got back to me. "Lou," he said, "I talked with Carl. He's also eager for you to go to Education and Labor. I do think we can get you on there. I can't get you any seniority. Chisholm and Clay also want Education and Labor, and they've got strong backing. I can get you on, though. But . . ." he hesitated a moment. "First you have to do something for the Democrats."

"Oh. What's that, Charlie?"

"You've got to agree to go on HUAC."

The House Un-American Activities Committee was precisely the last committee I would ever want to go on. That committee was notorious for its relentless pursuit of suspected communists and for its vicious interrogation methods. Its members were the House face of the McCarthyism that infected the Senate and did so much damage to innocent people. Their whole history was an embarrassment.

"Charlie, you've go to be kidding. I just signed a petition to have that committee abolished."

"Louie, maybe you can do that better from the inside. The Democrats need a lawyer with your kind of experience in constitutional and civil rights law to go over there and stir things up. You're the right guy who can stop them from doing some of the things they do."

There wasn't much to think about. Refusing Charlie wasn't really an option. "Okay," I said. "Those guys see a communist behind every tree. But if I have to do it, I will."

I was thinking, What a situation, for me to have to sit on a committee with those people. But I agreed. So I was assigned to the infamous HUAC, and also to Education and Labor, behind Bill Clay in seniority. Bill was initially denied a seat there, but George Meany, president of the AFL/CIO, intervened for him—back in Saint Louis Bill had represented the Plumbers and Steamfitters, Meany's union. When Meany heard that Wilbur Mills, the chairman of Ways and Means, had rejected Clay, he growled, "No hick from Arkansas is going to put me in short pants. I don't sit in the bleachers for nobody." So now there were two of us on the committee that Adam Clayton Powell had formerly chaired and from which he had done so much good.

I was, to say the least, an oddity at HUAC. The *New York Times* actually ran a picture of me with the surprised caption: "Negro Appointed to Serve on HUAC." I believe, in fact, that I was now occupying the seat formerly held by Richard Nixon, a ruthless red-baiter in his congressional days.

The head of the committee was Richard Ichord from Saint Louis, a staunch conservative and anti-communist. I wasn't necessarily expecting to be welcomed there, but the fact was that Ichord and everyone else on the committee treated me with the utmost politeness and respect. Their political views might have been inimical to mine, but there wasn't a trace of hostility. They were all southern gentlemen. At one point I invited Carl to testify on communism in the cities. Everyone expected fireworks. But when Carl came in you would have thought they were all long-lost friends. They just turned on that southern hospitality for him. Nevertheless, I did work to abolish HUAC (which had been renamed the House Internal Security Committee) from the inside, and two or three years later we succeeded in doing just that.

Nixon, my predecessor on HUAC, was, of course, now president. And he was making problems for those of us in the Congressional Black Caucus right from the start. Nixon was a complex man. The fact was that he appointed some blacks to high positions in his administration, two at HUD and, notably, Art Fletcher as assistant secretary of labor, who became known as the father of affirmative action. But at the same time he went about dismantling Lyndon Johnson's War on Poverty programs, this at a time when black adult male unemployment was twice the national average and youth unemployment three times the average.

One of Nixon's first acts was an attempt to kill the Job Corps. I had an important and effective Job Corps program in my district headed by Mrs. Zelma George. Zelma George was a person of considerable stature in Cleveland and beyond. She had done her undergraduate work at the University of Chicago and had earned a PhD in sociology at NYU. She had served as adviser to President Dwight Eisenhower's administration, as an alternate delegate to the UN, and as a member of the Corporation for Public Broadcasting. When Nixon decided to shut down Job Corps she called me. "Lou," she said, "I want you to save my Job Corps." That's what I heard when I went on a tour of the facility, too. I especially recall the pleading, tearful look of a young white girl who said, "Please save us, Mr. Stokes."

Because of the success of the program and because of Mrs. George's prominence in the community, the Job Corps situation was receiving a great deal of media attention. This was my first real test as the district's representative. Everyone was watching to see if I'd be able to do something about the administration's shut-down intentions.

We fought Nixon hard on that, and won, at least in part. In the end the administration was able to eliminate Job Corps programs in some places, but our Cleveland program survived.

Nixon went after not just the Job Corps but the Office of Economic Opportunity, which coordinated Johnson's social programs, and he did succeed in killing that. He created a southern strategy, slowing down school desegregation and attempting to gut enforcement of the Voting Rights Act. He nominated two southern justices to the Supreme Court, Clement Haynsworth and Harold Carswell, both of whom had bad records on civil rights and desegregation. Their nominations were defeated, but only after sharp battles. Nixon's general attitude toward black problems and black people's struggles to live decent lives was what came to be called "benign neglect," a strategy proposed by his adviser Daniel Moynihan. I found that simply infuriating, treating us as if we didn't exist. To all of us, benign neglect meant that the administration had simply decided to ignore the problems of crime, unemployment, inferior schools, lack of health care, and other elements of social malaise that plagued our districts.

The upshot of all this was that the Congressional Black Caucus was determined to meet with the president in order to make clear to him the devastating effect his policies were having on our constituencies. Charlie Diggs, who was at that time still our chairman, contacted the White House and requested a meeting, but it took two months before a letter came back from a low-level staff assistant denying the request. We kept pursuing a meeting but made no headway. Moynihan was against it and John Ehrlichman, Nixon's adviser for domestic affairs, told *Newsweek* that the administration wasn't going to "permit opportunists to use the presidency as a grandstand." In the eyes of the White House we were, apparently, opportunists looking to grandstand.

I took Nixon's refusal to meet as an insult, not just to us as black representatives but to all the people we represented. In January 1971, on the afternoon of the State of the Union message, Bill Clay and I were on the floor talking about Nixon and his upcoming speech. I said to Bill, "You know, I really think we ought to boycott the president tonight. If the president won't meet with us, then we ought not meet with him. When he walks in this chamber he ought to see a sea of white faces. There shouldn't be a single black in that audience. That might get the message through to him about what he's doing to us."

Clay jumped on the idea instantly. Here's his memory of what happened then:

"As soon as Stokes suggested it I went to the phones at the back of the chamber, a battery of phones in the little lunch counter they had back there. I started calling everybody I could think of, all the members of the CBC and all my other contacts. I asked them to make calls about it to their contacts and organizations, then I put together a press release. By nightfall it was all over the world. Black folks ain't coming to this meeting."

That night the only black congressperson in the chamber for Nixon's speech was Massachusetts senator Ed Brooke. Brooke was a moderate Republican who had not joined the Congressional Black Caucus. I had talked to him about it and he said, "Lou, I'm the CBC on the Senate side. Let's leave it at that." Brooke and I became good friends; over the years we often worked together on bills in Appropriations Committee conferences. There wasn't all that much difference between us on most issues, but he had a far different political situation from the CBC members. Brooke was representing a state with a 3 percent black population. We were all coming out of majority black districts. We were much more vocal, more militant. We had a black base to back us up on anything we did, which he did not, so he had to do things differently.

The next day newspapers all over the world reported that America's black congressmen had boycotted the American president. The Soviets exploited it as blatant proof of capitalistic racism. The news was especially harmful in Africa, where Washington and Moscow were jousting for influence in newly liberated African countries. The day following Charlie Diggs got a call saying that President Nixon would meet with us. He just needed a little time to get it together.

We took that time to also get ourselves together. Diggs appointed a group of people—he called it "the black cabinet"—to organize the preparation of a document we could present to the president when we met. We were fortunate to have around us in the private sector top African American experts in a host of areas—economists, sociologists, lawyers, psychologists, political scientists, civil rights activists—and they all wanted to be a part of what the CBC was doing. Diggs took advantage of that and had them work with our staffs to draw up what came to be known as the "Black Manifesto," a sixty-point document recommending action to address the urgent problems of black communities, each point supported by in-depth research and data.

The document began: "Mr. President, we sought this meeting out of a deep conviction that large numbers of citizens are being subjected to intense hardship, are denied their basic rights, and are suffering irreparable harm as a result of current policies." Our recommendations ranged from jobs programs to a guaranteed income system, the assurance of adequate health care for all, the enforcement of affirmative action regulations to assure that minority contractors have equal opportunities, the strengthening of early childhood education programs, and a range of other initiatives focused on alleviating the insupportable conditions affecting so many in America's inner cities. "Our people are no longer asking equality as a rhetorical promise," we wrote. "They are demanding the only kind of equality that ultimately has any meaning—equality of results."

On March 25, 1971, we finally met with the president, the thirteen of us along with White House staff and members of Nixon's cabinet departments, including Secretary of Labor George Romney and OMB director George Schultz. The meeting took place in the Oval Office, and from the moment he walked in Nixon demonstrated his formidable political skill. One by one he went around the conference table where we were all standing and said a few appropriate words to each of us. He knew who we were, he knew something about our districts, he knew little bits and pieces of our personal lives. "How's Mayor Stokes doing?" he asked me. "How are his programs progressing up there in Cleveland?"

When we sat down and Charlie Diggs presented his preamble, Nixon said, "You know, if I were black I'd be just as angry as you are about what's happening around our country today." Then he asked to hear from us and sat there listening patiently as one of us after the other spoke briefly to one of the points in our document. I asked for the immediate release of $800 million that had been appropriated for social programs but had not yet been made available. When we were finished he turned to Assistant Secretary of Labor Art Fletcher.

"Art, what do you think of what these gentlemen have just said?"

"Mr. President," said Art, "I've been saying for months that this is what black America wants. And nobody's been paying any attention to me."

At the end Nixon instructed his staff and cabinet people to look closely at each of our suggestions and demands. Diggs asked him for a reply within two months. "We do need action," Nixon said. "We can't promise to do everything, but we'll do as much as we can."

Several good things did follow that meeting. In 1969 Art Fletcher had drafted the so-called Philadelphia Plan that mandated the inclusion of minorities in government contract work. The construction unions especially had kept their memberships almost completely white. "They are," said Art, "among the most egregious violators of equal opportunities laws." The city of Philadelphia was 30 percent black, but blacks made up only 1 percent of these unions' members. The plan required minority hiring. It was promulgated by executive order. But the Philadelphia unions opposed it in court, claiming, among other objections, that the administration had overstepped its constitutional authority. Fletcher was ready to put the plan in place in other cities but was holding back pending a court decision. Some months after our meeting a three-judge panel decided that the law was constitutional and enforceable. The White House pressed hard for it, as did the caucus. So that was a positive. Another executive order provided for federal support of minority businesses, and that too was welcome.

But the two-hundred-page reply we eventually received from the White House in effect only documented the administration's positions. Even the minority workers and business enterprise affirmative action plans had originated earlier. There wasn't a single new initiative addressing any of our sixty points. "In reality," the CBC said in our response, "[Nixon's document] constitutes less a response than a reply, couched predominantly in the form of bureaucratic reports intent on justifying the status quo." We weren't going to be satisfied with rhetoric, Charlie Diggs had told the president. And this report was a model of rhetoric substituting for action, two hundred pages essentially worth nothing. A runaround.

~⌒~

One of the major subjects addressed in the CBC's "manifesto" was foreign policy. In 1968 Nixon had campaigned on a promise to end the Vietnam War, for which, he said, he had "a secret plan." I had made ending the war a central element in my own campaign for Congress, and almost every other caucus member was strong in opposition to the war, none more so than Dellums, representing the antiwar militants in Berkeley, California.

Not only was the war a tragic foreign policy mistake, it was eating up huge amounts of money at a time when urgently needed domestic programs (most urgently in our communities), so sparse to begin with, were being cut back by the administration. "We call upon you," our manifesto read, "to effect disengagement from Southeast Asia. . . . We call for drastic reduction in our military expenditures, and the redirection of these funds to finance much needed domestic programs."

At first I was part of a small group of congressmen vocally opposed to the war. We spoke in public forums, at universities, to the media. Some of us, including New York's brilliant Allard Lowenstein and Ed Koch, who later became New York's mayor, held a candlelight vigil on the steps of Congress. I was one of the plaintiffs in a suit we filed against Nixon for conducting the war without congressional approval. In my speeches on the floor I was as forceful as I knew how to be. On the eve of the massive Moratorium to End the War demonstrations in October 1969, I reviewed the myths and mistakes in judgment that had gained us not the promised victory but a quagmire that had already swallowed up tens of thousands of American lives.

If we are able to accept the reality of this massive, misdirected military effort, I said, then "maybe we will be able to at last direct our thoughts to where they should have been all along—with the critical domestic problems facing this nation. The war has been costly in many ways. Over 225 million dollars in federal tax money has been spent on the war *from my district alone.* We could have used that money in Cleveland . . . for food, schools, clothing, homes, transportation, and to combat the poisoning of our environment. The only memorial to that money now is several hundred

Cleveland boys dead or maimed and a few burned-out villages. It was not worth it."

But instead of Nixon's supposed plan to end the war, we had gotten a deeper involvement, increased B-52 bombing campaigns, the Cambodian invasion, and many thousands of more deaths with no discernable progress. There was every reason to think that the 1972 presidential election was going to be a critical test for the war effort.

Well before 1972 I had given serious thought to how to handle my district as far as presidential primary elections went. The Twenty-First District sent eight Democratic delegates to the nominating convention. In the normal course of affairs candidates would run their slates in the district and the winner would pocket those eight delegates. But I thought, why let them do that? Why not take the eight delegates ourselves? Conventions were often horse races with fierce competition for delegate votes. If I had the delegates myself, I could sit down with candidates and say, Well, here's what we want for our eight votes.

In the 1972 presidential primary I ran my own slate, which meant that I myself was running for president in our district. I won and took those votes with me to the convention. With a few exceptions, I continued to do that throughout my tenure, using the Twenty-First District Caucus as my presidential vote-getting platform. These presidential races gave our people some real understanding of the value of their vote. They saw that they could have me sit in Florida or San Francisco or Chicago, wherever the convention was, and be able to negotiate something on their behalf from a person who might well become president of the United States.

We educated the people in our district. We worked at it. We wanted the Twenty-First to be the most politically powerful district in the state. The way we changed the usual business made people understand that we ourselves have power. We know it. We understand it. We're going to utilize it. We voted so heavily that we always had those eight delegates, which was based on the voting tally in the district. So we always got the maximum.

To get ahead of the story a bit, in the following election—1976—Jimmy Carter was running for the nomination. So was Mo Udall from Utah. Udall came into Cleveland and we talked. I explained to him that it was important that our people in the district take advantage of their political power. "Because of that," I told him, "I'm going to run as the candidate here. Assuming I win, I'll carry the delegates to the convention. At the convention you're going to need votes. We'll sit down and talk at that time."

Udall said, "Fine. I understand that, I respect it. I won't run a slate in your district."

Later when Governor Carter came along, he called me up one night. "Lou, this is Jimmy Carter. I'm running in your state. I'd like your support for my slate."

"Governor," I said, "I'm glad you called. I appreciate it. But what I'd like to ask is that you not run a slate in my district." And I explained to him why. "I'd really like to ask you to stay out of my district. When we get to the convention you and I can sit down and talk."

"Oh no, no," said Carter. "You know, I promised my people that I would file and run in every congressional district."

I said, "Okay, Governor." And we hung up.

So he filed a slate and I filed a slate. I beat him three to one. Carter won the state, but he lost my district.

Back in Washington the Ohio delegation put on a reception for him. Well, I thought, I ought to go. We had never met personally, so I thought, he probably doesn't know me. I went over and introduced myself.

"Hello, Governor, I'm Louis Stokes."

"I know who you are," Carter said. "You gave me a good ass-whipping in your district."

In 1972 George McGovern was running. But so, that year, was Shirley Chisholm. Her candidacy was legitimate enough, but quixotic. She had no money and no organization. She appeared to believe that she would generate substantial support from women, young people, and minorities in general. But I saw her as having absolutely no chance of becoming president of the United States or even gathering any meaningful number of delegates.

My perspective was that the plight of minorities, the poor, the disadvantaged in America was such that we could not play games in terms of how we could help resolve the problems that daily beset them. So when you think about trying to solve these problems you have to be serious about the means by which you attack them. You start that endeavor, if at all possible, with the presidency. I thought, If I'm serious about doing something for my people, then I have to place my energy in support of a realistic possibility, which Shirley was not. As a consequence, I was going to utilize my political position to support someone with an actual chance of becoming president. We had to be practical about our voting power instead of heading off on a tangent.

My eight delegates weren't that many, but when I got to the convention in Florida that year I was able to work with Bill Clay, who had six, and Walter Fauntroy, who brought thirteen with him from the District of Columbia. Together that was a significant bloc of votes. It enabled us to sit down with McGovern and negotiate with him for some of the things we needed.

George McGovern, we believed, was the one Democratic candidate who did have a chance. He announced that he was in favor of the Congressional Black Caucus's sixty-point program that we had presented to Nixon. He was fully committed to ending the war, a burning necessity. So, along with Clay and Fauntroy, I supported him and did what I could to lobby others for his benefit.

Of course, as it turned out, McGovern's candidacy did not resonate with the majority of the American people. We were stuck in a deadly war. We were stuck with the progressive hollowing out of what we considered critical social programs. Nixon's continuing presidency was disheartening, to say the least.

It's a commonplace that politicians need to put aside personal feelings to most effectively further the interests of their constituents—no permanent friends, no permanent enemies, just permanent interests, as Clay had put it. But I was not an accomplished politician, and as far as Nixon went, I never did learn that lesson. He was someone I truly disliked. He was sleazy. He was profane. He was a man who, in my opinion, would do anything for his personal aggrandizement. I believed his policies were at heart racist. He represented, I thought, the worst of our society. At the same time, he was a master at the art of exercising political power. He was able to manipulate Congress better than any president I served under, which included Presidents Ford, Carter, Reagan, George H. W. Bush, and Bill Clinton. He also had a subtle grasp of foreign policy, and I give him credit for that. But I was not surprised when Watergate broke and the investigation began to reveal the level of the man's immorality and disregard for the law and his office.

I was one of the first members of Congress to call for Nixon's impeachment. After the Saturday Night Massacre in which Nixon fired Special Prosecutor Archibald Cox, which precipitated the resignations of Attorney General Elliot Richardson and Deputy Attorney General William Ruckelshaus, I spoke on the floor in behalf of the CBC:

> The Congressional Black Caucus . . . is dismayed and shocked by the actions of Richard M. Nixon. . . . The decisions to discharge Archibald Cox and abolish the office of Special Prosecutor were both irresponsible and unconscionable. . . . The end result represents not only an insult to the intelligence of American citizens but an assault on established governmental institutions and more fundamentally on the Constitution itself. . . . Watergate and all its associated criminal activities, the shady campaign contributions and payoffs

and Nixon's bevy of illegal impoundments of critical social program funding only serve to strengthen the position that Richard Nixon should—and must—be removed from office.

The Watergate scandal broke in 1972. By then I was into my second term in Congress. As chairman of the CBC I had precipitated Ron Dellums's report on how we could most effectively leverage our power. The caucus had accepted Dellums's conclusion—that we needed to devote ourselves to gaining meaningful places in the House committee system. My own path to doing that started by trying to learn everything I could about the sometimes arcane practices and procedures of this august deliberative body I was now part of.

I was fortunate in this regard to have mentors who cared about me and the advancement of my career. One was Hale Boggs, the House majority leader from Louisiana. He went out of his way to be warm and talk with me about civil rights and other issues. Jack Brooks from Texas was another. Brooks was one of a very small handful of southern representatives who voted for the 1964 Civil Rights Act. Mo Udall of Utah and Jim Wright of Texas were also good friends and counselors to me as I began to learn my way around, as was Phil Burton from California.

Burton and Carl were friends. "Just follow what Phil does," Carl had told me. "You won't go wrong doing that." "Carl told me to look out for you," said Burton, and he did. One day we were working on a bill on the Education and Labor Committee, where we were both members. I was looking at the bill as a lawyer and telling people the legal requirements of what we were doing. Phil came over to me and took me aside. He whispered, "Lou, Lou, you're absolutely right about the legal things. But that isn't what we're trying to do here. You're right legally, but you're wrong politically. Just back up."

I absorbed those kinds of lessons. I watched my mentors in debate, the same way I used to watch Norman Minor argue a case. They talked to me about how no matter how passionately you believe in what you are arguing for on the floor, it is your responsibility to be collegial in the manner in which you address the person you are debating: "the member with whom I disagree so heartily on this occasion, although he is my friend and someone for whom I have great respect." I learned from that. I stood up, but I didn't do it with rhetorical fireworks. I tried to maintain a sense of civility. People knew I would fight them all day long if I had to, but it was my natural inclination to try to get along and work things out. And as time went on that lesson served me well.

In those first years, when I was trying to learn everything I could as fast as I could, no one was more important to me than Charlie Vanik, my fellow Ohioan and predecessor as representative of the Twenty-First District. Vanik was a true mentor. He went through all the nuances of the House with me; he talked to me about people and positions and personalities and how best to relate to the many fellow representatives I was dealing with. His office worked with my office to see that I would be part of relevant legislation. He was with me on the floor when I made my maiden speech.

At the beginning of my second term he came to me and said he thought it was time for me to make a move to go onto the Appropriations Committee. That was almost unheard of, for someone to go onto that hugely powerful committee after only one term. "I think we can get you on there," Vanik said. "There's never been a black member on Appropriations. It's time to make that move and we think you're the right person to make it with. Besides, the party owes you for going on HUAC. You did them a big favor there. Appropriation's the committee that's going to make a difference for you and for the district. You've got that poor district, Lou. You have to do everything you can to help your people. You'll be able to do exactly that if you're on Appropriations."

Charlie initiated the drive to get me on there. But we still had to do the political work, which was for me to lobby members to get their support— which I did, and which he did, too. Right up until the processes screeched to a halt when Charlie began taking heat from some of his political allies back in Cleveland.

The Democratic machine back home was not in the least pleased with the steps Carl and I had taken to move Twenty-First District political workers and voters out of their traditional obedience to the party. In particular, they felt that the last thing the party should do was to reward me by giving me a highly coveted and influential seat on the Appropriations Committee, not when back in Cleveland I was attacking and defeating Democrats.

As a result, Charlie told me that unless Carl and I changed our political approach in Cleveland he wasn't going to be able to push the Appropriations appointment for me any longer. That set up something of a battle. Neither Carl nor I were going to go back on the Twenty-First District Caucus. So we had to figure a way to pressure Vanik to get him to stay with the plan and not let Cleveland politics interfere with national politics.

I was fortunate that the *Plain Dealer* entered the fray on my side, since the paper was mostly far more critical of me than not. But in an editorial they attacked Vanik for mixing local with national politics. Of course, having an additional Ohioan on the committee would be a big advantage for the state, which was likely the reason they took up the cudgel. Charlie Diggs played a big role as well. He and Vanik were good friends; they had come in together as freshman representatives in 1955 and they had great respect for each other. Diggs wrote Vanik a letter saying that what we were doing in Cleveland was what the district needed, and that should not by any means take away this historic opportunity to put the first black member on the Appropriations Committee. The CBC followed that with their own similar letter. That was a theme Vanik could hardly ignore. Nor could Majority Leader Carl Albert, who put his weight behind my appointment "in the interest of unity and harmony within the Democratic Party." After that Charlie thought better of his opposition and went back to supporting me for the seat.

So at the beginning of my second term I was graciously welcomed onto the Appropriations Committee by its chairman, George Mahon, a long-serving, stately Texan who assigned me to two subcommittees: Treasury/Post Office and the District of Columbia, neither considered particularly important. But I was sure that in time my chance to move up would come.

Meanwhile, this was my second historic appointment as an African American—the first being HUAC. I did not yet have the ability to bring real power to bear on legislation, but I was being recognized as someone who was moving quickly, which boded well.

CHAPTER 9

Assassination Committee

WHEN MEMBERS serve on Appropriations, Rules, or Ways and Means, they are ordinarily prohibited from taking seats on other committees. The big committee posts are considered too significant to allow time for other work. But in 1974 an act was passed creating a standing Budget Committee to provide an independent analysis of the yearly federal budget and reconcile differences between the president and Congress. As part of the political maneuvering over the budget act, several slots on the new committee were assigned to Appropriations Committee members.

When the Budget Committee was established a number of people, including Phil Burton, suggested I run for one of the seats. "We've heard that Jamie Whitten is running," Burton told me. "He's bad enough where he is." Whitten was a smart, old-line, segregationist southern politician, the author of the infamous Whitten Amendments that would have prevented the use of federal funds for busing in order to achieve integration in schools (though later in his career Whitten became considerably more liberal). So I did run, and together with Burton and some others I began lobbying for support. When word got around about that, Whitten came to me and said, "Why don't you go ahead. I've decided not to run for it." So now I was on Budget as well as Appropriations and Education and Labor. My plate was filling up quickly.

In 1977 Tip O'Neill campaigned to become Speaker of the House. Tip was a New Deal–style Massachusetts liberal who had come out against the Vietnam War early on, breaking with the party leadership. He had also been one of the first to call for Nixon's impeachment as the Watergate scandal unfolded. He was a strong advocate for universal health care and jobs programs. We had a lot in common. I did everything I could to support him in his quest for the job.

Tip was not one to neglect those who had helped him in one way or another, which now included me. "Louie, my pal," he liked to call me. Over his years as Speaker he furthered my career on several important committees, the first of which was the House Select Committee on Assassinations.

Carl Albert, O'Neill's predecessor as Speaker, had established this committee chiefly at the request of the Congressional Black Caucus. What had happened was that Coretta Scott King had talked to Walter Fauntroy about allegations that had come to her attention regarding the FBI's involvement in Martin Luther King's murder. Rumors had been floating around for years about this, but now a black Memphis policeman was claiming that he had been taken off security duty guarding King just before King was shot, which suggested there was some kind of high-level, possibly FBI, intervention.

The context here was that the Church Senate Committee on Intelligence Activities had recently published their report on the illegalities the FBI was involved in. The report revealed that the agency had been targeting King for years, subverting his activities, spreading false information and scurrilous rumors about him, bugging his phones and those of his colleagues. King's FBI tormentors had sent him an anonymous letter, repeating many times that he was "done," he was "finished," and urging him to commit suicide. "The 'neutralization' program continued until Dr. King's death," the Church report stated. "As late as March 1968 [a month before the assassination], FBI agents were being instructed to neutralize Dr. King because he might become a 'messiah' who could 'unify and electrify the militant black nationalist movement' if he were to 'abandon his supposed 'obedience' to 'white liberal doctrines' (nonviolence) and embrace black nationalism."

It was against this background that a group of us accompanied Mrs. King to talk to Speaker Albert about her contentions, urging him to establish an investigative committee. Albert agreed to do it, but the idea almost immediately opened an unexpected Pandora's box. Once it was known that the Speaker was considering a special committee, people who had never been able to get Congress to investigate the Kennedy assassination tried to piggyback on it. That might have had some cogency. Even more conspiracy rumors and theories about Kennedy's death than about King's had been in the air, many of them claiming FBI or CIA collusion. They had spawned a thriving cottage industry of assassination books and articles. Then other people began urging that the yet-to-be-established committee should include the Robert Kennedy assassination in its purview, which led to requests that the Malcolm X and George Wallace shootings deserved attention as well. A few began insisting that the Abraham Lincoln assassination had never been fully resolved, either.

In the end it came down to House politics. Albert saw that if John F. Kennedy's death weren't included in this, he wouldn't have the votes. So the House Select Committee on Assassinations was established to investigate Kennedy's murder as well as King's.

Albert named Thomas Downing of Virginia as the committee's chairman. Downing had been the leading advocate for reinvestigating the Kennedy assassination; he had been pushing that for years. Like many people he was skeptical of the Warren Commission's conclusions, and he was firmly convinced that a conspiracy was responsible, most likely involving Cubans. Thirteen other members were empaneled for the committee, including Walter Fauntroy, Yvonne Braithwaite Burke (also a CBC member), and myself.

As chief counsel Downing hired Richard Sprague, an assistant district attorney in Philadelphia who had become nationally famous for his successful prosecution of United Mine Workers president Tony Boyle for the murder of Jock Yablonsky, Boyle's competitor for the union presidency. Sprague had garnered a striking record of homicide convictions in Philadelphia. He was known as a smart, tenacious, aggressive prosecutor.

Sprague was a highly credible choice as counsel. Downing, though, was a strange choice as chairman, since he was a lame duck due to leave office at the end of the term, which he did. To replace him, Albert named Henry Gonzales of Texas. Gonzales and Sprague began feuding almost immediately over Sprague's proposed budget and investigative tactics, and shortly after he took on the chairmanship Gonzales summarily fired Sprague.

In this area Congress operates on the principle that staffers should be seen, not heard. As one longtime member advised me early on when I asked what titles to give to my senior staff, "Don't worry about that, Lou. There are only two types of people on Capitol Hill: members and clerks." Gonzales must have found Sprague insufferable. When the media asked him why he had fired Sprague so precipitously, Gonzales said, "When I walk out on my front porch and see a snake, I don't ask questions, I just stomp it."

So the first chairman, Downing, hadn't done anything, and now the second, Gonzales, had gotten into this public furor with his chief counsel. The committee had barely begun to work and already it was in disarray. People who didn't want any investigation to begin with were calling it a farce. Nothing had been done and nothing was going to be done. The Scripps Howard newspapers around the country began running editorials with the caption "Kill It." Their writers denounced the committee and the reasons for its formation. Kill it, they said, don't fund it, let it die a natural death.

Although Gonzales had fired Sprague, Sprague refused to go, insisting that only the committee as a whole had the right to fire him. Gonzales couldn't stand it. Sprague was, he said, "unscrupulous," "unconscionable." Fed up with the situation and buffeted by the press frenzy, Gonzales now resigned. That upset quite a few House members. They resented that a committee chairman would have to resign over a squabble with a staff person whose job should have been to do what Gonzales wanted him to do. They didn't like that at all. It set a bad precedent. So even members who might not have had much interest in the committee one way or another began questioning whether it ought to be funded. The thing was beginning to seem like an embarrassment.

Shortly after Gonzales resigned, Fauntroy, Yvonne Braithwaite Burke, and I were in my office discussing this distressing state of affairs when I got a phone call from the new Speaker, Tip O'Neill.

"Louie, my pal."

"Hello, Mr. Speaker."

"Louie, you're on the Assassinations Committee. There's a vacancy in the chairmanship and you have the seniority. I'd like to appoint you as chairman."

"Mr. Speaker, are you sure this is something you feel I can do?"

"Sure, I feel like you can do it!"

"Well, if you want me to do it, I will."

But as soon as I got off the phone and went back to Yvonne and Fauntroy, one of them said, "Lou, you sure about this? You know they're trying to kill the committee. You may want to rethink accepting the chairmanship. If they kill it you don't want to be sitting at the head of it. A dead committee that was supposed to be looking into the assassination of Dr. King? With you as chair?"

"Hmm," I said. "You've got a point."

We were now in a new term. The committee had to get funding. Scripps Howard was attacking relentlessly. Nothing was being done. The scandal between the chairman and the counsel was still making waves. There was serious doubt as to whether the committee actually would get the money it needed, and if it didn't it would simply expire.

Congress was in session just then; O'Neill had called me from his chair at the podium.

"I'm going to talk to the Speaker," I said.

When I went down to the floor Tip was presiding. I stood in the well for a minute before he saw me and invited me to come up.

"Louie, what is it?"

"Mr. Speaker, I'm not sure I want to accept that chairmanship after all."

"Really? Why not?"

"Mr. Speaker, you know about this committee's difficulties. I don't want to be presiding over a dead horse."

"What do you mean?"

"I mean that if this committee isn't going to be funded I don't want to be sitting in the chair when that happens."

"Louie, I wouldn't do that to you. I'll make sure you get whatever you need."

"Okay, then," I said. "Your word's good enough for me, Mr. Speaker. If that's the case, you've got yourself a chairman."

Tip O'Neill was a powerhouse, but I knew that though he wanted to do it, there was so much opposition to this committee that getting the funding was going to be a problem. So once he appointed me the first item on my agenda was to figure out a strategy. The other members agreed with me that we ourselves would have to go to work and politic this in order to get the funds and save the committee. There was a lot of sentiment in the House to just let these dogs lie. But there were other people equally determined that you couldn't just leave allegations out there that the FBI had killed the president of the United States.

Chris Dodd of Connecticut led the funding effort. He put together the strategy and really went to work. We all had meetings with different members of Congress and sometimes group meetings where we'd invite two or three members to talk with us, to explain the situation, what we were up against, and how badly we needed their cooperation. We explained the scope of what we needed to do, we gave assurances that we were going to handle our investigations with the utmost credibility and professionalism, in a way that would reflect well on the House. We offered to answer any questions they had. I also fired Sprague, and this time he went. I think our approach here helped restore confidence that under my chairmanship the committee would carry out its work thoroughly and impartially.

Under the rules establishing the committee we only had eighteen days before the original funding measure expired—eighteen days to change the mood and get support. It was an uphill fight, but in the end we succeeded in getting ourselves funded. For the first time, the committee was on stable footing.

Once we had the funding my next order of business was to find a chief counsel. My initial thought was to see if we could get Archibald Cox, the Watergate special prosecutor who had been fired by Nixon in the famous Saturday Night Massacre. But Cox declined my request. So did former Supreme Court justice Arthur Goldberg. With that, I asked Chris Dodd to draw up a list of candidates. After interviewing the most promising of them, I settled on Robert Blakey.

Blakey was a law professor at Cornell who had drafted the RICO Act and other criminal investigation law while counsel to James McClellan's Senate Subcommittee on Criminal Laws and Procedures. Blakey had served under Robert Kennedy in the Justice Department and had a distinguished history in criminal investigation and judicial proceedings. He seemed to me the right person. He had the skills, the integrity, and he was known and respected on the Hill. What I particularly liked was hearing him say, "Mr. Chairman, if I were to accept this job we would have to work together very closely, almost like husband and wife. I want to be honest with you, I'm going to need to check you out, just as you are checking me out."

"Okay," I said. "You do that."

Apparently I passed muster, because shortly afterward he came back and said, "Congressman Stokes, I'd like to take this job with you."

Given the fiasco with the two previous chairmen and Sprague, the previous chief counsel, I needed most importantly to establish the committee's credibility. Given his reputation, Bob Blakey went a long way toward that goal. I hired him for the job, which meant that he would oversee the committee's day-to-day operations and serve as the key staff strategist.

I then divided the committee into two subcommittees, one for the King investigation, one for Kennedy. I appointed Walter Fauntroy to chair the King assassination subcommittee and Richardson Preyer of North Carolina for the Kennedy.

Everyone on the committee understood what a daunting task we had in front of us. President Kennedy had been dead for fourteen years, Dr. King for nine—plenty of time for witnesses to die or disappear and evidence to be lost or destroyed. Over time memories fade and trails grow cold. Beyond that, sifting through the chaotic maze of rumors and theories presented a prodigious challenge by itself. Self-styled experts had picked apart skeins of evidence and constructed elaborate cases for their own suppositions, which they espoused relentlessly, often with religious fervor.

All this had to be approached systematically and efficiently, in particular because the House had given us a time limitation of two years. I had a deep background in murder cases from my years as a defense attorney, and Blakey was a highly competent administrator and investigator. I was sure that if we had been given these cases when they were hot, we would have had an excellent shot at solving them. Attempting to do that so long after the events was going to be far more challenging. And yet what could be more important than resolving in the most authoritative way possible the murders of these two men, one the nation's president, the other a towering African American hero who had done nothing less than change the course of American history?

I was prepared to bear the burden of this responsibility, but I was also aware of the potential downside. Right from the start the previous chairmen had made a mess of these investigations. With all the conspiracy theories that had swirled around for years, something like a circus atmosphere hovered over these gravest of national events. Against this background, our work had to be seen as ultimately credible. We had to bring to it a thoroughness and intelligence that would put its integrity beyond question. Whether or not we would be successful at that was going to have a lasting impact on me and whatever my reputation might turn out to be. And it wasn't lost on me that I was going to be judged not simply for my performance per se, but for my performance as a black man. I knew that a veil of prejudice overlaid whites' perceptions of black people's abilities. The damage from any kind of failure, or even perceived failure, would be far more than personal.

We knew that 85 percent of Americans believed that Lee Harvey Oswald was not a lone shooter, that he was part of a conspiracy. The Warren Report had left too many unanswered or incompletely answered questions. The Church Senate committee report, which had revealed the FBI's long war against Martin Luther King, had also described the CIA's attempts to kill Fidel Castro. Mafia bosses Sam Giancana, a successor of Al Capone in Chicago; Johnny Roselli, one of his associates; and Santo Trafficante, a

Miami don, had all colluded with the CIA in assassination plots against Castro. So it seemed plausible to some that Castro would have wanted to take revenge or to get Kennedy before Kennedy got him. Or again, Oswald had spent time in the Soviet Union; perhaps he had been recruited by the KGB. Exiled Cubans were also suspect. Kennedy had not backed up the Bay of Pigs invasion with air strikes, which had contributed to the death or capture of over a thousand CIA trained Cuban expatriates. Cuban exiles certainly had their reasons to go after him. Kennedy had a long-term affair with one of Giancana's girlfriends. Did the Mafia feel he had to be eliminated? Then there was Jack Ruby, Oswald's killer, a nightclub owner close to mob figures. Then there was the so-called magic bullet that had, according to the Warren Commission, passed through Kennedy's throat and Governor Connally's wrist and into his thigh, even while remaining more or less pristine. Unlikely, many thought. The air was thick with these things, and more. We needed to sort them out.

I had told Bob Blakey that we needed to get the best criminal investigators and forensic scientists available. Accordingly, we contracted with leading independent experts in the fields of forensic pathology, ballistics, photography, acoustics, and neutron activation analysis. Our field investigators were former homicide cops, detectives, and criminologists led by Eddie Evans, a retired New York City detective supervisor who in his twenty-two years with the department had interviewed tens of thousands of suspects and witnesses. I had never met a more skilled interrogator. These teams did extraordinary work conducting technical studies, sifting through leads, tracking down people and evidence, interviewing persons of interest, and cutting through apparent enigmas.

There was, for example, the umbrella man theory. The Zapruder film had shown a man on the grassy knoll lifting up and opening an umbrella just as the president's car passed by in front of the Book Depository. He was the only person among the crowd of onlookers with an umbrella—that day in Dallas was bright and sunny. It seemed that he might have been signaling the shooter, or perhaps he himself was the second shooter. A CIA agent had testified to the Church Committee that the CIA had in fact developed an umbrella weapon. Books had been written about the umbrella man, with illustrations showing how the gun could have been deployed in the raised umbrella.

Fifteen years later, our investigators tracked down the umbrella man and brought him in to testify in front of us, with his umbrella. His name was

Louis Steven Witt. He had never before been questioned by the police or other government investigators. What was he doing on that sunny day on the grassy knoll with an umbrella?

Louis Steven Witt turned out to be a mild-mannered, charming individual. He testified that he had been out for his usual lunch break walk from the insurance company where he worked. He had heard that President Kennedy's motorcade was going to come through the center of town, so he was walking in that general direction, with his umbrella, which he had brought along specifically to heckle Kennedy with.

Witt didn't particularly like Kennedy; he said he didn't think too highly of liberals in general. He had also heard from somewhere that umbrellas were a sore point with the Kennedys. It had something to do with their father, Joseph Kennedy, who was ambassador to England in the years leading up to World War II and was in favor of appeasing the Nazis. England's prime minister, Neville Chamberlain, had appeased Hitler at Munich, and Chamberlain was usually depicted carrying an umbrella. So the umbrella was a symbol of appeasement. Witt had heard that a group of JFK hecklers somewhere had opened umbrellas in front of Kennedy, which had annoyed the president. He was a little vague on all this, but he had decided that opening an umbrella in front of Kennedy would be just the thing, even though he felt stupid and awkward carrying an umbrella on such a nice day. He had been pretty close to Kennedy's car when the president was shot, but he hadn't seen it because he "had the stupid umbrella opened" in front of him.

"Did the umbrella have a gun in it?" I asked.

"No," he said, a little incredulous at the question.

"Did it have a dart gun it?" (One theory was that the umbrella man had shot Kennedy with a paralyzing dart, which set the president up for the assassin's bullet.)

"A dart gun? No, it didn't have a dart gun."

"Would you open the umbrella, please."

He didn't want to open it. We were in open session; photographers were there. He didn't want his picture in the newspapers opening the umbrella. He was already embarrassed enough, he said. So was his family. I asked a staff person to open it. When she did, it fell apart. The hearing room filled with laughter. It was a cheap, fifteen-year-old umbrella, quite apparently not an assassin's weapon.

We dealt with the umbrella man theory. We dealt with the magic bullet theory. Conspiracy practitioners were particularly obsessed with this subject since the Warren Commission's study of the autopsy results was not thor-

ough, plus the records had been sealed, which had led to all sorts of specula-
tion about a cover-up. In addition, the Zapruder film seemed to show that at
least one bullet had hit Kennedy from the front rather than, as the autopsy
report stated, from behind.

To reexamine this subject we first had all the autopsy and related evidence authenticated by a team of forensic anthropologists, forensic dentists,
and radiologists. Then we impaneled a committee of nine of the country's
leading forensic pathologists, eight of whom were chief medical examiners
in major cities. Among them they had performed over a hundred thousand
autopsies. Our investigators reenacted the shooting, duplicating the trajec-
tory, the type of bullet, and the other forensic elements, using goats to show
that, yes, a bullet could penetrate two bodies through the path that bullet
took and emerge relatively pristine. As a result of these investigations as well
as examinations of the witness interviews, and in some cases reinterviews
that we ourselves did, we were able to absolutely confirm the Warren Commission's conclusion about both the so-called magic bullet and the death
wound itself.

We looked hard at the Cuban theories. The revelations about the CIA's
Mafia-related plots to kill Castro were spectacular. Castro must have known
about at least some of them. How did they affect him? Castro had allowed
the Soviets to place nuclear weapons in Cuba aimed against the United
States, which had led to the Cuban Missile Crisis only a year before Kennedy was killed. He had, in other words, almost precipitated a thermonuclear
war. Would assassinating the American president have been beyond him?

We could find no evidence of Cuban involvement, but as part of our
investigation my staff initiated efforts to see if Castro himself would talk to
us. We were astonished and excited when word came back that he was willing. To my knowledge, no other head of state had ever subjected himself to
this kind of interrogation by another country, let alone about an assassination
of another nation's leader.

We hardly expected that Castro was going to somehow admit that Cuba
was involved. But we did think it would be most interesting to hear what he
had to say. We thought it would be good to get him on record about that. We
were even more interested in getting his understanding of the nature of the
situation between the two countries. We thought there was value in opening
a window on the relationship between himself and Kennedy and Cuba and
the United States. I personally thought that had extremely great value.

On April 3, 1978, I sat down with Fidel Castro in his presidential office.
Subcommittee chairman Richardson Preyer was with me, as were Chris

Dodd, Blakey, various other staff, and an interpreter. Castro had his own advisers and staff and his own interpreter.

I wasn't sure how this was going to work; a meeting like this was unprecedented. But I decided to handle it as I would any other interrogation. How Castro was going to handle it, I couldn't say.

After some pleasantries and a number of introductory questions and answers, I got to the point, though indirectly. I asked not whether he knew about any involvement of his government, but about what he thought of assassination as a political tool in general. I meant to open him up on the subject.

It did not take much to open up Fidel Castro, who was famous for speaking for four or five hours at a stretch. The man was not naturally reticent. But he was extremely intelligent and extremely sharp; he understood instantly what I was really asking him.

"It was really something inconceivable," he said, "that we could have the idea of killing the president . . . that would have been a tremendous insanity." The Cuban revolutionaries were "an intrepid people," he said. "But we have not proven to be an insane people. The leaders of the Revolution do not do crazy things."

Castro went on at length to describe how his entire effort from the Bay of Pigs to the Missile Crisis and beyond was to protect Cuba from an American invasion. "We have always been extremely concerned to prevent any factor that could become an argument or a pretext for carrying out aggression against our country." He understood all too well that if American might were ever unleashed against Cuba, his country would be demolished. His revolution would be a page in a history book instead of the driving force in a living nation.

"Who could have operated and planned something so delicate as the death of the United States president? . . . From an ideological point of view it was insane. And from the political point of view it was a tremendous insanity. I am going to tell you here that nobody, nobody ever had the idea of such things. What would it do? . . . That would have been the most perfect pretext for the United States to invade our country, which is what I have tried to prevent for all these years, in every possible sense." He felt, he said, that "this committee here" [namely, my colleagues and I] "is giving the impression that we are being judged, that we are being tried."

Castro also gave an appreciation of Kennedy. The president was, the Cuban leader said, an adversary, but a known adversary, so someone they were growing comfortable with to a certain extent. He felt fortunate that Kennedy had been president during the Bay of Pigs invasion. "If the 1960 election had not been won by Kennedy, but Nixon instead, during the Bay of Pigs the United States would have invaded Cuba. There is no doubt that we appreciate very highly that Kennedy resisted every kind of pressure to have the Marines land in our country. Nixon himself was in favor of that."

Moreover, Castro believed that Kennedy was in the process of reevaluating the American relationship with Cuba. "I can tell you," he said, "that in the period in which Kennedy's assassination took place Kennedy was changing his policy toward Cuba. . . . You could see indisputably that a new trend was coming." In fact, at the very moment he learned of the assassination, Castro was speaking with a French journalist, Jean Daniel, whom he believed was delivering a back-channel message from Kennedy. "One of the things I regretted the most was that I was convinced that Kennedy was starting to change . . . and that I was here talking to that man who was bringing a message from him." Castro was, he said, "saddened" by Kennedy's death, even "bitter" about it.

By May 1978 we had managed to draw our investigations to an end and were preparing to issue our final report. We had done a thorough forensic analysis of the bullet evidence and the fingerprint evidence performed by leading experts using technology not available fifteen years earlier. We had brought in photographic evidence specialists and forensic anthropologists to verify all the extant pictures of Oswald and Kennedy relative to the event. We had impaneled nine forensic pathologists to review the methodology and accuracy of the original autopsy. We had examined all the most apparently plausible conspiracy theories as thoroughly as possible. We had reviewed the Warren report to determine both its flaws and its accuracy.

We were about to close our hearings and deliver our report. Our draft conclusion was that there was no conspiracy and that Oswald acted alone. But at the last moment our investigators were drawn to the existence of a motorcycle policeman's Dictabelt tape recording of that day's events. It had been stored with the mass of Warren Commission material, but we couldn't ascertain whether they had ever listened to it.

The tape was recorded on a Dictabelt machine commonly used by Dallas motorcycle officers. We commissioned the Cambridge, Massachusetts, technology research firm of Bolt, Beranek and Newman to analyze the tape for us, the same firm that had analyzed both the Watergate tape with its famous eighteen-minute gap and the tape of the Kent State National Guard killing of four students during a Vietnam War demonstration. When their analysis came back it showed that four shots, not three, had been fired that day, three from Oswald's rifle and a fourth from the vicinity of the Grassy Knoll. Dr. James Barger, who headed the BBN team, testified that the probability of the report's accuracy was 95.6 percent. This was explosive. If there was indeed another shooter, that meant there had been a conspiracy of some kind. Oswald had not acted alone.

We immediately ordered a review of the BBN findings by other acoustic scientists, Mark Weiss and Ernest Aschkenasy of Queens College. Their work corroborated the BBN analysis. Then, in order to be as certain as possible, we went to Dallas and, with the help of the Dallas Police Department, reenacted the shootings with microphones placed along the motorcade route through Dealey Plaza.

When these test patterns were then compared to the suspect sound patterns on the Dictabelt, they were found to match. That is, all the relevant sound patterns identified on acoustical criteria in the laboratory analyses were found to match the echo patterns of test shots fired in Dealey Plaza. The odds of this happening if the sounds were not gunfire were remote.

Most of us on the committee now concluded that there had to have been a fourth shot; in other words, a conspiracy was involved. In the end it was clear to us that we could not simply ignore two scientific studies of the tapes done by leading acoustics experts. In our findings we wrote:

> Scientific acoustical evidence establishes a high probability that two gunmen fired at President John F. Kennedy. Other scientific evidence does not preclude the possibility of two gunmen firing at the president. . . . The committee believes, on the basis of the evidence available to it, that President John F. Kennedy was probably assassinated as the result of a conspiracy.

It is worth noting that subsequent to our report, examinations of the Dictabelt evidence took on a life of their own. In our final report we had urged the Justice Department to review all of our findings for accuracy and pursue any elements they believed required further investigation. The one area they did follow up was the tape analysis. We turned the Dictabelt material over to them, and they submitted it to the National Academy of Sciences and its Research Council Committee on Ballistic Acoustics. The NAS conclusion, issued almost two years after our final report, disputed the BBN and Queens College conclusions. Some years after that, a British analysis published in the *Journal of the Forensic Science Society* corroborated the BBN and Weiss/Aschkenasy studies. As I write this, thirty-seven years after the publication of our committee findings, the debate is still alive.

We had concluded that President Kennedy was "probably assassinated as the result of a conspiracy." But we were unable to name the co-conspirators. In fact, we had succeeded in dismissing the conspiracy theorists' favorite suspects. But though we could not identify the co-conspirators, we did name the categories from which the co-conspirator could have come. In our findings, for example, we concluded that organized crime was not involved in the assassination. But we did not discount the fact that individual members of organized crime could have been involved. The same with the anti-Castro group, and others.

I was proud of the work our committee did. Of course, conspiracy theorists are still busily arguing cases. Their devotion to this subject is, simply, remarkable. No one, it seems to me, is ever going to finally close the curtain on the killing of the country's thirty-fifth president. But my committee's investigation, which we conducted with so much care and seriousness, bringing in the top experts of the day to assist us, has never been refuted. It still stands as the landmark study of this signal event in the nation's history.

When Oliver Stone's movie *JFK* came out, I did not rush out see it. But as it gathered momentum and notoriety, I felt I needed to look at what he had done. In the theater I sat and watched as the film flagrantly falsified factual material and fictionalized history in order to assert that our government itself had killed the president. The film created a myth around sinister government operations and deep official duplicity, a massive, secret, concerted plot by the CIA, FBI, Secret Service, and military intelligence all working together in the interest of the military industrial complex, which stood to lose vast sums of money because a peace-loving President Kennedy was planning to pull America out of the Vietnam War. As the man in line to succeed Kennedy, Vice President Lyndon Johnson was the designated benefactor for the war industry. The assassination, in other words, was a coup d'état. This spiderweb of secret controllers, the movie implied, was also responsible for the assassinations of Martin Luther King Jr. and Robert Kennedy because they too favored peace and the downsizing of the military, to the detriment of war capitalism.

For its part, the Warren Commission supposedly covered up or obtusely ignored evidence of the ongoing iniquity at the heart of the combined national security agencies. But the movie also suggested that my own committee was somehow in agreement with its thesis, citing our conclusion of the probability of a second shooter.

It was true that the Warren Commission had fallen short in various regards. Our report had detailed those failings. But there was not a shred of evidence that their investigation was conducted with anything other than integrity and certainly no evidence of anything resembling what Stone's movie claimed. I was astounded that someone could have distorted the factual evidence and record in the manner he did. To exacerbate the movie's insidious effect, Stone himself was appearing in any number of media venues to maintain his blatantly false theory of conspiracy.

Some time after the film was released, Stone asked to meet with me. I deeply resented the fact that he had perpetrated this false understanding of American history. Needless to say, he never saw fit to consult with me while he was planning or making the movie, and he must have known that our investigations refuted his thesis on one point after another (he had even featured the umbrella man as a signaler for the assassins). Still, I did agree to meet with him.

The meeting didn't last long. My secretary buzzed me telling me that he was here and I told her to show him in. When he came through the door he had a contingent of photographers with him. Lights were flashing all over the place; it was a propaganda stunt. When they had gotten what they came for, he and I had a more or less civilized chat. I did not tell him that I thought he was an insidious prevaricator, though perhaps I should have.

I could not let the movie stand, though. I could not accept having the work we had done discredited by some movie so distortive of the facts. I simply could not have people think that I presided over a committee that was somehow complicit in a cover-up of such a heinous crime.

One essential claim of the film was that the federal government had destroyed or hidden information revealing the conspiracy's existence, sealing secret files on the pretext of national security. We, of course, had sealed many files, over eight hundred boxes of them, which we had sent to the National Archives. We had done that not to hide evidence, but under a House rule that required all investigative committees to seal any files that might affect living persons. Our files included raw data, that is, unsubstantiated testimony that could defame people. They contained names of informants and others who gave us information on the basis of our promising complete confidentiality. They contained CIA documents, which we used, but which could not be made public without the CIA's approval.

But I understood that sealed records invited suspicion of my committee's motives. When I got in touch with Bob Blakey about this, he agreed to draft legislation that would create a blue-ribbon panel to be appointed by the president, which would sit for five years. During that five years the panel would release every bit of evidence related to the assassination of President Kennedy from whatever source, wherever it was, in FBI offices, CIA offices, Secret Service offices—wherever, including in particular our own committee files. Anything that could be released without infringing on individuals' constitutional rights or damaging their reputations. I introduced this legislation, which passed and became law in 1992.

Over a period of five years a voluminous amount of material was opened to the public. Nothing released in that five-year period changed a single thing in our conclusions.

CHAPTER 10

Martin Luther King Jr.

The cause of death was a combination of extensive hemorrhage and blood vessel injuries as well as damage to the nerves and spinal cord of Dr. King. The medical pathology panel was not able to be specific as to whether the cord was actually cut and transected completely, but the closeness of the missile track through this area of the body would have caused significant damage to the spinal cord, even if it was not mechanically cut in half because of the lines of force emanating from the bullet as it struck the spine bones proper.

—Testimony of Dr. Michael Baden, forensic pathologist and Chief Medical Examiner City of New York, on behalf of the medical examining panel of the Committee

THE "MISSILE," that is, the soft-nose bullet, had been fired from a Remington 30.06 rifle found with a bundle of other items in the doorway of a store adjacent to a rooming house, a window of which was opposite the balcony of the Lorraine Motel in Memphis, where Martin Luther King Jr. had been staying. The rifle and other items in the bundle had fingerprints on them that belonged to James Earl Ray, a longtime criminal and escaped convict who was arrested in London after a sixty-five-day police hunt. The police and FBI investigations had determined from the fingerprints and many other pieces of convincing circumstantial evidence that Ray had been the killer, and Ray had pled guilty to the crime in exchange for a ninety-nine-year sentence, by which means he had avoided a trial and potential death sentence. By 1978, when our committee was established, Ray had been in prison for ten years. He had been, so he maintained, framed and coerced into confessing to Dr. King's murder. He was, he claimed, a "patsy" for the real killer.

The committee and its investigations had been precipitated by suspicions about FBI involvement in Dr. King's murder. I was aware of the FBI's hatred for King. I had heard the allegations and the information about the black Memphis police officer who had supposedly been taken off security duty for him. But these were allegations and suppositions. I didn't know the facts. But we needed to find out. I was chairman, and I was completely prepared to let the chips fall wherever they were going to.

Given the deep suspicions about the FBI and CIA, my first order of business was to send chief of staff Bob Blakey to work out our relationship with the agencies, knowing exactly what the conspiracy theorists would make out of our investigations if we did not have complete access to all files—not to mention that in order to pursue everything out there, our efforts demanded total compliance from the FBI, conspiracy theorists or no conspiracy theorists. After some difficult negotiations we executed an agreement with the FBI, the CIA, and the Department of Justice that opened up for our study all documents, classified as well as unclassified. This was in regard to both the Kennedy and King investigations. The FBI archives alone yielded more than 1,500 volumes of unsanitized memos, correspondence, field reports, exhibits, and raw investigative notes. The CIA's data came to in excess of 21,000 files. We reviewed it all. We also reviewed all relevant documents from the National Archives, the Secret Service, the IRS, the Defense Intelligence Agency, and the Department of Immigration and Naturalization, as well as all police records from both Dallas and Memphis.

James Earl Ray himself was an eighth-grade dropout who had made a lifetime career out of burglary, theft, forgery, and strong-arm holdups. Ever since his imprisonment he had been claiming that he was stampeded into pleading guilty. But Eddie Evans and others on our investigative team thought otherwise. Eight days of intensive interrogation at Brushy Mountain Penitentiary had convinced them that Ray was a dyed-in-the-wool liar, a man with no regard whatsoever for truth.

Evans, the former NYPD detective and detective supervisor, was as skilled an interrogator as I'd ever seen. Each time he returned from Brushy Mountain he gave me a written report. Then we would sit down and discuss his findings in detail. Ray claimed he had been coerced into confessing. But after all of the work by Evans and his colleagues, it seemed clear to me that regardless of his lack of education, Ray had a shrewd, conniving mind. I believed that he had pled guilty in order to avoid a trial and a likely trip to the electric chair, then he had begun a campaign to extricate himself from the life sentence by proclaiming his innocence and demanding a trial—

especially pertinent because conspiracy theorists gathered like flies over the King killing, all of them claiming either that someone else had done it or that Ray was only a pawn in a larger plot. One of these theorists was Mark Lane, an attorney who has made a career out of writing dramatic "exposés" of government nefariousness, including *Code Name Zorro* alleging an FBI conspiracy and government cover-up of the King assassination ("Zorro" was the FBI's code name for King). After hiring and firing a number of lawyers, Ray retained Lane to represent him in front of the committee, which he now saw as a forum to demonstrate his innocence and thus give him a potential lifeline out of prison.

Ray's own plot line concerned a mysterious "Raoul," no last name, an elusive criminal mastermind who had purportedly befriended Ray and took him on as an associate in various drug smuggling and gunrunning activities. It was Raoul who instructed Ray to buy a rifle with a telescopic sight—apparently, Ray thought, as a gunrunning sample. It was Raoul who had told him to rent a room in a rooming house opposite the Lorraine Motel where King ordinarily stayed when he was in Memphis. When Ray did that, Raoul then told Ray to take himself somewhere else. It was Raoul, according to Ray, who then shot King from the rooming house and disappeared, leaving a bundle with the rifle and other items, Ray's fingerprints on them, in an adjacent doorway for the police to find, setting Ray up as the fall guy.

Raoul had sandy hair or dark hair or dark hair with a reddish tint. He spoke with a Spanish accent or a French Canadian accent—Ray's stories changed with various tellings. No one had ever seen Raoul and Ray together. Even though in Ray's tale he and Raoul worked hand in hand over an extended period in several countries, Ray knew nothing at all about him other than his first name.

Eddie Evans was a past master at interrogation. Instead of simply dismissing Ray's tale as a transparent fiction, he intimated to Ray that the committee was there to help Ray prove his innocence. The fact was that Evans did want to ascertain if there might be any truth to Raoul's existence. If not, he wanted to keep Ray talking until all the holes in his story revealed themselves.

~⊙

We looked closely at every scrap of a lead we could in regard to Ray's story. We were equally relentless when it came to the FBI itself. We meticulously reviewed each relevant FBI file, including all those that touched on the agency's scandalous COINTELPRO operations targeting King and his work. We did extensive interviewing of FBI personnel. We found abundant evidence of illegal FBI harassment, defamation, and subversion, what could reasonably be characterized as a paranoid vendetta by J. Edgar Hoover against King. In my opinion, the FBI's many-years-long assault on King created a poisonous moral climate in which it was possible for others to not only contemplate killing King but consider it a justifiable act. "Did responsible officials at the FBI intend by their conduct to bring about Dr. King's death?" I asked at one of committee hearings. "Should the FBI bear some responsibility for the death of Dr. King?"

Yet with all this we did not find a single shred of evidence that suggested the FBI, any FBI surrogate, or any other government agency was culpable in the assassination. Nor was Ray himself an FBI puppet. Nor did the black Memphis police officer's story hold up, the one whose report that he had been taken off King's security just before the murder had triggered the King family's appeal for an investigation.

That was an especially sad story. Detective Edward Reddit had been on a surveillance detail watching King, but word about his activities had leaked out to black militants, then to others in the African American community. After the shooting, afraid of being ostracized by his own people, Reddit had put out the story that he had actually been on security duty for King stationed at the firehouse across the street from the Lorraine Motel, and that he was suddenly and inexplicably removed from his post, which allowed the assassination to go forward. As our interrogators burrowed more and more deeply into his account, though, Reddit broke down and started crying. The truth was, he admitted, that he had not been stationed at the firehouse to provide security for King but to surveil him, and he did not want the black community to know that, so he had concocted the security story. There was no truth to it. The FBI had not conspired with the Memphis police to have Reddit removed.

There was, simply put, no government conspiracy. Moral responsibility for the death, yes, I thought to myself. Direct responsibility, no.

Another large dimension of our investigation concerned other conspiracies rumored and alleged by the theorists. The FBI's original investigation of the assassination was deficient in this area. With so much evidence linking Ray to the killing, the agency had single-mindedly pursued him and largely ignored the possibility of others' involvement.

There were, we discovered, twenty-one extant conspiracy theories that were not obvious flights of fantasy. Tracing these down took our investigators all around the country. All but one we debunked without too much difficulty.

The one credible account had to do with a large monetary reward for King's murder offered by two Saint Louis men, one an attorney, the other a businessman. We picked up a lead on this from an FBI report that had been misfiled and ignored until our investigators noticed it. According to an FBI informant, the two Saint Louis men had tried to hire him as a hit man.

Unfortunately, as we traced the report down, we found that neither of the two men was still alive. They had both died of natural causes. But though those two were dead, our investigators were able to locate the purported hit man they had approached. Under a grant of immunity, he testified in front of us. In his account, which we succeeded in corroborating, he had been offered $50,000 for the hit but had turned down the contract.

A thorough analysis of the informant's and moneymen's links turned up the fact that the informant's brother-in-law had been James Earl Ray's cellmate in a Missouri prison. A prison doctor in that same Missouri State Penitentiary was an associate of the businessman, and this doctor had had contact with Ray when Ray was assigned to duty in the prison infirmary. It was, we learned, commonly believed among the businessman's associates that the hit money was a standing offer. In addition, the two Saint Louis men had had ties with white supremacists associated with the American Independent Party, which had run Alabama's segregationist governor George Wallace for president in 1968. American Independent Party associates in Saint Louis often gathered at a Saint Louis bar owned by Ray's brother John, who visited Ray in prison.

All this was inferential, but it led us to conclude that it was likely Ray had learned about the hit offer in prison. It was just a year prior to the assassination that Ray had escaped from that Missouri prison, hiding in a bread truck.

Eddie Evans's team of investigators began to track down Ray's movements as a fugitive. Ray was forthcoming about these, as well as about some of his activities: the locksmithing course, the bartending school, the dancing lessons, the plastic surgery to his nose, the trip to Canada, the volunteer work for George Wallace's presidential campaign. On July 13, 1967, in Alton, Illinois, Ray's hometown, two men in stocking masks robbed a bank of $27,000, most of it in twenty-dollar bills—this was two-plus months after Ray's escape. The robbery was unsolved, but Ray and one of his brothers were in Alton at the time and circumstantial evidence pointed at them. Within a day or two of the robbery Ray left for Canada.

Our investigators were able to track down and calculate Ray's living expenses and purchases—all paid for in twenty-dollar bills—almost to the penny. They learned his aliases: Harvey Lowmeyer, John Willard, Raymond Sneyd, Ramon Sneyd, Henry Gault, Eric Starvo Galt. Then, as they traced Ray's movements in the weeks prior to the assassination, they noticed a peculiar pattern. Ray's movements in those days mirrored King's own, from Los Angeles to Selma to Atlanta to Memphis.

Ray was an inveterate newspaper reader, and news items about King related his appearances and forthcoming activities. It suddenly became clear. Ray was following King. He was stalking him.

Given Evans's work with Ray, I felt I had an excellent grasp of how this man's mind worked. On the one hand, he was a petty criminal, but he was inventive and deceptive, cunning in that way, a habitual and proficient liar. He may not have been the brightest bulb, but like many practiced criminals he believed implicitly that he could outwit those pitted against him.

Given what we knew, not only our grasp of the facts but also of Ray's psychology, Blakey and I decided that the best way to demonstrate his guilt to the American public would be through cross-examining him at the televised hearings. Under skillful enough questioning, Ray would convict himself, revealing his duplicity, the unbelievability of his so-called alibi, and by contrast the solidness of the evidence against him. He would hang himself in the web of his own lies.

I decided to do the questioning myself. We had other first-rate lawyers on the staff, but I was a veteran at these things, and I was chairman. I felt a responsibility to handle this myself.

But before I got at Ray in public I wanted to meet him face to face, to test him out and get a personal sense for his state of mind, his manner of expressing himself, the level of his commitment to his fabrications. I wanted to peer as far as I could into this person's head and heart.

Ray was incarcerated at Tennessee's maximum-security Brushy Mountain Penitentiary, which was where Evans and his other investigators had interviewed him. Ray had thrown a considerable scare into us earlier in the committee's work when he and six other inmates had pulled off a daring escape. Brushy Mountain was located in a particularly rugged, remote section of Tennessee's thickly wooded Cumberland Plateau. Few escape attempts had ever been made from there, and none had succeeded. But on April 23,

1977, two prisoners had staged a fight to divert the guards, then Ray and his accomplices had scaled a wall on an improvised ladder. The last of the escapees had been shot, but Ray and the other five had made it into the forest.

When Blakey told me this news my first thought was, Oh my God, we have to get him back, and we have to get him back safely. The guards had shot one of the escapees. All we needed was for them to kill Ray. We needed him back and we needed him alive. The thoughts of what the conspiracy crowd would make of anything else were too awful to contemplate.

Tennessee's governor, Ray Blanton, had formerly been a representative with me in the House. While there he and I had formed a good working friendship. As soon as Blakey told me, I called him. "Ray, whatever you do, do not kill him. We need this man alive."

"I understand completely," Blanton said. "Don't worry, we'll get him."

A few minutes later I was on the line with the warden, who gave me the same assurance. "We'll get him," he said. "Those guys aren't going far. They'll never make it out of the countryside up here."

They didn't. Two days later, the warden called back. "We've got him," he said. "Other than some scrapes and bruises he's just fine."

I prepared for my encounter with Ray by going over all the transcripts of our staff's interviews with both him and others. I pored over the thick briefing book that laid out the evidence—the material evidence and the minutely reconstructed accounts of Ray's activities, travels, and expenditures, from the time he escaped the Missouri prison to the moment he was arrested at London's Heathrow Airport after robbing a bank in London to finance his continuing flight.

I had a last briefing with Eddie Evans. By the time I sat down with Ray I felt I knew the man better than he knew himself. Ray was unaware that our investigators had carefully compared his version of his movements against accounts of witnesses who had interacted with him as well as against the trail of evidence he had left behind—motel and laundry receipts and other items that pinpointed the locations and timing of his travels. I knew the story he had concocted, and I knew the truth.

Prior to meeting him I also paid a visit to Memphis. I saw the Remington 30.06 rifle. I handled it, the murder weapon that had killed one of America's noblest sons. I stood in the bathroom where Ray had stood. I looked out the window where he had taken aim. I saw the unobstructed view of the Lorraine Motel balcony. It was an unsettling experience, full of anguish and bitterness. It took me back to King's funeral services at Ebenezer Baptist in Atlanta and our own memorial for him in Cleveland, to the picture embedded in my memory of Carl with tears streaming down his face. And now I was going to see the killer himself.

At the time we originally launched our investigation, I assumed that King's assassination had been the act of an enraged, virulent racist. I had a good deal of certitude about that, no doubt in common with many other Americans. Yet the record of Ray's interaction with blacks was much different from what I expected. He had gotten into a scuffle with some black sailors in Mexico; he had volunteered for George Wallace's political party. But he wasn't a member of any white supremacist group, and he wasn't someone who baited blacks. He may well have had a deep-seated dislike of blacks; I believe he did. But nothing in his life appeared to have been driven, or at least solely driven, by race hatred.

Looking back on his upbringing, his disjointed, piecemeal life of short-lived jobs, failure as a soldier, his burglaries, robberies, mail frauds and forgeries, the picture that emerged was of a small-time criminal drifter, always living on the edge, always looking for his next score. Necessity, desperation, and greed were what drove James Earl Ray, never more than when he was living the fugitive life of an escaped convict, scratching to keep himself alive, with a big-time bounty hanging out there somewhere for the man with enough guts to go for it.

Bob Blakey, Eddie Evans, and some other staff were with me at Brushy Mountain when Ray was brought in. He was an ordinary-looking individual, five foot eight or nine, thin, pale, narrow, close-set eyes in a narrow face. There was nothing really distinctive about him, neither in his person nor his manner, except that he was studiously polite and pleasant. Eddie Evans had told me that he was unfailingly polite with him, too, even though they had spent many hours together, with Eddie "trying to pull his eye teeth," as he put it. So there Evans was, and here I was, both of us African American, and from Ray there wasn't a whiff of racism. I knew, of course, that he knew his case depended on his being able to handle me. I looked at him and thought, the man's a lifetime con artist, and here he is trying to con me. On the other hand, I was suppressing a tide of emotion myself, sitting there opposite this small-time nonentity who had shot Martin Luther King to death.

In any event, his attitude made for a decent-enough interview rather than a hostile confrontation. As I ran through my questions Ray was open, ready to acknowledge everything that he had told others, everything he knew we knew or surmised we knew about his history and about this case. But he adamantly denied he had killed King. He harbored, he claimed, no racial animosity; he had never done anything out of race hatred. He had a good explanation, he said, for all of our evidence. I discussed with him his previous interviews, his claims, the books that had been written about him. I talked with him about some of the evidence, the rifle purchase, the white Mustang in which he had fled Atlanta. I touched on his travels, careful not to rouse suspicion of the fact that we had detailed evidence of where he had been and when he had been there.

I was at Brushy Mountain with Ray for almost four hours. By the time I left I knew just how I was going to handle him on the stand.

We called Ray to witness in a hearing room of the Rayburn Office Building on August 14, 1978, almost two years after the Assassination Committee was established, a year and a half after I took on the chairmanship. Since I was going to conduct the examination, I needed someone else to chair the session. Walter Fauntroy was head of the King subcommittee, but Richardson Preyer had seniority over him, so for the Ray testimony I asked Preyer to take over.

Richardson Preyer had been a judge on the federal bench prior to his election to the House. He was a jurist at heart and brought a powerful sense of command and credibility to whatever he did. Preyer was just the person we needed in the chair for this, not only to handle Ray, slippery as he was, but especially to control Mark Lane, Ray's attorney. Lane was a true character, a conspiracy theorist par excellence and a high-drama loudmouth known for his brash and obstreperous behavior.

Ray's appearance was going to be dramatic. After the assassination he had been the center of a media frenzy and then again after his capture. He had granted interviews to journalists, books had been written about him, and he had loudly proclaimed his innocence. He had been in prison now for ten years, but the year before he had done an interview on CBS and another for *Playboy*. He was a presence in the national consciousness, the mystery man who may or may not have killed Dr. King. And now he was going to get the hearing he had been clamoring for, on national television.

"Before calling the witness," Preyer announced, "the Chair wishes to make a statement regarding the security precautions to be observed with this

witness. . . . The Marshals have asked the committee to emphasize the following rules and the Chair states that they will be strictly observed. Anytime
that Mr. Ray is standing or being escorted to and from the witness table,
absolutely no one in the room is to stand. Let me emphasize that again. . . .
No one in the room is to stand. . . . No one is to move until the Chair gives
permission. Any person violating the rule will be summarily removed."

People sat. An air of expectancy quickened the hearing room. Then the
marshals led him in. Wearing a loud, checkered jacket and a striped tie, his
hair brylcreemed and swept up in a pompadour, James Earl Ray looked
exactly the epitome of the petty con-man criminal he was.

He raised his right hand.

"Do you solemnly swear the testimony you will give before this committee will be the truth, the whole truth, and nothing but the truth, so help you
God?" Preyer intoned.

"Yes, sir," said Ray.

"Mr. Ray," said Preyer. "I understand you have a statement you are prepared to read to the committee." He looked at Ray, expecting him to start.
But before he could Mark Lane jumped in, asking for the others on his
defense team to be seated with him and Ray.

"They're in the audience," said Preyer. "You won't have any difficulty having reference to them. . . . The Chair declines your request."

Ray has been mistreated, said Lane, beaten and put in solitary confinement.

That's a question for the Marshals, said Preyer, a collateral matter, not
before the committee today. "We are here for one purpose—one special purpose—and that is to hear the testimony of Mr. Ray. . . . You as counsel are
here to advise him as to his constitutional rights." Preyer paused and stared
at Lane for a moment. "All right, if Mr. Ray is ready to proceed at this time
we are ready to receive his statement."

"Mr. Preyer," said Lane. "Under rule 3(5) I wish to make an objection . . ."

"Mr. Lane," said Preyer.

"I will be very brief, Mr. Preyer," said Lane.

"Mr. Lane! . . . We are here, again, to hear the testimony of the witness."

"I wonder if as a last request we might be given a small cup so that we
might have a drink of water on occasion," said Lane.

"The staff will make cups available," said Preyer.

Preyer was unruffled by all this. But it was clear enough that he was going
to need a lot of fortitude to stomach Mr. Mark Lane.

Ray finally began.

"My lawyer, Mr. Lane," he said, "has just examined three FBI documents which provide further evidence of possible FBI and Memphis police complicity in the murder of Dr. King."

He went into a long recitation about a Memphis police officer/FBI agent who had arrived at the scene of the fallen King shortly after the shot, the relevance of which was less than apparent.

"On this other matter," Ray went on, "there is an article in the *Washington Post* . . . The article quotes a congressman . . . saying that a certain member of the committee is intending to nail me to the cross. . . . I anticipate there will be many FBI informers up here testifying. Most of them are paid informers. And some of them even have, you might say, a license to kill."

With this warning about his possible impending death at the government's hands, Ray began reading his statement:

> The statement I am about to give is essentially the same testimony I would have given the trial court in Memphis, Tennessee, in 1969 if that court would have had the fortitude to have ordered a public trial into the murder of Dr. Martin Luther King, rather than making an in-chambers deal with the attorney who was allegedly representing me, Percy Foreman, and capitulating to the wishes of the dominant commercial publishing companies and the companies' special relationship with the intelligence communities. In essence I would have told the trial court and jury that I did not shoot Martin Luther King Jr.

He had been, in other words, railroaded into a guilty plea by a conspiracy of his lawyer, the judge, publishing companies, and "the intelligence communities."

Back in 1969 Ray had stipulated to his guilt. As part of a guilty plea, the presiding judge is required to *voir dire* the defendant. Is the defendant being pressured into his plea in any way? Does the defendant know he has the right to a jury trial? Does he know he has the right of appeal for a new trial, the right of successive appeals to the Court of Appeals, then to the state Supreme Court, then to petition the Supreme Court of the United States?

We had the transcript of that 1969 *voir dire* in the record:

> JUDGE: Do you understand that you have those rights?
> RAY: Yes, sir.
> JUDGE: You are entering a plea of guilty to murder in the first degree, as charged in the indictment . . . Is that what you want to do?

RAY: That's right.

JUDGE: Do you understand that you are waiving, which means giving up, a formal trial by your plea of guilty? . . . You are also giving up your right to 1. Your motion for a new trial, 2. Successive appeals to the Tennessee Court of Appeals, and the Supreme Court of Tennessee, and 3. a petition to review by the Supreme Court of the US. . . . You are waiving and giving up all these rights?

RAY: Yes, sir.

JUDGE: Has anything besides your sentence of 99 years in the penitentiary been promised to you to get you to plead guilty?

RAY: No. No-one has used pressure.

JUDGE: Are you pleading guilty to murder in the first degree because you killed Dr. Martin Luther King . . . ?

RAY: Yes, legally guilty. Uh huh.

JUDGE: Is this plea of guilty to murder of the first degree with agreed punishment of 99 years in the state penitentiary, freely, voluntarily, and understandingly made by you?

RAY: Yes, sir.

JUDGE: Is this plea of guilty on your part the free act of your free will made with your full knowledge of its meaning and consequences?

RAY: Yes, sir.

[I pointed out to Ray his stipulations in the *voir dire.*]

So, there's no really, no big guilty, big deal about maneuvering a defendant into a guilty plea . . . all guilty pleas are not made in heaven.

My plan was to deal with the claim of a coerced plea. Then I intended to establish that this was not a man whose word meant anything. He had, for example, told different stories of the assassination and his role in it to different people, on record—one to Dan Rather of CBS.

"As you best recall your testimony to Dan Rather," I asked, "was it truthful?

"I don't recall," he said. "I wasn't under oath."

"You gave an interview to *Playboy* magazine," I said. "Was the substance of the answers you gave to their interviewer the truth?"

"Well," he said, "it was intended to be the truth. Of course I can always make errors in recollection."

"Our staff people visited Brushy Mountain Penitentiary," I said. "[They] expended somewhere in excess of forty hours taking testimony from you. . . . Would you say that that testimony is truthful?"

"Well, when the committee's counsel, Mr. Robert Lehner, started interrogating me, he made a point that nothing I said would be under oath . . ."

I wore away at his story about Raoul, whom nobody else had ever seen
and whom he had described differently at different times. Raoul, he said, was
the real killer, a man who had initially approached him at a bar in Montreal
about smuggling contraband, the man at whose request he had purchased the
murder weapon.

"What was Raoul's full name?"

"I don't know."

". . . During a period of nine months you and Raoul were together in
three different countries, ten different cities, twice in Birmingham, twice in
Atlanta, so you knew this man pretty well, didn't you?"

"I never made no effort to know him too well. Usually I don't like to
know too much information of someone else's business. That's an easy way
to get killed."

"This is a man whom you were in business with, weren't you?"

"Yes, but it was not a legitimate business."

". . . Mr. Ray, doesn't it seem unusual to you . . . that there is no one
who can substantiate the fact that they ever saw you with this mysterious
Raoul?"

". . . I really don't know, sir. The FBI has released various documents to
Time magazine, United Press International, and I have another paper here
where they locked up considerable documents in the National Archives and
this committee has made no attempt to get these documents out of the
Archives. Possibly there would be information there which would substantiate what I am testifying before this committee. . . . In fact, in 1974 in a *habeas
corpus* hearing, we attempted to subpoena FBI documents."

"Mr. Ray, I can say to you that this committee has reviewed every FBI
document that you have made reference to including every FBI document
related in any way to this case, and in none of those documents have we ever
found any reference to Raoul."

Raoul had not only never been seen by anyone, he had never left any fingerprints on anything—on the murder weapon, for example. But Ray had. I
asked him about the discarded bundle containing the Remington rifle and
the other items.

"Now, isn't it true that the items found in that bundle belong to you?"

"I think all the items except three or four articles belonged to me."

"Do you want to tell us what the three or four were that did not belong
to you?"

"Well, I think there were three cans of beer in there. I believe my finger-prints were found on one. I don't use beer and I never recall buying any of it. I'm kind of mystified how my prints got on it."

I led him through his journeys, showing that he had been in the same cities Dr. King was in leading up to the killing, an all but impossible concat-enation had he not been stalking King.

"Did you follow King?" I asked.

No, he hadn't.

"You stayed in Atlanta until March 28, didn't you?"

"That is correct."

"Then you went to Birmingham. . . . This is when you purchased the 30.06 rifle?"

"That is correct. Yes, sir."

"Now you said in your statement to us here that after purchasing the rifle you didn't return to Atlanta. Isn't that true?"

"That is correct, yes."

"Do you want to change anything at all about that statement?"

"No, I don't want to change that one regardless of how many documents you have up there. I know I didn't return to Atlanta. If I did, I will just take the responsibility for the King case here on TV."

What Ray didn't know was that we had evidence that on March 31 he had paid rent in an Atlanta rooming house. We also had receipts dated April 1 from a laundry just down the block from the rooming house.

I entered the laundry receipts into evidence.

"Have you had a chance to look at this laundry receipt document, sir?"

"I have."

"And would you tell us the date on there?"

"April 1, 1968."

"And what is the name of the laundry?"

"Piedmont Laundry."

"And does a name appear on that receipt?"

"Eric Galt."

He had put his laundry in under the name of Eric Galt, one of his aliases. I adduced the laundry logbook, which also showed the date.

"Does it refresh your recollection as to whether or not you were in the laundry on April 1st?" I asked.

"No," said Ray. "It convinces me that I wasn't in there."

"I think these documents will speak for themselves," I said, "and we will move on."

None of this flowed without continual interruptions from Mark Lane. Ray's statement that if we could place him in Atlanta after March 28 he would "take responsibility for the case on TV" made Lane throw up his hands and cover his eyes. The laundry receipt and logbook that showed exactly that caused an explosion of interruptions and demands for maps, calendars, and transcripts of testimonies, the laundry clerk's, the rooming house manager's. I had, Lane said, confused the witness. He suggested that we had given him false documents. We finally recessed so he and Ray could examine the evidence, and so the rest of us could take a break and have a quiet lunch.

Lane's behavior throughout Ray's testimony was simply over the top, outrageous.

> LANE: We believe we were given a doctored document.
> CHAIRMAN PREYER: This Committee produces no "doctored" documents.
> LANE: We have a defendant here [Ray] and a prosecutorial organization.
> PREYER: This is not a trial. There are no prosecutors here. There are no defendants. This is a legislative, fact-finding hearing. We are here to hear Mr. Ray's testimony. . . . We are not here to hear arguments by counsel. The chair warns you. . . .
> The chair will not allow continuous interruptions, Mr. Lane. . . .
> We warn you for the second time, Mr. Lane. . . .
> The chair has the authority to order you to leave the courtroom if you are interrupting orderly proceedings. . . .
> That is enough, Mr. Lane!

If not for Preyer's masterful control, Lane's continual disruptions over irrelevancies might have become simply intolerable. The man was straining every ounce of inventiveness he could muster to obfuscate, delay, and sow confusion. Of course, in a sense he was doing what any good defense lawyer would try to do in a situation where all the evidence is against his client, who in addition is revealing himself as an inveterate liar. That is to say, he was muddying the waters, only in a far more antagonistic and persistent way than would have been permitted in a court of law.

Preyer, meanwhile, wanted to bend over backwards to demonstrate the absolute fairness of the hearing, as did I. As chairman he did a remarkable job of squaring the circle, allowing everything he could in order to maintain the assurance of openness and transparency and preclude any notion of cover-up or secrecy, while at the same time keeping Lane from creating the train wreck he was striving for.

But even with Preyer's adroit handling, Lane's obnoxiousness threatened at times to overwhelm the proceedings. Whenever I went back to the floor of the House during committee recesses, members who were watching our proceedings on television would tell me they wanted to tear Lane limb from limb. It was my business to maintain a completely calm and fair-minded presence, but Lane was so aggravating that at one point I scribbled a note to myself thinking that a moment would come when I would just have to let him know what I thought of him. The hearings were almost thirty years ago as I am writing this, but I've kept the note:

> Mr. Lane, is there no low to which you will not stoop? You, sir, are the most despicable purveyor of filth and lies I have ever encountered. Your crass pursuit of self-aggrandizing publicity is only exceeded by your incompetent representation of your client.

But the moment never did come, and I'm glad it didn't. I caught myself once or twice recoiling with disgust, but it was involuntary and I don't believe the hearing room audience or the television cameras picked it up. I wasn't the main object of their attention.

Once Ray had presented his notions about the FBI–publishing industry–intelligence community–defense lawyer–trial judge conspiracy against him and had woven his tale about the invisible Raoul, he had one last defense—his alibi.

At the time of the shooting Ray was, he said, at a gas station trying to get a tire fixed on his white Mustang.

> STOKES: I want to know where you were when Dr. King was killed.
> RAY: I believe I was in the service station, but I'm not positive.
> STOKES: . . . What is your best recollection?
> RAY: My best recollection, I would be in the service station or just leaving it.
> STOKES: . . . What service station?
> RAY: . . . I can't think. It was one of the major brand service stations, but I can't give you the exact name.
> STOKES: Do you know the name of it or you don't know the name of it?
> RAY: I never checked the name of it out.

We looked at the area service stations. No one had seen a white Mustang needing a tire fixed, or any white Mustang. A *National Enquirer* article had quoted a Memphis resident who said he had seen Ray and his car at a Texaco station at the time of the murder. We deposed the Texaco owner and his son who had been working at the station then. Neither had seen a white Mustang. We deposed the *National Enquirer* witness. He had fabricated the story at the request of a friend who wanted to get a book contract.

The *Cleveland Plain Dealer,* rarely in my corner on issues, reported the hearings this way:

> ### STOKES SKILLFULLY CUTS DOWN RAY'S STORY, DISCREDITS LANE.
>
> For ten years James Earl Ray has been demanding a chance to tell his side of the story of how King was shot: now he probably wishes he never poked his head out of his cell, for Stokes, his committee and his staff simply devastated Ray and his sensation-seeking lawyer, not with a sledge hammer, but with a scalpel so sharp that much of the time Ray and Lane didn't feel a thing until they saw their own blood.

That was a satisfaction, and other major media stories from around the country echoed the *Plain Dealer.*

~⌒

The committee concluded in our final report that Ray was indeed the lone assassin. There was no credible evidence that anyone other than he himself had pulled the trigger.

At the same time, we believed that others had to be involved, if not in the assassination itself, at least as accessories to Ray's act. Our suspicions here fell on two of Ray's brothers, John and Jerry, both with criminal backgrounds, both of whom had been in contact with him during the pre-assassination months, providing him, we concluded, with funds from the Alton bank robbery and other advice and help. There was, then, a conspiracy, if not the kind of sinister government plot so beloved by Mark Lane and by others more recently.

The murder of Dr. Martin Luther King Jr., like that of President John F. Kennedy, will never be a closed affair. All doubts will never be answered. Associated enigmas of one sort or another simply cannot be solved. Deep suspicions of the FBI, CIA, and other government institutions are a built-in dimension of our national psychology. But we on the House Special Committee did our work thoroughly and with the utmost integrity. On the essentials of how these tragedies happened, our cases rest on their merit.

One painful postscript to the King investigation took place in 1997, nineteen years after we had closed down our committee and issued our final report. Despite our findings, the King family continued to harbor reservations about Ray's culpability. So did others, including Walter Fauntroy. Walter had chaired the King investigation subcommittee and had concurred fully with our conclusions. But over time his thinking had changed. Then Martin Luther King's oldest son, Dexter, decided to visit Ray in the prison hospital where he was in the last stages of liver disease. Dexter's interview with Ray aired on national television.

"Did you kill my father?" Dexter asked Ray.

"No, no, I didn't," Ray answered.

"I believe you," said Dexter, "and so does my family."

Other prominent people whom I respect made their own similar statements. Walter Fauntroy in particular was one of the finest colleagues I ever served with.

When NBC broadcast Dexter King's meeting with the dying Ray, they said, "Now Ray will never have a chance to tell his story." But of course he did tell his story, at length and under oath. The nation saw it; the nation read about it. The facts were clear to me then, as I think they were to almost everyone. They are clear to me now. Ray stalked King. Ray bought the gun. Ray fired the gun. Ray's prints were on the gun. The evidence is circumstantial. But in law school they teach that if you go to bed at night and there's no snow and you wake up the next morning and there is snow, you don't have to have seen it snowing to know that it happened. The circumstantial evidence tells you it undoubtedly did.

Dexter King looked Ray in the eye and said he believed him. I also looked Ray in the eye, and I saw who was there—a petty criminal, a liar, and an assassin.

CHAPTER 11

Moving Up the Ladder

TIP O'NEILL, my pal and benefactor, appointed me to other committees that had national consequences, though none with the same kind of lasting importance as the Assassinations Committee. One of these was a committee to investigate the American invasion of Grenada in October 1983.

Grenada was a tiny Caribbean spice island known mainly as one of the world's largest nutmeg producers, to the extent it was known at all. Our problem with Grenada was that its socialist prime minister, Maurice Bishop, had been displaced in a coup, then murdered along with five of his cabinet members. The coup leaders were hard-line Marxist members of Bishop's own party.

There were two items in Grenada of interest to the Reagan administration. One was the construction of a new airport with a runway capable of handling large jets. The other was a medical school whose students were almost all Americans. Cubans were building the airport, and there was concern in the administration that many of them were Cuban military and that the airport was intended for use as a transit point for the shipment of Cuban and Soviet arms to Latin American revolutionaries. As far as the medical students were concerned, the chaos accompanying Maurice Bishop's removal and murder made it possible that they might be in harm's way, or possibly might even be taken hostage.

Those, at least, were the administration's fears. It's probably fair to say that not many in Congress shared them to any great degree. Reagan had talked about the Cuban presence in several broadcasts, but whatever threat the Cubans might have constituted didn't seem particularly imminent, and what might be taking place on a tiny speck of a place in the Caribbean was hard to think of as threatening America's national security.

The television set in the House cloakroom was ordinarily tuned to CNN. On October 25th, suddenly CNN came on with breaking news. The United States had invaded Grenada with contingents of Marines, rangers, and Special Forces. Most members reacted with disbelief. It seemed preposterous that the United States would invade a place like that, with no discussion, no forewarning, with the Congress kept completely in the dark about it, with no declaration of war, no advice and consent. Nothing.

As the story unfolded, the administration announced that fears of a communist takeover had unsettled various other Caribbean nations, which had asked for U.S. help to quash the threat. Administration spokesmen also emphasized the precarious situation of the American medical students.

The invasion, featuring the armed might of the United States versus a country with no army at all, took three days to achieve its objectives. In that time a worldwide tidal wave of criticism erupted. The UN General Assembly voted 108 to 9 to condemn the United States for "the armed intervention in Grenada which constitutes a flagrant violation of international law." Britain's Margaret Thatcher was beside herself with anger—Grenada had achieved independence from the United Kingdom in 1974 but was still a member of the British Commonwealth. Tip O'Neill was deeply skeptical of Reagan's motives. The invasion was "gunboat diplomacy," he said, launched for political reasons. Shortly after the invasion O'Neill organized a House panel to go to Grenada to do a firsthand investigation.

The fourteen-member bipartisan panel was headed by majority whip Tom Foley, a sign of O'Neill's seriousness about this potentially unconstitutional use of American force. Ron Dellums and I were among the other members. As far as I was concerned we were there to examine the justification for this armed intervention. Was there actually a threatening Cuban military presence? Were there signs of an arms buildup that could have menaced other countries? Were our medical students truly in some kind of danger?

Our first night on the island I went to sleep in the hotel listening to sounds of sporadic gunfire. We had thought the situation had calmed down completely, but apparently that wasn't the case. The next day and those following, however, were uninterrupted by any kind of violence. We were able to look at the relevant sites, talk to people, including the Cubans our soldiers had taken prisoner, and check in with the medical students.

Our inspections and discussions confirmed, at least for me, that this invasion was unnecessary and ill advised. It sent a bad message to the rest of the world about American interventionism and a bad message to Congress and the American people about the unauthorized use of military force. The Cubans may have been soldiers as well as construction workers, but they didn't constitute any sort of coherent military presence. They were mainly a bunch of guys standing around in their shirtsleeves.

The Cubans had, or so we heard, stockpiled arms on Grenada for potential distribution to Cuban-supported Latin American revolutionary movements. We inspected the warehouse where these arms were stored, but what we saw was old, dilapidated equipment of questionable usability. Much of it looked as if it was falling apart. We also talked with quite a few of the islanders. That was interesting. Some of them were extremely articulate, speaking with a kind of clipped British accent. They did talk tough, but as we spoke with more and more people and began to understand conditions on the island, what emerged was that Grenada was a place where there was almost nothing to do. Except for its nutmeg farms, Grenada was a sleepy, sun-drenched backwater where there was no work to be had and lots of time for idle people to stand around and talk philosophy, politics, and revolution. Grenada did not seem a likely cog in a Cuba-Nicaragua totalitarian axis. It also didn't seem to me that any of the eight hundred or so American students had ever been in any kind of danger. That hypothetical scenario was nothing more than a fabricated justification for the invasion.

When we got back to Washington on November 7 the entire panel met with Speaker O'Neill. Most had arrived at a different conclusion from mine. Foley told O'Neill that in the opinion of most of the panel, in light of "the tension and danger on the island, it could not be said with any confidence that there was not a potential threat to American lives and the lives of other nationals. . . . Under the circumstances, the president acted correctly to protect American lives."

I dissented strongly from that opinion, along with Ron Dellums. Don Bonker from Washington also expressed his strong doubts. "The evidence," I told a press conference, "is that not a single American child or a single American national was in any way placed in danger, placed in jeopardy, or placed in a hostage situation during the entire period prior to the invasion. Under those circumstances, I do not believe the invasion was justified."

⌒◦

A few years later I served on another committee that investigated a far more serious abuse of power, one that had the potential to trigger the impeachment of President Ronald Reagan. This was the Iran-Contra affair.

Iran-Contra was an intricate piece of secret foreign policy adventurism that in the mid-1980s linked together two areas of national concern: the Middle East, where Ayatollah Khomeini's Iran and Saddam Hussein's Iraq were locked in a mutual bloodbath, and Nicaragua, where the Contra guerrillas were waging an armed struggle to overthrow the Sandinista regime of Daniel Ortega.

Regarding the Contras, beginning in 1982 a series of bills called the Boland Amendment (after Massachusetts Democrat Edward Boland) were passed that prohibited the CIA and the Defense Department from providing military assistance or funding for use by the rebels against the Nicaraguan government. In the Middle East Congress had banned all arms sales to Iran, which had been designated a terrorist state. But these prohibitions did not keep certain elements of the government from pursuing both arms sales to Iran and military aid to the Contras.

These were separate and distinct situations. CIA director William Casey and Admiral John Poindexter, the national security advisor, were ideologically dedicated to furthering support for the Contras—who were fighting against the communist Sandinistas—and they were searching for ways to circumvent the Boland Amendment. In the Middle East, Iranian-backed militants in Lebanon had abducted a number of Americans, including the CIA's Beirut station chief, William Buckley, AP bureau chief Terry Anderson, and Presbyterian minister Benjamin Weir. Ronald Reagan was deeply committed to doing everything possible to get these and the other hostages back, even if it meant considering paying ransom for them in some fashion by dealing with the abductors' sponsor: Iran. This despite the publically maintained policy of not negotiating with terrorists and hostage takers.

Because of his emotional engagement with getting the hostages back, Reagan was receptive when told there was a possible approach to the problem by having the Israelis transfer weapons to Iran in return for the hostages' release, weapons the United States would then replace. This would work around the prohibition against the United States selling weapons to Iran, since technically it would be the Israelis doing it. The idea originated in Poindexter's office.

Poindexter and Marine lieutenant Oliver North, a National Security Council staff person, then conceived the idea of diverting the money Iran would pay Israel into the hands of the Contras. The CIA's Casey took the lead in arranging shell organizations and secret bank accounts to facilitate these transactions and in overseeing the operation. In all of this the three men, Casey, Poindexter, and North, worked in the greatest secrecy. They were in effect making and carrying out national policy on their own, hidden from the State Department, the Defense Department, and Congress, and, possibly, from the president as well.

These clandestine activities—selling arms to Iran and funding the Contras—gathered momentum in 1985. By that time I was a senior member of the House Intelligence Committee, headed by Lee Hamilton, the powerful representative from Indiana. Although our mandate was to oversee all intelligence activity, we were given no notice of what was going on. But we were starting to pick up rumors and bits and pieces of information. As a result, in the summer of 1986 we called in Oliver North to answer questions. North came, an erect, soldierly individual, handsome in his uniform with its rows of battle ribbons, with a no-nonsense air about him and a direct gaze that conveyed honesty and trustworthiness. We asked him in particular about the Contras. What did he know about Contra operations? Had he given any military advice or other assistance to them? He looked us straight in the eye and said, No, he had not.

But a secret operation of this magnitude, involving intermediaries, money sources, bank accounts, Israelis, Iranians, Nicaraguan revolutionaries, CIA operatives, and at least one or two assistants to the principals, could not stay forever sealed off from the outside world. Something was bound to blow.

Something did. On October 5 a plane carrying supplies to the Contras was shot down over Nicaragua. The crew perished except for one, Nicholas Hasenfus, who parachuted safely but was captured by the Sandinistas.

The Sandinistas claimed Hasenfus worked for the CIA. In a press conference in Managua Hasenfus said that he himself believed he was working for the CIA. Shortly afterward, Casey came to talk to the chairmen and ranking members of the House and Senate intelligence committees. No, he told us, every bit as straight-faced as North had been. It wasn't true. The CIA had no involvement with Hasenfus or the supply plane.

A month later another story broke. A Lebanese magazine ran an article claiming that the United States was shipping arms to Iran. By this time the Intelligence Committee knew that something illicit was going on. When we demanded to be briefed, leaders from both the House and Senate committees, myself included, were invited to the White House to meet with National Security Advisor Poindexter. My memory is that Casey was in the room for that meeting, but I do not recall that he said anything.

The meeting was scheduled for thirty minutes. Poindexter came in smoking a pipe. He casually read for us a "Finding" signed by the president a year earlier authorizing the CIA to withhold notification of the Iran arms transfers from the committees. This was so outrageous that some of us were temporarily speechless. But then the questions began to pour out. As they did, Poindexter put on the greatest single performance of slow-motion obfuscation I have ever witnessed. He emptied his pipe; he packed his pipe with tobacco; he carefully tamped it down. He lit it. He gazed at it thoughtfully. He put it back in his mouth and sucked on it. He looked up at us and gave us a couple of nonanswers. Then he went back to his pipe and lit it again. It was enraging and mesmerizing at the same time. When our thirty minutes were up we walked out knowing no more than we did when we came in.

That meeting with Poindexter was in early November. Within a few weeks the entire scheme came apart at the seams. Ollie North and his secretary, Fawn Hall, had shredded everything in their files about Iran-Contra, but somehow one handwritten memo slipped through, what came to be known as "the diversion memo." In this memo North had spelled out the diversion of the Iran weapons sale monies to the Contras. It was the smoking gun. The facts were now out. The president was going to have to make a statement; that is, the affair was going to go public.

On November 25 President Reagan held a press conference, together with Attorney General Edwin Meese. Yes, Reagan said, between $10 and $30 million had been diverted to the Contras from Iran weapons sales. He himself had not known about it. No one had done anything illegal, but National Security Advisor Poindexter had resigned and his assistant, Lieutenant Oliver North, had been fired.

In early January 1987 both the House and Senate intelligence committees launched investigations. Then the two committees merged in order to pursue one rather than two investigations. Our staffs worked together, and our joint panel held hearings for forty-four days. We reviewed many thousands of documents and examined witnesses from the NSC, CIA, FBI, Justice Department, and other involved persons, most in open hearings, a smaller number behind closed doors.

We uncovered many heretofore unknown facts about the arms shipments, money transfers, and the individuals who bore responsibility, even though we were significantly impeded by large numbers of missing documents and equally large numbers of improbable memory lapses. Various witnesses obstructed our investigation through their strange inability to recollect key meetings and conversations, but the most egregious witness was Oliver North, who succeeded in turning the investigation into patriotic theater in which he was the star performer.

The committee had granted North immunity. The majority felt that his testimony would be the key to unraveling the conspiracy, and especially to understanding President Reagan's involvement. Without immunity North would be a difficult, adversarial witness. There was a general conviction among most panel members that granting immunity would not jeopardize any criminal prosecution that might flow from our investigation—a conviction that I and several others did not share and to which we objected.

So North testified under immunity. He appeared before us, and before the television cameras, in uniform, making the same kind of impression he had made on our intelligence committee almost a year earlier, when he had looked us straight in the eye and lied through his teeth about the Contras. Now, in front of the joint Senate/House investigation panel, he exuded the same aura. He was the very image of the upright, brave soldier, dedicated to defending the United States of America at all costs.

He opened by expressing his disbelief that the committee could be investigating the actions of such American heroes as Admiral Poindexter and CIA director Casey, and by implication, himself. We should instead, he said, be investigating ourselves and the role of Congress. He was here to tell the truth, he said, "the good, the bad, and the ugly."

"I am going to walk from here with my head held high," he told us, "and my shoulders straight because I am proud of what we accomplished. I am proud of the efforts that we made. And I am proud of the fight that we fought. I am proud of serving in the administration of a great president."

To many Americans watching the hearings on television, North was indeed emerging as a hero. He may have done illegal things. He may have conspired with others to pursue a separate foreign policy, in essence setting up a secret government within our government. He may have illicitly shredded documents and manipulated secret funds and hidden his activities and those of his fellow conspirators behind a smokescreen of evasions and lies. But there he was, an upright, four-square, honorable soldier—the epitome of an American patriot.

I listened to this day after day and took as much of it as I could stomach. The thought that this man was hiding behind his uniform, his love of country, his supposed reverence for the law and the Constitution was just too much to bear. A person like this portraying himself as a great American—and succeeding at it for many in the national audience—was intolerable. Man, I found myself thinking, I have to show this for what it is, this shameful masquerade, the dishonor of it, in particular when so many have struggled so hard to truly grasp the rights bestowed by our Constitution and laws.

North had begun his testimony on July 7. By the time he finished, I had truly had it. A week later I addressed him directly:

Colonel North, at the beginning of your testimony you told us you came to tell the truth, the good, the bad, and the ugly. I want to commend you for keeping your word. It has been good; it has been bad; and it has been ugly.

I suppose what has been most disturbing about your testimony was the ugly part. In fact, it has been more than ugly. It has been chilling, in fact, frightening. I'm not talking about just your part in this, but the entire scenario. About government officials who plotted and conspired, who set up a straw man, a fall guy; officials who lied, misrepresented, and deceived. Officials who planned to superimpose upon our government structure a layer outside our government, shrouded in secrecy and only accountable to the conspirators. I could go on and on, but we both know the testimony, and it is ugly. In my opinion it is a prescription for anarchy in a democratic society.

In the course of your testimony I have thought often about the honor code in the U.S. Naval Academy [North was an Academy graduate]. For nineteen, almost twenty years I have been appointing young men to that Academy. I have always taken great pride in these appointees, knowing that they would be imbued with the highest standard of honor, duty, and responsibility toward their government. . . . But more than that I think of the young students all over America who are sitting in civics and government courses.

You have said many times that you worry about the damage these hearings are creating for the United States around the world. I worry, Colonel, about the damage to the children of America, the future leaders of our America. I worry about how we tell them that the ugly things you have told us about in our government is *not* the way our government is conducted. That it is *not* our democracy's finest hour.

Then lastly, Colonel, I was touched yesterday by the eloquence of Senator Mitchell who spoke so poignantly about the rule of law and what our Constitution means to immigrants. . . . Senator Mitchell's words meant a great deal to another class of Americans, blacks and minorities, because unlike immigrants they have not always enjoyed full privileges of justice and equality under the Constitution. . . .

If any class of Americans understand and appreciate the rule of law, the judicial process and constitutional law, it is those who have had to use that process to come from a status of nonpersons . . . to a status of equality under the law.

In fact, Colonel, as I sit here this morning looking at you in your uniform, I cannot but remember that I wore the uniform of this country in World War II. In a segregated army. I wore it as proudly as you do, though our government required black and white soldiers in the same army to live, eat, sleep, and travel separate and apart while fighting and in some cases dying for our country.

Because of the rule of law, today's servicemen in America suffer no such indignity.

Similar to Senator Mitchell's humble beginnings, my mother raised two boys. She had an eighth grade education and was a domestic worker. One son became the first black mayor of an American city—Cleveland. The other sits here today as chairman of the Intelligence committee of the House of Representatives.

Only in America, Colonel North. Only in America.

And while I admire your love for America I hope too that you will never forget that others love America just as much . . . and they will die for America just as quickly as you will.

That afternoon our phones lit up. Telegrams poured in, thousands of messages. By and large people loved me for tearing North down that day—black people in particular. The idea that this individual, who had broken the law, who had subverted the Constitution, who had set up a separate government hiding in the shadows—the idea that this individual might personify what it meant to be American, inimical as it was to so many Americans, was particularly so to those who knew so well what the values embodied in the Constitution truly meant.

North aside, it was Attorney General Ed Meese who was the leading obstructionist. His testimony was crucial, in particular because it bore so closely on what President Reagan knew and when he knew it. As the scandal was nearing the breaking point, Reagan had asked Meese to undertake an investigation. Meese had done that, but he had forsaken his role as attorney general, the country's top law enforcement officer, in favor of his role as Reagan's friend and political adviser. This was by itself an extraordinary dereliction of duty, an arrogant and contemptuous disregard of his sworn constitutional responsibilities. Then there was his testimony, as often a non-testimony of "I don't recalls" and misrememberings, as actual testimony.

Meese did not remember, and Poindexter, the man with the pipe, swore that he had not informed Reagan of the diversion of Iran weapon monies to the Contras. Many of us felt that was dubious, but there was no way to disprove it. Given the piles of shredded evidence, other critical documents that we never got to see even though we had subpoenaed them, and testimony so shot through with forgetfulness, we never could determine the truth of President Reagan's involvement or noninvolvement.

It was a close call as to whether the president was complicit. Most signals pointed in that direction. But if we concluded that he did know, we would have had to go after him. Watergate had taken place a little over a decade earlier, but the trauma of that event still loomed large in people's minds. Nobody wanted to go after another president. Doing so would have created an explosion of poison between Congress and the executive branch. Everyone on the committee was leery of going that route. There was simply no appetite for it.

The committee's final report condemned those who had perpetrated Iran-Contra:

> The Iran-Contra affair was characterized by pervasive dishonesty and inordinate secrecy. . . . The covert program of support for the Contras evaded the Constitution's most significant check on executive power. . . . In the Iran-Contra affair, officials viewed the law not as setting boundaries for their actions, but raising impediments to their goals. When the goals and the law collided, the law gave way. . . .
>
> The committees make no determination as to whether any particular individual involved in the Iran-Contra affair acted with criminal intent or was guilty of any crime. That is a matter for the independent counsel and the courts. But the committees reject any notion that worthy ends justify violations of law by Government officials; and the committees condemn without reservation the making of false statements to Congress and the withholding, shredding and alteration of documents relevant to a pending inquiry. . . .
>
> Administration officials have, if anything, an even greater responsibility than private citizens to comply with the law. There is no place in Government for lawbreakers.
>
> Who was responsible? . . . At the operational level, the central figure in the Iran-Contra affair was Lieutenant Colonel North, who coordinated all of

the activities and was involved in all aspects of the secret operations. North, however, did not act alone. . . . North's conduct had the express approval of Admiral John Poindexter, first as deputy national security adviser, and then as national security adviser. . . .

Nevertheless, the ultimate responsibility for the events in the Iran-Contra affair must rest with the President. If the President did not know what his national security advisers were doing, he should have. It is his responsibility to communicate unambiguously to his subordinates that they must keep him advised of important actions they take for the Administration. The Constitution requires the President to "take care that the laws be faithfully executed." This charge encompasses a responsibility to leave the members of his Administration in no doubt that the rule of law governs. . . .

> "Our Government is the potent, the omnipresent teacher. For good or for ill, it teaches the whole people by its example. Crime is contagious. If the Government becomes a lawbreaker, it breeds contempt for law; it invites every man to become a law unto himself; it invites anarchy."
> —Supreme Court Justice Louis Brandeis

I concurred with the majority of the panel in these conclusions. But Peter Rodino, Dante Fascell, Jack Brooks, and I felt that something more was needed. We needed to highlight the profound harm the perpetrators had done to the concept of constitutional government both in their illegal actions and in their behavior during the hearings. The White House had failed to produce documents necessary to the committee's investigation. The NSC had interfered with the ongoing investigation of Iran-Contra. Worse, the duly constituted law enforcement agencies had accommodated the NSC and the attorney general's office. Attorney General Meese in particular served both the president and country badly. Our "Additional Views" were attached to the committee's final report:

> Meese was particularly evasive. He simply did not pursue what was going on as the country's chief law enforcement officer. The attorney general's contention that he had no reason to believe there was any possible criminality involved is belied by the facts.
>
> Meese testified in his deposition 340 times that he either did not know, did not recall, or had no recollection. . . .

Our nation has painfully learned from past experience that a democracy cannot exist where those responsible for enforcing the law can be manipulated for criminal purposes.

Oliver North was indicted by a grand jury on sixteen counts. He was convicted in federal court on three, including aiding and abetting the obstruction of Congress and shredding documents. John Poindexter was convicted of five counts of lying to Congress and obstructing congressional committees. Both men's convictions were eventually overturned on the grounds of the immunity granted by the special investigating committee—which I had objected to at the outset. CIA director William Casey never testified and was not charged, although he was the gray eminence behind the conspiracy. The day before he was scheduled to appear before the committee, he was admitted into Georgetown University Hospital for surgery on a malignant brain tumor. The surgery left him unable to speak. A few months later he was dead.

A year before the Iran-Contra affair began percolating, I had gotten a call from the National Conference on Soviet Jewry. They were organizing a visit to the Soviet Union for a number of Congress members to meet with Jewish refuseniks to see what could be done to help them get out of Russia.

The background was that in 1974 my friend and colleague from Ohio, Charlie Vanik, had sponsored an amendment to a trade bill together with Senator Scoop Jackson. The so-called Jackson-Vanik Amendment denied most-favored-nation trade status to countries that restricted emigration, which applied to most of the Soviet bloc countries, most especially to the Soviet Union itself. Many Soviet citizens wanted to leave, but none more than the USSR's Jews, who suffered from vicious state-led anti-Semitism. Those who tried to emigrate lost their jobs, their apartments, and educational opportunities for their families, and they all too frequently suffered imprisonment.

The plight of the Russian Jews was of great concern to the American Jewish community. I knew a good deal about the issue. I had been in close contact with Cleveland's Jewish community, or at least with some of its outstanding representatives, going back to my early days as an NAACP lawyer. A number of Jewish attorneys were on our Legal Redress Committee, including Harry Lehman, who had prepared the briefs for the Supreme

Court redistricting case that brought me to Congress. Others I had gotten to know just in the ordinary course of my law practice. I was also close friends with Rabbi Arthur Lelyveld, who had been to Mississippi to do voter registration and was so badly beaten there. Art was on our NAACP board. Martin Luther King had spoken at his Cleveland synagogue.

Then there was Sam Miller, probably the greatest philanthropist I have ever known. I was friends with Albert Ratner and Mort Mandel and his brothers, Jack and Joe, and with Dick Bogomolny. These were not only hugely successful businessmen; they were, one after the other, people who embodied the spirit of charity. Most of them came out of poverty themselves. Sam Miller's family had lived at Sixty-Third and Woodland, not far from where I grew up. They were impoverished immigrants. Miller didn't speak English until he was seven.

These men knew what it meant to be poor, and they acted accordingly, giving whatever help they could to those in need. My district, of course, the Twenty-First (the Eleventh later on, when I got redistricted) was extremely poor. One of the things I did as a congressman was throw a giant Christmas event each year for the most impoverished area of the district. We gave away turkeys, fruit and candy baskets, toys, sometimes hams. We collected good used clothing and hung it on racks for people to take what they needed.

The event grew so big that we had to move it from our original venue, Cuyahoga Community College, to the Public Auditorium. The entire exhibition space would be filled with people. Many mothers would walk up to me and say, "Congressman, I want to thank you. If it weren't for you my children wouldn't have had any Christmas." It hurt your heart to see that kind of poverty and to see families who were that appreciative.

Through all the years I did this, Mort Mandel and Sam Miller and Dick Bogomolny made it possible. All I had to do was call and tell them what I needed to put it on. There'd be no talk, no discussion; they'd just send a check.

So I had that kind of relationship with these Jewish men and with people like Rabbi Lelyveld and Harry Lehman as well as with others in the Jewish community. Then one year I was redistricted so that my district included a large segment of Cleveland's Jewish neighborhoods. I had, I was told, the largest Jewish district outside of Chicago. And so, with the relationships and friendships I had developed over the years with the lawyers, the civil rights people, the philanthropists, with all the things we had done together, it was important to me to see that that community got the best representation they could possibly get.

Then in 1985 the National Conference on Soviet Jewry called about visiting the Soviet Union. Barbara Mikulski from Maryland and several other congresspeople were going. Would I be interested in joining them?

It was a memorable visit. In our Moscow hotel a severe, silent old woman sat at a table in the corridor on each floor, watching who came and who went. We were told to be careful of what we said; the rooms were almost certainly bugged. During the daytime we were visitors. We went to the museums, we saw Lenin's mausoleum, we toured some hospitals. But in the dead of night our real visits began. We were picked up and taken to the homes of refuseniks, where small groups would be gathered to talk with us. Our drivers took circuitous routes, watching for cars that might be tailing us. In our meetings people described the conditions they lived under once they applied for exit visas: dismissals from work, revocation of living permits, refusal of medical care, harassment by the KGB. They talked about the bullying their children were subjected to, the opprobrium they themselves experienced, the religious persecution they suffered.

When we came back to Washington we presented petitions to the Soviet embassy on behalf of these refuseniks, petitions with hundreds of thousands of signatures on them. Subsequently I became co-chairman of the Congressional Committee for Soviet Jews and gave speeches on the floor of the House, focusing a spotlight on the conditions they suffered under and often detailing the plight of specific individuals and families:

> Why should there be a classless class called "refuseniks"? A class of people created and defined solely by the fact of their having applied to emigrate and been refused, thereby sentencing them to social and economic purgatory. Why should the Soviet Union prohibit family reunification, repatriation, or simple emigration? These are rights guaranteed by the Helsinki Accords and other international agreements to which the Soviet Union is a party.

I was proud that Cleveland welcomed as residents many of the Soviet Jews who were released, including a number of musicians who joined the Cleveland Symphony Orchestra. One of those, the violinist Lev Polyakin, became the orchestra's assistant concertmaster.

Participating in this endeavor was one of the most exciting experiences I had in Congress, and one of the most meaningful. It gave me the opportunity to help with the liberation of human beings from suffering, which put me in the company of longtime human rights campaigners like my traveling companion, Barbara Mikulski, and with Congress's great champions of human rights, Dante Fascell of Florida, John Porter of Illinois, and California's Tom Lantos.

During this period I was also serving as chair of the House Committee on Standards of Official Conduct, better known simply as the Ethics Committee. This was another Tip O'Neill appointment, one that I did not seek. Ethics is, in fact, a committee no one joins happily; it's always more dreaded than sought after. Serving on Ethics means sitting in judgment on your fellow members, not something anyone is eager to do. But Tip asked me, and I accepted. Somebody has to do the job, I thought; it's an essential function, and my background as a criminal law attorney gave me the experience and skills for it. Plus, a seat on Ethics would put me back in touch with the law, my first love.

Beyond that there was a widespread feeling that the chairman at the time and some other committee members were going after people for partisan, even vendetta-like reasons rather than strictly for suspected malfeasance. Because of that the committee had fallen into deep disfavor, and a movement was gaining momentum to scrap it altogether and go to some other form of oversight.

My feeling was that we didn't need something else. Congress, I believed, should be able to police itself. What we needed was an attitude of fairness and the determination to extend to members the protections they were entitled to. I thought I could help renew that perspective. If I was taking a seat on this committee I was going to do everything in my power to conduct business independently and equitably, with no leaking and no partisanship.

Don Edwards from California was leading the drive to abolish the committee. Edwards was a former FBI agent and a respected voice of conscience in the House. When my appointment went through I was happy to hear that he had decided to drop his effort. He apparently believed that a chairman with a strong commitment to civil liberties and rights would be able to back down any committee members who might want to use his or her position for personal or political ends.

I went onto the committee during Abscam and chaired it for the last part. Abscam (for "Abdul Scam") was an FBI sting operation that involved agents masquerading as wealthy sheikhs, hence "Abdul." It embroiled seven congressmen, one senator, the mayor of Camden, New Jersey, and several other local politicians. The scandal was unique in American history, given the number of congress members involved. At this writing Abscam is thirty-five years behind us, but its convoluted scheming, exotic elements, and flamboyant characters have made it an ongoing source for books and movies. Along with Teapot Dome and Watergate, Abscam has taken its place on the top rung of Washington corruption scandals. It may have been the single most disgraceful episode in the history of the U.S. Congress.

At the beginning of February 1980, news broke on television that an FBI sting operation had caught members of Congress taking bribes from a phony Arab sheikh and FBI agents posing as businessmen in return for promising help on development schemes, including casino projects in Atlantic City. The bribery transactions had been videotaped. One of those involved, Michael Myers from Pennsylvania, had stuffed the cash into his pockets and said, "You're going about this the right way. Money talks and bullshit walks." Another, John Jenrette of South Carolina, told the disguised FBI agents, "I've got larceny in my blood. I'd take it in a goddamn minute." Richard Kelly of Florida claimed he only accepted the money as part of his own investigation of corruption.

Watching the tapes sparked feelings of revulsion and anger, probably for congress members even more so than for the public. It was deeply upsetting that the people involved had cast this kind of light on the institution that so many members truly loved and respected.

When we had parallel cases with the Department of Justice, as we did here, they would ask us to hold back so that we wouldn't in any way influence the outcome of their investigation. So we did. We opened our own inquiry but held it in abeyance pending the outcome of the Justice Department's findings.

The case itself was interesting. Some congressmen had discussed projects with the undercover businessmen and sheikhs but had not taken any money. The FBI actors, though, were good, so conversations were cordial, and even though an individual hadn't taken the money, he may have said things that seemed compromising. John Murtha, the powerful congressman from Pennsylvania, was one of these. The videotape showed him eager to bring investment money into his district, but turning down the suggestion that he accept cash in return for helping one of the Arab investors obtain American residency status. "I'm not interested," he said, ". . . at this point." After discussion we concluded that Murtha had not violated any laws or regulations and we absolved him of any wrongdoing.

Murtha was a Democrat. So were five of the other seven congress members who were eventually convicted and served prison terms. One of these—

Pete Williams—was a senator. Of the six House members, we expelled two and two resigned. We were in the process of recommending the expulsion of the two others but they failed to be reelected, which put them outside our purview.

As we moved into our own inquiry Republicans were calling for the appointment of outside counsel and investigators. Since most of those indicted were Democrats, there was a feeling on the Republican side of the aisle that a Democratic-controlled Ethics Committee wouldn't take appropriate action. I met with O'Neill and the other Democratic leadership determined that we should keep the investigation in the committee. The end result was that we did do that. I worked closely with Floyd Spence, the Republican ranking member, and I believe the actions we took demonstrated that the committee could function in a nonpartisan way, that we were fully capable of policing our own regardless of who might be brought before us.

I pursued that course through my entire tenure as chairman. Among other things, I insisted that there be absolutely no leaking. My predecessor had used that tactic to destroy several careers, but I made it crystal clear that anyone who leaked would be dismissed from the committee. I remember once being more or less dragged into a press conference about one of our cases and answering every single question with "I have no comment." I expected the same from other committee members.

Several other situations we considered provoked national headlines. In the House page sex scandal two representatives, Gerry Studds of Massachusetts and Dan Crane of Illinois, were accused of having sexual relationships with seventeen-year-old pages, Studds with a boy, Crane with a girl. This was a high-profile, potentially explosive situation, and I was fortunate to get Joe Califano to serve as our committee counsel. Califano had been President Lyndon Johnson's top domestic aide and had served as HEW secretary in the Carter administration. He was a distinguished figure, highly respected by both parties as a man of utter integrity. Interestingly—given the Studds allegations—when Califano was HEW secretary he had gotten rid of the Public Health Service's definition of homosexuality as "a mental disease."

Studds and Crane both admitted the activity. Crane was deeply apologetic. Studds was a more complex case. During the course of the inquiry he talked about how difficult it was under any circumstances to fulfill all the responsibilities of private life and public life, let alone both at the same time—especially when a person is gay, he said, "as I am."

While the House has certainly had other gay members in its history, Studds was the first to come out openly. His relationship with the page represented, he said, a serious error in judgment. But he also insisted that it was consensual and that the investigation itself raised serious privacy issues. While Studds considered it a judgment error to have been involved with a congressional subordinate, he did not believe he had done anything improper and he rejected our finding that he had.

We found that both Studds's and Crane's relationships had in fact been consensual, and on consideration we recommended to the House that they be reprimanded, a less serious though still forceful action. The full House rejected our recommendation, though, and voted to censure each of them, a harsher measure that requires the member to stand in the well of the House while the Speaker reads the reprimand. Crane faced the House as Tip O'Neill read it out. "I want the members to know how sorry I am," he said. Studds faced the Speaker, his back to the other members. Given the moment, it was as strong a statement as he could make. Crane failed in his next election bid. Studds was reelected to six more terms before his retirement.

The other high-profile case that came before us while I was chairman involved Geraldine Ferraro, Walter Mondale's vice presidential running mate in the 1984 election. The origin of this was a complaint against her by the Washington Legal Foundation, a conservative lawyers' group. Because of their political orientation and their litigiousness, I knew we had to handle the allegations with kid gloves.

Ferraro's husband, John Zaccaro, was a real estate investor in New York, and although Ferraro herself was listed as a partner in his firm, she had not included her husband's holdings in her congressional financial disclosures. When the charge of impropriety was made the press had a field day. Ferraro was the first woman to be nominated as a presidential or vice presidential candidate, and this was the first time a spouse's finances had become an issue in a presidential campaign. Ferraro was also the first Italian-American nominee, which gave rise to the usual innuendos about mafia connections. When John Zaccaro refused to disclose his tax returns, suspicion spiked as to whether he and his wife really did have something to hide. He reversed himself some weeks later and did make his tax filings public, but by that time the damage had been done to Ferraro's campaign.

The Democratic nominating convention was in full swing when the story broke. Ferraro knew that the issue was likely to come before the Ethics Committee at some point, so she called and asked me to come over to her hotel to talk. She told me there that charges of illegality or impropriety were strictly political; she dismissed them as having no basis in any actual violation. It was a brief meeting that didn't leave me feeling one way or another. If the case did come before us, we would pursue it just as we would anything else, whatever the potential consequences.

The case did, of course, make its way to us, but later in the campaign, by which time it was clear that the Mondale-Ferraro ticket was far behind Reagan and his running mate, George H. W. Bush. By the time we completed our investigation, Ferraro and her husband had released everything and had paid almost $60,000 in back taxes their new accounting firm had found were owed due to an error made by their previous accountants. We found that Ferraro was in fact guilty of a "technical violation" of the House disclosure regulations. Her assets and liabilities and her husband's were extensively intermingled, whether she was knowledgeable about her husband's business or not. But we didn't have the finding ready until after the election, which Reagan won in a historic landslide. At that juncture Ferraro was out of Congress, so beyond any sanctions against her we might have pursued.

In the Ferraro case as in all the others that came before us, I kept in the forefront of my mind that I had an obligation to the House and to the public, but also to the member under investigation. I saw it as my job to do a thorough investigation, ascertain the facts, then have the committee agree on the facts and determine a punishment. I was not prosecutorial. I tried always to be fair and judicious.

At that same time I ran educational programs for the members to help them keep clear of entanglements. We sent newsletters discussing certain circumstances that had come up, things members had done and should not have, so that other members could avoid making the same mistake. I made our staff available if there were any questions about legality or ethical propriety under the House's standards of conduct. Quite a number of members did come to us for advice or clarification. My purpose had been to get them to talk to us before, not after, they engaged in something questionable, but more than a few reversed the order I had in mind.

I credited the House leadership, Democratic and Republican, for keeping their hands off our proceedings. Floyd Spence, the ranking member, and I worked together closely to develop strategies to handle even the most politically charged cases that came before us. As a result, under my chairmanship I believe the committee built a reputation for even-handedness that even the most partisan House members respected. Everyone knew there would be no leaking and no one was going to be targeted for political reasons. Because of that they allowed us to do our job. Even Tip kept his hands off. He never questioned me about anything we were doing or sought to intrude in any way. The most I heard from him was, "Louie, how are things going over there?"

"Fine, Mr. Speaker," I'd tell him. "They're going just fine."

Ethics is a committee no one wants to serve on. Intelligence is a committee everyone wants to serve on. The limit, though, is six years, so at intervals fresh faces come on. Intelligence is attractive; a seat on this committee gives you access to all the nation's most tightly held secrets. From here you see our government's foreign and domestic security endeavors up close. Because the committee controls the intelligence budget, members also have the power to prevent or cut back or expand a variety of covert activities.

In the mid-1980s a vacancy came up. By that time I had done HUAC for the Democrats. I had gone to Grenada. I had done the Assassination Committee for Tip. I had served on Ethics for him. Now I went to him and said I'd like the vacant Intelligence slot. Tip leaned back in his chair and regarded me for a moment. "Louie, my pal." he said. "Forty members have asked me for that seat. But if you want it, you've got it."

I served on the Intelligence Committee for six years, first as a member, then as chairman. There is an obscure, private elevator in the Capitol Building that has only one stop: the Intelligence Committee room. The room is guarded. No one but members are permitted inside. Visitors with special approval are escorted during their visits. As chairman, every morning the first thing I did was take that elevator to the room and sit down with the daily intelligence briefing. The briefing describes American clandestine activities all over the world. It is never boring. There are things in it you are glad to know and things you wish you didn't know. There is nothing you can share, other than with members of the committee. The knowledge is an awesome burden to carry.

When I was on the committee there were allegations about the CIA's activities in supporting dictators. There were ongoing discussions about Executive Order 12333, which banned the CIA from assassinating foreign leaders or other foreigners. We engaged in extensive debates on whether or to what extent the budget for intelligence activities should be disclosed. But I always held the workings of the committee very close to my chest. I think my constituents took pride that I chaired that committee, but they understood I was not going to speak to them about anything of substance, despite their curiosity.

One significant function of the committee was budget oversight. All the agencies that fell under our purview would send their executives and rel-

evant staff to our regular budget hearings: CIA, NSA, FBI, military intelligence, and others. These hearings gave us a chance to weed out activities we
believed were inappropriately funded.

Our hearing room was small, and typically the agencies would bring fifteen or twenty people in to testify, sometimes more. They'd all sit down in
front of the ten members of the committee, and all of us together would fill
the room. Invariably, I would be the only African American in the chamber,
a fact the crowded setting seemed to magnify. Every morning during those
hearings I would find myself facing a roomful of white people—almost all
males; extremely few white females, and more or less zero minorities.

It just stuck out—a white crowd, composed of upper level agency officials,
and me. I would ask, "Are there any minorities who are part of your agency?
If there are, at what level are they?" And invariably the minority employees
would be at clerical level or below.

It was embarrassing, the only black person in the room sitting there asking white people about why they had so few African Americans or other
minorities. But I felt it was my obligation to raise these questions. So I did.

"Mr. Stokes," I'd hear. "You are absolutely right, we should be doing a better job. It's an area where we have great concerns. We do make a strong effort
to recruit minorities."

"Well, where do you go?"

"We go to the historically black colleges and universities."

"That's good. What happens there?"

"Our problem is that we have to compete with the private sector. We
can't pay the same kind of money, and the good minority candidates are very
attractive. They choose to go elsewhere."

I listened to that over and over and over. When I became chairman of
the committee I pulled my staff people together to see if we couldn't address
the problem. One of my top staffers took the lead on this, and we developed
a program that would tie capable minority and other disadvantaged students
into the agencies from the time they graduated high school. Our concept was
that we would identify students whose high school GPAs qualified them for
the country's top-tier universities. We would offer those selected students
four-year scholarships to the schools where they were accepted in return for
a four-year commitment after graduation to the agency that had adminis-
tered the scholarship. In addition, during their undergraduate years we would
have them come into the agency as summer and short-term interns so that
relationships would be established. They would become familiar with the

agency and the agency would become familiar with them. After graduation they would merge into the system easily, and in this way we would be able to create a pipeline for minority employment in the country's intelligence community.

Those were the basics of the program. We had no idea how the agencies might respond; this was going to be something completely new to them. We decided we would start off with two, the CIA and NSA. I got the legislation passed as part of our funding bill with no objections. So it became law.

Then we approached the two agencies, but neither wanted it. These were two organizations that needed to do a lot about minority employment and were always telling me how hard they were trying. But then when we offered them a program, it seemed they actually weren't all that interested after all. NSA did have several black employees at a higher level, but only a few. I don't think CIA had any at all. And they didn't want the program.

Trying to move the issue ahead, I talked with an African American woman who was at a deputy level at NSA. Minnie Kenny was dynamite, one of those individuals so talented it makes you wonder. She was a top cryptographer, adept at many languages, also a forceful personality. Kenny became the liaison between NSA and CIA on this. She eventually got both agencies to accept the program, though they did so reluctantly.

But though they dragged their feet at first, after they had experience with our initial group of students their enthusiasm level shot right up. These students proved to be superior, smart, curious, and engaged. Before long the agencies were fighting over them. We started with the CIA and NSA, but soon we had it working at the FBI, the Defense Intelligence Agency, and a few others.

What I was demonstrating was that if you really want to do something about minority employment, you can devise a means by which to do it. These students were not only minorities, they were disadvantaged minorities. Many of them would never have gone to college had it not been for this program.

My own motivation here went back to the earliest strategic decision of the Congressional Black Caucus, to leverage our influence on the committees to which we were assigned, no matter whether or not there was only one of us. Ron Dellums had started us off in that direction, and the others and I had embraced the strategy. I was the only African American on the Intelligence Committee. As I saw it, I didn't have the luxury of being there in that position without trying to create change. It wasn't easy sitting there in that white sea. I was the only black person, yet I was the one who had to raise questions about discrimination against people like me, against people who looked and sounded like I did. I didn't worry about it. But it was embarrassing that I would have to do this myself, uncomfortable and awkward.

I did have allies, of course. One colleague from Virginia, Dan Daniel, intervened on more than one occasion. I'd have my questions lined up and he'd say, "Lou, give me your questions. Let me do this."

He took my questions and went down the list, one after the other. He did that understanding that it looked much better for a white person to be asking those questions than for me to have to ask them. And it was very effective.

Many other colleagues supported my efforts. This was especially the case as I gained seniority on the powerful Appropriations Committee. Carl Albert had appointed me to Appropriations as a second-term congressman in 1971. Twenty years later I was named chairman of the Appropriations Subcommittee on VA, HUD, and Independent Agencies. It had taken two decades. When I was first appointed to Appropriations I was the lowest-ranking Democrat. But as passing time brought with it retirements and election losses, even deaths, I finally had the seniority to assume a subcommittee chair. I had now become a so-called cardinal, one of the thirteen subcommittee chairmen who among them controlled all of the money that flowed through the House of Representatives. If there were positions in the House where it was possible to say that you had arrived, being an Appropriations Committee cardinal was most definitely one of them.

CHAPTER 12

Cardinal

THE APPROPRIATIONS subcommittee chairmen, the cardinals, are singled out. They are highly respected; they control the money. They are addressed regularly as "Mr. Chairman." "Mr. Chairman, I have this problem." "Mr. Chairman, I'd be grateful for your help." And when they are able to help members with their bills, people are appreciative. They remember. And down the line if the chairman comes to them and says, "I need your vote this afternoon," the answer is a quick, "Mr. Chairman, you've got it."

On my subcommittee, VA, HUD, and Independent Agencies, I was going to be handling $91 billion of the total federal budget. That was the kind of power I had never exercised before, power to help my constituency and launch or advance programs I felt were essential to the nation's well-being. To say I was looking forward to my new job would be a considerable understatement.

Then early one morning the phone rang in my office. Ohio's two senators, John Glenn and Howard Metzenbaum, were on the line. "Lou," said Glenn, "we have a vacancy on the federal bench in Cleveland. We'll advise the president on it, and we want to give you the opportunity to step in, if you would want to accept it."

I thanked them. Ordinarily a federal judgeship is something a person jumps at without having to mull it over too long. But I told them I needed to give it some consideration. I'd get back to them.

The Appropriations subcommittee's purview included NASA, veterans' hospitals, the Environmental Protection Agency, housing—key areas where I could make a real difference. But a federal judgeship was a lifetime appointment. For two decades now I had been raising money and campaigning for reelection every two years. If I took the judgeship I could put all that behind me. I'd have none of the headaches of politics, the bickering, jockeying for position, the fighting with obstructionists and people whose values were in the wrong place. Instead I'd be home with my family. I'd be fully engaged with the law. My life would have some tranquility to it, for a change. Besides, I was sixty-four years old, an age when many people are thinking about retiring. Not that I'd be retiring if I took the judgeship, but the stress of constant legislative work with all its lobbying and persuading and debating would be gone. And I'd been working, when I thought about it, for fifty years straight—even more. Ever since I was a twelve-year-old paper boy.

On the other hand, what did I come down here to Washington for in the first place? Wasn't my purpose to do as much good for the people of my district as I could? Why would I close down that endeavor at exactly the point where I could do the most for them and for minorities and poor people around the country? They had elected and reelected me, the people of my district, twelve times now. The seniority I had was due to them. Didn't I owe them as much loyalty as they had shown me?

I remembered what Charlie Vanik had said to me not long after I first arrived. "Lou, if you're ever going to be able to do real good for your district, you have to get on a committee where you can get some money into the programs they need." It had taken me twenty years to get to the point where I could truly do that. And if I left now? There were no other black representatives ready to follow me, no one who had the seniority to step into a chairmanship like this.

I talked to a few friends about it. I talked with Jay. In the final analysis it came down to figuring out what I wanted to do at that stage of my life. Did I want to secure my own personal career with a judgeship and take myself out of the political world, have the prestige of the bench, have a staid but comfortable life? As appealing as that was, I decided against it. The thought of the things I could accomplish as an Appropriations cardinal was just too overwhelming. Jay agreed with me, which made it easy. I could never have had the kind of career I did without the counsel and advice and support she'd given me in every major decision I had to make, and this one was no different. I opted to take the chairmanship.

From the beginning I looked at my role on Appropriations as a mechanism to do things that would improve the lives of my constituents, bring projects into my state, and put money into the national programs of special concern to me. The historically black colleges, for example, were always walking a financial tightrope, without the large endowments that support many mainline private institutions. They needed federal funding for scholarships, facilities, and research. I worked hard to get budget requests in for them, including the oldest of them, Howard University, the only black land-grant college with an ongoing federal appropriation, and Morehouse School of Medicine, the first predominantly black medical school in a hundred years. My position on Appropriations helped assure a level of assistance to these schools that they might not otherwise have had. Over time I became something like a congressional godfather to them.

I did my best to funnel money into early enrichment and ongoing education programs for disadvantaged and minority youth: Title One grants, Head Start, and the TRIO initiative that provided student services and support to middle schools, high schools, and colleges with large numbers of low-income students, veterans, and students with disabilities, programs like educational counseling and Upward Bound, Upward Bound Science and Math, and Veterans Upward Bound.

NASA was one of the seventeen independent agencies my subcommittee oversaw. In 1993 President Bill Clinton began pushing for funds to build a new international space station. Specifically, he was requesting $15 billion. He was asking for support from both me and Barbara Mikulski, my counterpart in the Senate.

I was ready to do this for Clinton. But NASA was another one of these agencies that employed extremely few minorities and extremely few females in any of its upper-level jobs. I was going to support the $15 billion, but I wanted minority contractors to get an appropriate share of it. When we readied the funding bill I put an amendment on it—the so-called Stokes Amendment—that provided for 10 percent to be set aside for minority contractors on all NASA programs. In the end I had to compromise on the percentage, down to 8 percent instead of 10. But that 8 percent was consequential. Money suddenly became available for qualified black and other minority contractors.

A wonderful woman joined me on that amendment, Louisiana representative Lindy Boggs, Hale Boggs's wife. Lindy Boggs was an exceptional person, pure southern class. She supported me, but she also wanted women included. Lindy Boggs was highly respected. With her quiet, sweet, southern drawl she could sway anybody. Even her adversaries found it almost impossible to oppose her. There was a little screaming and shouting—though not at her—but in the end we did get the money Clinton wanted.

We had in the Cleveland area NASA's Lewis Research Center (later renamed the Glenn Research Center, for John Glenn), one of the space agency's major research facilities. Dr. Julian Earls, an African American radiation physicist, was a top scientist and administrator at Glenn, revered throughout NASA. But despite his reputation, he was regularly denied promotions it seemed obvious he should have had.

As chairman of NASA's oversight committee I worked hand in glove with NASA director Dan Goldin on many major projects, and we got a lot done together. Along the way I brought to his attention that I wanted to see an African American as head of the Cleveland facility, and we talked about Dr. Earls. Earls did eventually get the appointment, which he richly deserved, and he did a great job leading a center with twenty-four specialized research units and almost two thousand employees, but he went through a lot.

I went through some memorable unpleasantness myself as we were negotiating the additional NASA funding Clinton was asking for. Mikulski and I met with the president several times to go over his proposal, which was controversial because it was additional to the approved NASA budget and took money from other programs various members wanted to move forward. As his special liaison to Mikulski and me, Clinton appointed Vice President Al Gore.

For one of the morning meetings the two of us had at the White House with Vice President Gore, I had my chief of staff, Dick Mallow, drive me over. The guards stopped the car at the entry gate and saw me in the passenger seat. Mallow, who is white, said, "This is Congressman Stokes. He has a meeting with the vice president." The guard asked for my identification, mine, but not Mallow's. Then he said, "Open the trunk." Mallow popped the lid. "Just a minute," said the guard, and a moment later another guard brought up two dogs to sniff the car. Now, they are not supposed to do that to a member of Congress. The established protocol is that once they establish your identity you go right in. But he did it, I felt surely, because I'm black. The guard took my identity—not my white driver's. Then he brought over the dogs.

I was seething, angrier than I had been over anything in a long time. When I got inside Gore was sitting there with Barbara Mikulski. I told him what had taken place. Gore was outraged as well, and embarrassed on top of it. He had some people go out immediately to check into the situation. When I asked Barbara what had happened when she drove up she said, "Nothing, they just waved me in."

The incident instantly brought me back to the fact that we still live in a society where as a black man, no matter how high you go and how much you accomplish, you are still somehow different, somehow suspect, subject to petty indignities and slights, and, if you are unlucky, to far more dangerous confrontations. There I was, chairing a committee, and the president of the United States is asking me to appropriate $15 billion for him, and I'm treated as someone who needs to have dogs sniff his car. It was insulting beyond words. It made me think: Do not forget who you are. You are Lou Stokes. And you are still black.

That incident stayed with me as a kind of signpost, not that I needed one. Racism is in the atmosphere we breathe, whether or not we are conscious of it; and it goes without saying that African Americans are far more conscious of it than white Americans are. It is present in our institutions, and it is present in the embedded legacy of hundreds of years of slavery, segregation, relegation, and impoverishment.

The tragic consequences of racism show up in communities of color, impossible to ignore, and most particularly impossible for me to ignore as representative of my own Cleveland community. I saw, for example, that in Cleveland large numbers of middle school black kids were failing to pass ninth-grade math and as a result were not progressing through to tenth grade as they should have been.

Here was just one of those social maladies, many of which could be fixed or at least ameliorated if we only gave them the proper attention and resources. In this case I called John Hairston, the external affairs person at the Glenn Research Center. "With all those NASA scientists, engineers, and aeronautical people you've got out there," I said, "we just cannot have black kids unable to pass math exams. Your people have some responsibility to come in here and help those kids in the inner city."

He agreed. Then I called Dr. Jerry Sue Thornton, the president of Cuyahoga Community College. I told her the same thing. "A college like yours with all those fine instructors in science and engineering. I think you and John Hairston ought to sit down and figure out a program where we can utilize all that skill out at NASA and at your institution. Develop a program where we can give these kids what they need in terms of STEM subjects."

They followed up. The program they developed was conducted on Saturday; it still is. It's ongoing. One component is that the kids have to bring their parents with them. They spend most of the day on Saturday. Instructors take the kids out to NASA, put them in the cockpits of planes and simulators. They show them what it is to fly. They teach the math and science that go into it. The NASA people take buses furnished with equipment out to the schools.

The program became so popular that NASA director Goldin said, "We need to make this national." So we put money into it and created SEMAA, the Science, Engineering, Mathematics and Aerospace Academy. SEMAA started in Cleveland but became a nationwide endeavor located in schools, community colleges, and science museums throughout the country. To date almost half a million students have gone through the program.

I worked equally hard at bringing funding into another national program, the National Science Foundation's Alliance for Minority Participation (after my retirement it was renamed the Louis Stokes Alliance for Minority Participation. or LSAMP). LSAMP is similar to SEMAA in that it concentrates on nurturing an engagement with the STEM subjects—science, technology, engineering, mathematics—and fostering college studies in those areas for students from underrepresented populations. Another program called the Bridge Program supports LSAMP students in bridging the gap from undergraduate to graduate school. That program has graduated thousands of students all over the country, a great many of whom have become practicing scientists and engineers, teachers and professors.

Perhaps the most devastating inequality that afflicts the black and other minority populations is inequality in health care. Martin Luther King Jr. called it "the most shocking and inhumane of all injustices."

The statistics on health in the black community were, simply put, appalling. The average life span of black men and women was years less than that of white men and women. But that was just the gross manifestation. The factors that went into this shocking discrepancy came from almost every major medical specialty. Black babies died at more than twice the rate of white babies. African Americans with heart conditions were far less likely than whites to be diagnosed with advanced catheterization methods. Their blocked arteries weren't nearly as likely to be treated with angioplasties or bypass surgeries. If their organs failed, blacks had less of a chance of receiving transplants. If their joints failed they were less likely to get new ones. If they had various cancers they weren't operated on as frequently.

As a congressman I came to know the details of these disparities well, but you didn't have to be in Congress to see that the black community suffered from health problems in ways the mainstream didn't. You couldn't live in a black community and not be aware of it. People tended not to have primary care doctors; very few private doctors even practiced in the inner cities. People didn't have insurance. They didn't have money for medications. Often they went to emergency rooms for treatment of illnesses and injuries that should have been attended to much earlier.

I was always aware of these things, so when I did go to Congress, health care was very much on my mind. Fairly soon after I took office I became involved in efforts to provide support for black institutions with health-care programs: Howard with its medical school; Meharry with its schools of medicine and dentistry; Xavier with its pharmacy school; Tuskegee with its veterinary school. Howard was a special case since it had been chartered by Congress at its founding and received legislated federal funding, but each of these schools was in financial distress, and I and others on the Black Caucus made efforts to channel funding to them.

One day in 1975 or 1976 Andy Young approached me on the floor and asked if I'd be willing to meet with a Dr. Louis Sullivan. Dr. Sullivan, he said, was starting up a new predominantly black medical school in Atlanta, in Andy's district—the Morehouse School of Medicine, associated with Morehouse College.

A short time later Andy, Dr. Sullivan, and I were sitting down together over lunch. Sullivan explained to me that the last twenty years had seen a dramatic growth in the number of medical schools as a response to data that projected an acute shortage of doctors. The doctor shortage was especially marked in the South, and in the black community it was dire. Georgia, for example, had one white doctor for every 795 whites in the state, but one black doctor for every 13,810 blacks.

Despite this prodigious discrepancy, the Morehouse School of Medicine was the single new black medical school, not only in Georgia but in the country. But his school, he said, was coming on line just as federal funds for medical school expansion were drying up. Medical school expansion had been going on for almost twenty years, fueled by federal funding. Now analysts were saying the expansion had gone far enough, even too far. Many government aid programs were being curtailed or eliminated altogether. Consequently, Dr. Sullivan said, his need for funding was urgent. The new

Morehouse medical school's mission was to prepare minority primary care doctors for service in minority communities. It was not possible to exaggerate the need for black primary care physicians. Could I help?

With Morehouse still in the planning stage, Howard and Meharry were the only black medical schools. Between the two of them they were training more than half the country's black doctors and dentists. They were doing an excellent job, especially considering their sparse resources. But the number of minority health professionals they were graduating was a miniscule percentage of the need. Mainstream white schools had historically accepted only one or two black students at a time, if that. Schools in the South had accepted none, and schools in the North almost none. Now, with the civil rights laws and after Dr. King's death, that was changing. But the change was glacial. There were still few black students in the mainstream schools, and students at the best schools tended to go into medical specialties and subspecialties, not primary care. All of which meant that there simply were not enough doctors available to help alleviate the profound health-care deficiencies and suffering in minority communities.

I was taken with Dr. Sullivan's grasp of the problem and with the mission of his new school. I was able to generate a grant that provided money for Morehouse's first medical school building, which enabled them to move out of their trailers and rented space. When the building was finished they invited me down to Atlanta to take a look. My pride in that building was almost as great as Dr. Sullivan's. Morehouse School of Medicine asked me to give the commencement address for their first graduating class, and on that occasion they awarded me an honorary doctorate. My relationship with Dr. Louis Sullivan began over our lunch with Andy Young when Morehouse medical school was in the planning stages. Neither of us then could have predicted that more than a decade later he would become the first African American secretary of Health and Human Services, which enabled the two of us to collaborate in unprecedented ways.

By the end of the 1970s my engagement with health care had deepened considerably. Parren Mitchell from Maryland was chairman of the Congressional Black Caucus by then, and Parren had created what we were calling Brain Trusts to examine problems and generate legislative proposals addressing significant needs in the black community. He had first established Brain Trusts on housing and small businesses. Now Parren asked me to set up a Health Brain Trust.

My work on health care had by that time given me a host of contacts with health officials in the minority community, with organizations that worked with minority communities, and with the historically black colleges and universities. With that background my staff and I identified potential Health Brain Trust members from around the country: doctors, dentists, nurses, medical scientists, social workers, sociologists, psychologists, administrators, lawyers, and others. We invited them to Washington for an initial gathering, then looked at issues that needed attention and set up working groups and scheduled meetings. David Satcher, who some years later would be named surgeon general, was a Brain Trust member, as was Louis Sullivan. The Health Brain Trust gave me something like a broad-based think tank I could draw on for studies, background information, and testimony on health-care bills, those I initiated and others that came before my committees.

During this period the subject of disparities in health care was emerging as a national issue, not just a black issue. I was doing everything I could to help open up the national consciousness about this. I wanted mainstream health-care professionals to understand the gravity of the situation and the level of human suffering it entailed. Every time one of the NIH institute directors or other NIH officials came before me I'd say, "You are coming here asking us to appropriate money for the Institute you're heading. Would you agree that black people have higher levels of hypertension than whites?" (Or higher rates of cancer, or heart disease, or other illnesses depending on which NIH division was there.) "Do you know why there are higher rates of this disease? Is it genetics, or biology, or environment? Or something else? Do you know why there are higher rates of death among blacks for almost every major disease? Do you know why that is? What are we doing to understand that? Tell me, what is your Institute is doing to address this specific problem among minorities?"

The NIH directors were extremely uncomfortable facing these questions, because the fact was that they were sponsoring extremely little research on minority health. Clinical trials specific to the black population were rare (the same was true regarding women). "Well, Mr. Stokes," I'd hear. "We think that if we put money into these programs generally it will help minorities, too, along with everybody else."

"No," I'd say, "that's not adequate. NIH should be looking at these things specifically, don't you agree?"

The fact was that I had a unique vantage point from which to do this. The directors knew that I was a strong advocate for NIH. I was always a forceful voice for increased NIH funding, and over the time I was involved the agency's budget doubled. People there understood that I had voted favorably on legislation that they needed, that I had lobbied for it. So when I said that what they were doing—or were not doing—on minority health didn't sit well with me, they knew I was saying that as a friend and not as an adversary—and that had a material effect. It enhanced the leverage I already had.

Had I not asked these and similar questions, they would not have come up. There was, simply, insufficient concern by my white colleagues. I needed to raise my voice about these things. I felt strongly that I needed to inject a concern about black lives into our deliberations.

There were, of course, white colleagues on those committees who knew and understood that I had to do what I was doing. They were representatives; they understood that like them I had a constituency to represent. Besides that, they agreed with me. There were occasions when they would come to me and ask what I wanted done on some issue, and they let me know they were going to support me.

One of these was Silvio Conti of Massachusetts, the ranking Republican on the Labor, Health and Human Services subcommittee. On one of the minority health bills I was working on with Lou Sullivan and David Satcher, Conti saw me fighting to get the money I needed. But the chairman and I were at loggerheads, the chairman saying to me, "Aw, Lou, we can't do that. We can't put that kind of money into this." As it was going back and forth Conti came over and sat down next to me. "Lou," he whispered, "what will you take on this?" I told him. A little while later when we came back to the subject, Conti said, "Mr. Chairman, I think in this area we ought to fund it at such and such a rate."

What was the chairman going to do then? He wasn't going to oppose his ranking member. That was the amount I had hoped to get out of it. The chairman said, "All right, all right." He looked at me. "Lou, I guess we'll put that in."

Meanwhile, I was sponsoring legislation to help the historically black colleges and universities, in particular those providing health-care education. When the Higher Education Act came up for reauthorization in 1981, I put in an amendment that provided financial support for the development of black graduate health profession schools. Morehouse School of Medicine was the first to receive assistance, then the others were folded into the program incrementally. Subsequently we were able to pass the Minority Centers of Excellence program that recognized and supported institutions that trained minorities for health service and the Research Centers in Minority Institutions Program, which funded the expansion of research and clinical facilities. President Reagan had drastically cut funding for the National Health Service Corps Scholarship Program, which provided tuition, books, and living grants for poor medical school students. His cuts affected needy white students as well as black, but proportionately they hit aspiring black students harder, since many of them would never be able to attend medical school were it not for these scholarships. I worked hard to refund this program, with some though not complete success.

In 1983 HEW Secretary Margaret Heckler became engaged with the problem of health-care disparities, and she appointed a blue-ribbon panel headed up by Dr. Tomas Malone, an African American PhD who was deputy NIH director at the time. The panel's report—the so-called Heckler Report on Black and Minority Health—was issued in 1985. In her introduction, Secretary Heckler wrote, "There is a continuing disparity in the burden of death and illness experienced by Blacks and other minority Americans as compared with our nation's population as a whole. . . . [This is] an affront to our ideals and to the ongoing genius of American medicine." Among its conclusions, the Heckler Report found that disparities in health care were resulting in 60,000 excess African American deaths every year.

With the prestige of this panel, and the secretary's imprimatur, the findings were immediately accepted. That added real weight to the concerns I was voicing about disparities. It gave those of us in Congress who were raising these issues the ability to speak with reference to an authoritative government study.

In 1988 George H. W. Bush succeeded Ronald Reagan as president. When the newly elected President Bush named his cabinet, the big surprise was his nomination of Lou Sullivan as HHS secretary. By that time Sullivan and I had worked on a lot of legislation together. We now had the chance to further up the ante.

Collaborating closely with the Association of Minority Health Professions Schools, which Sullivan had established in the late 1970s, my staff put together a bill we named the Disadvantaged Minority Health Improvement Act. This bill provided information and counseling services for low-income individuals in order to ameliorate many of the risk factors that were leading to such an excessive rate of minority deaths. It provided funding to coordinate and implement an integrated federal approach to minority health problems. It established funding for minority students to pursue careers in the health professions, directly addressing the Heckler Report's finding that minorities were grossly underrepresented in the health professions, and that the country needed far more minority professionals to help combat the health crisis facing black and other minority communities.

The Disadvantaged Minority Health Improvement Act was not as all-encompassing as I would have liked, but it was substantial. I introduced it in the House and Ted Kennedy did the same in the Senate. The bill was passed by voice vote in the House on October 10, 1990. The Senate passed it, also by voice vote, a week later. There were no dissenters. President Bush signed it into law on November 6. It was the first comprehensive legislation addressing minority health ever passed by the U.S. Congress. It was a landmark.

I took the lead in many of these health endeavors, but I had close collaborators and allies who were dedicated to the same goals as I was. Among these, Ted Kennedy, my counterpart in the Senate, stood out. Kennedy was a force to reckon with. If he was moving a bill on the Senate side, I was sure it was going to carry. One reason Kennedy was so effective was that he maintained respectful and often close relationships with people on the other side of the aisle, which I also found so important in my own dealings.

Kennedy was a delight to work with. So was Bill Natcher, who chaired the House Appropriations Committee. Natcher was from Kentucky. When I first met him he was head of the District of Columbia Committee. I thought of him then as someone who had something of a plantation attitude. But over time he changed. When he chaired the Subcommittee on Labor, Health and Human Services he seemed to realize that he had a much bigger role to play, and he stepped up into it, leaving his parochial southern thinking behind him. Every year he would introduce the Labor H funding bill saying in his ringing voice, "Mr. Speaker, this is the *peoples'* bill!"

By the time he assumed the Appropriations Committee chairmanship, Natcher was somebody with whom I could always discuss minority issues and know I was going to get thoughtful advice.

Bill Natcher was one of the true gentlemen of the Congress, a person of huge dignity. Whenever an especially tough bill came up on the floor, Tip O'Neill would put Natcher in the chair. Natcher had an intimate knowledge of rules and procedures, and he commanded great respect from Republicans and Democrats alike. Nobody was going to get out of line when he was in the chair. He could keep the kind of decorum no one else could.

Natcher and I became close friends. I thought of him as the epitome of what a congressman should be. Every night he would write notes and a little commentary about what had happened that day, which he would send to his grandchildren. The originals he kept in binders in his office. He showed me several of them once.

"Lou," he said.

"Yes?"

"See these? You're in here, you know."

Among other things, Natcher held the record for never having missed a vote—over 18,000 roll calls during his forty-one years of service. When he was extremely ill—he died in office—they would bring him in on a gurney from NIH to vote. He was an extraordinary man. No one meant more to me.

The year 1994 saw a historic midterm election, a landslide for the Republicans. Democrats lost fifty-four seats in the House, eight in the Senate. The last Republican majority in the House had been in 1954, forty years back.

With the new balance of power Newt Gingrich replaced Democrat Thomas Foley as Speaker. The Republicans came in riding a wave of unhappiness with congressional Democrats, many of whom voters perceived to have lost touch with the needs of their constituencies. Four decades in power had taken a toll on more than a few Democratic representatives' sense of service.

Gingrich, the new speaker, had promised voters action on a platform he called the Contract with America. Clinton called it the Contract *On* America, which was in my opinion an accurate characterization. Over all, the contract's consequences for programs that helped the poor and disadvantaged were devastating. "This is supposed to be a government of the people, by the people, and for the people," I said in one of my speeches. "We ought not forget the part that says *for* the people."

At the Congressional Black Caucus we mobilized our full force to oppose Gingrich's policies, which were so detrimental to our constituencies. But while this was a major battle, it wasn't as if Democrats and Republicans had never fought major policy battles before. In one way or another those conflicts were going to be worked out, as some of them were between Gingrich and Clinton, although only after Gingrich had precipitated two government shutdowns. At least as serious was the pervasive, poisonous, and long-lasting effect on the House's ability to work in an atmosphere of mutual respect and functional bipartisanship. Amity between Democrats and Republicans was hardly universal before Gingrich, but it wasn't uncommon, either. As speaker, Gingrich put an end to that. His tenure triggered the long, pernicious slide into the ferocious partisanship that has gone so far toward ruining decent, effective government from then until now.

Many have spoken about the rancor that has marked congressional relationships in recent times. Some, the hard-case ideologues, have no doubt
relished it. Many others, maybe most, have hated the dysfunctionality it has
brought to the business of legislating, which is the business Congress was
established to do. I had my own experiences with it.

While I was a chairing the VA, HUD and Independent Agencies Subcommittee, Jerry Lewis, a California Republican, was the ranking member.
Jerry's positions on many issues were contrary to mine, but despite that we
enjoyed an excellent working relationship. When the committee was considering a bill I would consult with Jerry to reduce as many areas of difference
as we could. When we finally made our recommendations or crafted the legislation, he didn't have to oppose me; we had already ironed things out.

Jerry and I traveled around the world together on committee business. We
had respect for each other, and over time we developed a warm friendship. I
know others in the House noted and referenced our relationship, the general
feeling being that we should all be able to work together in a similar way.

All that came to an abrupt halt as soon as Gingrich took over. With
the Republican sweep in 1994 Jerry assumed the chair of VA, HUD and
Independent Agencies and I became the ranking member. Suddenly he and
I were not consulting together any more. He didn't include me in helping
shape legislation; he stopped talking to me about issues. He simply began
imposing himself. I found myself having to oppose what Jerry was doing
legislatively in a way he had never had to do with me when I was chairman.
We were at odds in our committee hearings, butting heads instead of trying
to find common ground.

It became rancorous. I didn't understand it; I didn't understand why Jerry
had turned that way. We had worked closely together for a long time. We
had enjoyed a close personal relationship. What in the world had happened
to him?

Then one day Jerry asked me to have lunch with him. He explained to me
that Gingrich did not want Republicans to have any social relationships with
Democrats. He had basically banned it; we were likely violating the ban just
by having a meal together. Gingrich was insisting that Republicans carry out
the "Contract" and end any kind of consultation or contact across party lines.
Jerry apologized for this having caused a change in our personal friendship.
He asked that I be patient with him as he tried to restore the warm relationship we had had previously.

I respected that. It helped me understand my friend. But of course it
wasn't just Jerry. Gingrich was requiring this of all Republicans. We weren't

the only ones who were used to working in a consultative way with each other or who had friendships with each other at one level or another. Gingrich's baleful influence extended to the entire House. Prior to his ascendancy, as committee chairmen we would take ranking Republicans to conferences on bills with our senatorial counterparts. They had a seat at the conference table. Now, instead of inviting Democrats to participate, the new committee chairmen kept us out, then informed us what the conference had done. The opposite of what we had done with them.

Of course, the Republicans had been out of power in the House for forty years. Being in the minority in Congress is not a pleasant experience. I think what happened was that rather than them seeing that this was their chance to simply change polices and govern, they became vindictive and wanted to punish Democrats for their forty years in exile and for the things they perceived had been done to them during their time in the desert. Gingrich in particular had the perfect character to execute that type of vindictiveness.

Gingrich was speaker from 1994 through 1998. By that time he had alienated enough members of his own party that they forced him out of his leadership role. They were, he told the media on his departure, "cannibals."

In 1994 President Clinton appointed my brother Carl ambassador to the Seychelles, a beautiful archipelago nation in the Indian Ocean, a thousand miles east of Africa. Serving the country as an ambassador was in some ways a fitting cap to Carl's career, a boy from the streets, the projects, who had shown the way for black Americans to turn the struggle for civil rights into a full-blown participation in the world of mainstream political power. Carl is, still today, known as the first black mayor of a major American city. That isn't simply a label. It signifies a historic change in the country's political life. There was talk in 1967 of Carl being a viable vice presidential candidate. That was the first time, with Carl's election, that people began thinking seriously that one day there could be a qualified, capable, black candidate for president.

Carl carved out a path that has been followed by black political figures ever since, people who have been elected as mayors, representatives, senators, and of course President Barack Obama. Carl showed how black politicians could successfully reach out to white voters and demonstrate their qualifications, not on the basis of race, but on the basis of talent and vision. He was, in that sense, *the* pivotal African American political figure.

Carl was Cleveland's mayor for two terms. He decided not to run for a third, though. His second term had been marked by conflict, with the city council especially, but also with the newspapers and with the Democratic establishment, angered over the way he and I had taken the Twenty-First District Caucus out of the party. He was criticized every day by the *Plain Dealer* and the *Cleveland Press,* harshly and mostly unfairly. His family suffered from that and from the other pressures he was subjected to, and, as he said, "they didn't run for mayor, I did." When it was clear he was not going to have the money or the political support to bring about the changes he thought essential, Carl decided there was no point to running again. "I choose not to compromise with those who want to keep the system running as it is," he said. So he made his announcement and signed off.

Carl's next stop was New York City, where he became an anchorman for NBC News and won an Emmy for broadcast journalism. In 1980 he was offered a position as general counsel for the United Auto Workers Union of Ohio, with their 500,000 members. He was the first black general counsel for a major union. He did that for several years, then he ran for municipal court judge. I helped him with his campaign, which he won. He was on the bench for eleven years.

This was the municipal court, the lower court, which dealt with small crimes and misdemeanors, the court where both of us had gotten our start as lawyers, hustling cases. Carl became the administrative judge there, but he always took his turn presiding at hearings and trials. On the municipal court bench he dealt with prostitutes, hustlers, habitual drunks, criminally negligent landlords, husbands and wives whose disputes had gotten out of hand. His abilities, of course, were such that he could easily have presided over Ohio's Supreme Court, or something higher than that. But it was fitting that he spent those years dealing with the people we had grown up among, the ordinary, common people with their hard lives and their hard problems, trying to resolve the challenges they faced in their lives.

During Carl's eight years in New York our closeness wasn't what it had been. But when he returned to Cleveland we talked almost every day and had dinner together as often as we could. We talked about family and friends, but mostly our talk was political. Carl was still consumed by politics. He was a brilliant politician. He grasped the nuances of power and the essence of power. Back in the day he didn't have much respect for me as a politician, which was not incorrect. I didn't pretend to be a politician. I wasn't one myself and I didn't have much concern for politicians in general. But as my career in Congress progressed he began to respect my political abilities. Given his earlier disdain, that was a great satisfaction. It meant a lot to me. Earlier in my career people would often refer to me as "Carl Stokes's brother." Then, after I had been in Congress for a time, someone said to Carl, "Say, aren't you Lou Stokes's brother?" We laughed about that. "I guess that means you've arrived," Carl said.

In April 1995 Carl was back in Cleveland on leave from his ambassadorship. The Twenty-First (now Eleventh) District Caucus was having its annual boat ride on Lake Erie. Carl had promised he would come down and go with us; people loved having the chance to spend time with him. But as the departure time drew near he hadn't shown up. I was looking for him and finally saw him arrive. "Lou," he said, "something's bothering my throat. I need to go to the hospital and have it checked out."

When we got back from the cruise later that evening I called his home, but he wasn't there. When I called the Cleveland Clinic to check, they said he was in the emergency room, so I went down there to see him. They had examined him, he said; they were running some tests.

The next day we went back. The tests revealed esophageal cancer. A few days later we traveled together to New York to get a second opinion. Doctors there confirmed the diagnosis. The tumor, they said, was inoperable.

We planned a trip to Florida; a friend had offered him his home down there so that he and I could have some quiet time together. He told me that people were still after him for advice and consultation. "But all I want to do," he told them, "is sit around a pool and read and spend some time with my brother."

We never did get to do that. He became very ill a week before we were to leave and went into the hospital. He died there on April 3, 1996.

We held Carl's funeral at the Cleveland Music Hall. Very few churches in town could have accommodated the several thousand mourners who wanted to see Carl off. Bill Clay and his wife Carol came; Maxine Waters; Don Payne, who was then chairman of the Congressional Black Caucus; Secretary of Health and Human Services Donna Shalala was there representing President Clinton. Arnold Pinkney spoke. Jesse Jackson gave a moving eulogy.

When it was my turn I talked about how Carl had epitomized the classic American Horatio Alger story, but with a twist, not from rags to riches but from poverty to power. I could easily have said "rags" instead of "poverty." I had a photo in my house of Caldwell Gaffney and me when we were working our paper routes as kids. I was twelve, and Caldwell must have been fourteen. In this picture we were standing there with our heavy bags full of newspapers. Neither of us looked good. What we looked was poor. Our clothes were raggedy. My shirt had a hole in it. One day at my house Carl was looking at that photo. He stared at it a while, then told Jay, "You see those clothes Lou's wearing. After he wore them I had to wear them."

I told the crowd at the Music Hall that Carl had always been a leader. I had seen that from the time we were young. He never understood the concept of big brother/little brother. As long as he was able he wanted to be the leader, the big brother. I didn't mind that in him. I was never jealous of him; it made me proud that he was my brother. At the end of my talk I said, "Good night, little brother." I know he would have taken that in the spirit I meant it.

I retired from Congress in 1999. Carl had said on many occasions when we talked that you've really got to love politics. You've got to have fun at it, because you're certainly not going to make any money at it. I never did have the love for it he had; I was never consumed by it. But I did have fun at it, partly because he and I could talk about things. We talked about political people, what they did right and what they did wrong. We talked about strategy and tactics. I could get his opinion about things. Carl's passing left a void in my life. There was nobody else I could talk to like that. So now that was gone.

I had thought even earlier about leaving, but Carl had said, "Lou, you can't go yet. You've got other things you've got to do." So I stayed. But then Gingrich came in and I saw how mean-spirited Congress had become. Over the years I had learned to enjoy being a U.S. congressman. I went to work early every morning and worked long, hard days. Seven days a week, ten, twelve, fourteen hours a day. That was how I had done it. But I didn't feel any longer that I wanted to come to work, in a place where ill will and anger were the order of the day, where bellicosity pervaded the atmosphere.

I felt my age then—when Carl passed I was 71; when I finally retired I was 74. But I knew that if I left I could go back and resume my career as a lawyer, to do something that would give me contentment and enjoyment. I discussed it with Jay and my family. They all understood and concurred that if that was how I felt, this would be the right time to leave. So that's what I did.

On the last bill I ever worked on, just before I retired, a vote was about to be taken on the floor. Jerry Lewis, still the Republican chairman of my Appropriations subcommittee, asked the House to join him in a tribute to me and my service. It started with that. Three hours later there were still members standing in line waiting to speak.

Finally the Speaker said, "Listen, we've gone on three hours with this. We've got business to accomplish here." But after what had just happened I felt I needed to say something to my colleagues. Jerry yielded the floor to me.

This was, I told them, "the greatest day I have ever experienced in the House of Representatives. . . . I have been touched and moved in a way I will never forget." I couldn't help reciting then something about my life, which had never destined me to this place. "I have oftentimes," I told them, "sitting on the floor or standing in this well, pinched myself and asked if I was really here." I told them about my mother scrubbing floors and about Carl achieving the place he had achieved, both of us coming out of the projects and the streets. "I can only say to all of you," I told them, "that I am proud that I am an American. No matter what gripes we have, this is the greatest country in the world. The story I have recited to you today of the Stokes brothers could only happen in America. Only in America, Mr. Chairman. Only in America."

We voted. Then I left. As I walked out the door for the last time I thought, what a true honor this has been.

EPILOGUE

CHARLIE VANIK, my predecessor as the Twenty-First District's representative, was my most important mentor when I first came into the House. After he retired, Charlie had become a partner in the international law firm Squire Sanders and Dempsey, whose home office was Cleveland. Thereafter he would constantly tell me, "Louie, when you leave Congress you have to come with us at Squire Sanders."

When I retired Charlie had just left the firm—he was eighty-five or eighty-six by then. But he hadn't really left. He called them constantly, telling them they had to do this or that, just as he used to write me regular notes telling me what I ought to be doing. Charlie was an irrepressible character. When I told him I was retiring he called the Squire Sanders managing partner, John Lewis, insisting in his own unique way that they had to "get me."

John Lewis and I knew each other well; we had worked on various Cleveland projects together. Lewis was one of the city's movers and shakers, instrumental in (among other things) opening the city's law firms to blacks, Jews, and women. John had followed the firm's legendary managing partner, Jim Davis, who had been one of the city's leading business figures. As head of the Cleveland Bar Association, Davis had given a powerful speech back in the late 1960s telling not just the bar association but the city's entire business establishment that they had to address equal opportunity for all of Cleveland's citizens. I was a member of the bar association executive board at that time, along with two other African Americans, John Bustamante and Russ Adrine. Later Davis wrote that the three of us were the type of lawyer who should have been recruited into the city's law firms.

Squire Sanders recognized what an exceptionally good move hiring Charlie Vanik had been. Charlie brought them a high level of congressional expertise and knowledge, along with the great respect he had as a legislator. This gave them an entrée into government they had never had. Bringing me in would give them access to some of the same kind of experience and counsel. When John Lewis and Squires' chairman, Tom Stanton, came to Washington to talk to me, I told them I was ready to join. By then I was eager to return to a profession I loved more than I loved being a congressman. I wouldn't be going back as a trial lawyer, but I'd be around lawyers, working with lawyers. I'd be part of what I considered a great club. I was thrilled about it.

At the same time Case Western Reserve University was talking to me about coming to the law school to teach. But Darlyne Bailey, the dean of the university's Mandel School of Applied Social Sciences, also visited to talk about what they were doing in social work. I told her I was speaking to people at the law school about teaching. When she said, "I wish we would have a chance to bring you to the Mandel School," I said, "Well, that's something we can certainly discuss."

When I chaired the Appropriations subcommittee I had set aside millions of dollars for social work programs in Cleveland. Much of it had gone to community organizations such as Fairfax Community Development, the Hough Area Development Corporation, and the Saint Clair Superior Development Corporation. These organizations had done tremendous work in helping improve lives in Cleveland's inner-city neighborhoods. The Mandel School was one of the leading social work schools in the country. Joining the faculty there would give me a chance to talk with young, aspiring community social workers to help them understand the importance of advocacy, in particular the nature of the alignment between social work and legislation and the political realities behind those interactions. That appealed to me very much. So I opted to join the Mandel School faculty—where I have now been serving as visiting professor for fifteen years alongside such distinguished colleagues as Mark Joseph, Terry Hockenstad, David Crampton, and Dean Grover "Cleve" Gilmore.

So there I was, shortly after my retirement, at Squire Sanders and the Mandel School, and also on the radio. WEWS in Cleveland had opened up a spot for me as a political commentator, which I especially enjoyed doing.

In 2008 I was on the air when Barack Obama was elected president. I shed tears of joy that night.

Years after my retirement a friend asked what I was proudest of in my legislative career. I was proud of it all, I told him, but if one thing stood out in my mind it was what I had done to further health care, particularly minority health care. Looking back I have vivid memories of sitting on committees considering health-care legislation, taking testimony and asking questions of people from the health-care agencies and institutions: the HHS secretary, the surgeon general, the directors of CDC and NIH, the chiefs of NIH's various centers and institutes.

I would sit there, the only black on the committee, asking very pointed questions about minority health care, thinking, all these white people sitting here with me and I'm the only one who's going to raise these issues. I'd start and as soon as I did I'd see the eyes begin to roll. I could hear them thinking, *There he goes again. What is he talking about? What does this have to do with anything?* That was demeaning, but I had to disregard it. Just ignore it, I'd say to myself. No matter how they look at me, just ask what you have to ask and ignore it.

So I did what I thought I had to do. This went on for years, during a great deal of my tenure on one or another of the Appropriations subcommittees, twenty-eight out of my thirty years in Congress altogether. It was not comfortable for me, and it was not comfortable for those sitting there on the hot seat answering question after question from this black man about black people—at a time and in a context where they weren't thinking much about black people at all. But it turned out that over time those interactions had consequences. They helped change the way the health-care leaders and directors felt they had to focus their efforts, or at least broaden their thinking.

Then a most surprising thing happened. As the subcommittee on Labor, Health and Human Services was considering the last bill I would be part of, just before my retirement, Chairman John Porter said, "Lou, the heads of the institutes at NIH want us to construct a building named in your honor."

I knew that occasionally NIH recognized people with a building. I'd been out at the NIH campus for the dedication of the William Natcher and Silvio Conti Buildings. But the NIH institute heads who had approached Porter were the very people I had harassed and implored and pleaded with. For more than two decades I badgered and fought with them and brought issues to their attention they might rather have disregarded. And to have the heads of these institutions, whom I'd been beating up for so long, say *they* wanted a building on their campus named after me? What more emphatic answer could I have to the questions I was always asking myself during those committee encounters: Should I question this? Should I question that? But at the end, evidently it seemed I had done the right thing.

As the building was going up on the NIH campus I took a tour with John Ruffin, director of the Center for Minority Health and Health Disparities. The building site was busy and in one area we came across an African American mason, apparently in charge of the brickwork. We stopped for a moment to talk, and Ruffin asked, "Do you know who this gentleman here is?"

He did not. Ruffin and I had our hard hats on, not that he would have recognized me anyway.

"This is Congressman Stokes," Ruffin said, "the man this building is named for."

The man hesitated a moment. You could see in his eyes what it meant to him, that this building, which he was helping build, was being named for a fellow African American. "I'm glad to meet you, Mr. Stokes," he said. We shook hands. "I can tell you one thing," he said. "There will not be a single crooked brick on this building. If there is one crooked brick, it will be made straight."

I didn't know which of us was prouder.

I was immensely moved by the honor of having that building named after me, most especially considering that NIH decided to locate so much of its research on health disparities there. So it's not only the building itself that I am proud of, it's what takes place inside that building.

Since my retirement I have kept up my engagement with efforts to improve minority health care. For the last two years I've been co-chair of the Community Action Board of the NEOMED-CSU Partnership for Urban Health. NEOMED is the Northeast Ohio Medical University; CSU is Cleveland State University. Northeastern Ohio, like other urban areas, has a dearth of minority primary-care physicians, which is so detrimental to inner-city residents especially. The purpose of the NEOMED-CSU partnership is to develop a pipeline for students from high school through college through medical school. The students themselves come from the Cleveland public schools. NEOMED-CSU nurtures and supports them through their undergraduate studies and medical school in return for a commitment to practice in Cleveland's underserved neighborhoods. Along the way they become familiar with the health-care needs of urban areas, and when they have completed their residencies NEOMED-CSU helps them place themselves in the communities where they are most needed. We hope and intend that this might become a nationwide model, and we have allied the program with my old friend Lou Sullivan's Sullivan Alliance to Transform the Health Professions, a national endeavor to increase the diversity of the U.S. health-care workforce.

The NEOMED-CSU Partnership will eventually be able to graduate minority physicians at an almost unheard-of rate. Establishing the program on such a scale has taken an unconditional commitment from the two institutions and their presidents, Ronald Berkman of CSU and Jay Gershen of NEOMED. In my experience, alliances like this often run into trouble because of territorial issues and, frankly, the egos of powerful presidents. But Presidents Gershen and Berkman have worked together with a selflessness that I have found simply extraordinary.

My co-chairman of the Partnership's Community Action Board is Dr. Edgar Jackson, a leading physician and medical educator who had been chief of staff and senior adviser to the president of Case Western Reserve's University Hospitals. He is the first African American to have an endowed chair named after him. Sonja Harris Heywood is our executive director, a young, inspired, family medicine practitioner and professor at Case Western Reserve. It has been hugely gratifying to be involved on the cutting edge with individuals of their stature and commitment.

For me personally, the naming of the NIH's Stokes Building was a landmark. It reinforced the sense of accomplishment I took with me when I left Congress, especially reflecting back on how few of us there had been when I first arrived, how inexperienced we were in the art of governance, and how we had fought to establish places for ourselves and make an impact on the legislation that meant most to us and to our communities. For thirty years I had worked hard and, I hoped, in a way that honored the institution I grew to love.

I knew that my colleagues valued my service; it gave me immense satisfaction that they did. I believe that over the years those of us in the Congressional Black Caucus succeeded in establishing an understanding that black legislators were every bit as capable and dedicated as white legislators. I have no doubt that we changed perceptions in that regard. Over time we were no longer regarded as strange and semiforeign anomalies in the world of political power, but as a normal part of governance. When Tip O'Neill gave me the kinds of assignments and appointments he did, it was not because I was his pal or because I was black, it was because he understood I would carry them out capably. The same held true for the work other African American legislators were doing.

But although we might have carved out a place for ourselves in the world of governance, there were other areas where derogation was still the rule. I felt that; I still carry some bitterness about it. From a historical point of view, the most important committee I chaired was the House Special Committee on Assassinations. Our hearings were televised nationally from gavel to gavel. They precipitated volumes of newsprint. I was sensitive to the fact that I was a black American chairing this investigation into the deaths of President Kennedy and Dr. King, such huge events in our nation's life. But the media rarely noted that or referred to the committee as the Stokes Committee, as, for example, they typically referred to the Senate Committee on Intelligence Operations as the Church Committee, after its chairman, Frank Church.

I noticed that. Then, following our hearings, whenever there was additional news or developments, instead of coming to me for comment the media habitually went to Bob Blakey, my counsel. I noticed that, too. In similar situations, reporters commonly looked to committee chairs for clarification or commentary, not to committee staff. I had a high regard for Blakey's abilities. But he was not the spokesperson for the committee. When I turned on the TV and watched news about the work my committee had done, it wasn't easy to see it being discussed by the man who had worked for me as my counsel. It disturbed me to watch the media do this. It also disturbed me to see that Bob seemed to accept that it was his role to speak authoritatively about the committee's work.

Those feelings came to a head one night when I was watching Blakey being interviewed regarding my interrogation of Fidel Castro. This was one of the highest points in our investigation, an unparalleled event in international relations. They should have really come to me about that, I thought; it's appalling that they didn't. Then I was astonished to hear Blakey say about Castro, "I looked him directly in the eye and said, 'Did you kill the president?' And he said no."

I remembered the Castro interview minutely. Blakey had never said such a thing. No one had, and Blakey himself had played an extremely small part in that day's questioning of the Cuban leader. Why in the world was Blakey drawing attention to himself with such a statement? And why was he taking on the role of the committee's spokesperson to begin with? Why had he lent himself to that?

Of course, Blakey wasn't responsible for the media approaching him. But the question rankled: Why did the media think they should go to Blakey, to the white lawyer rather than to the black chairman? I would have been annoyed by this had I been a white chairman of so significant a committee and the media had gone to my lawyer instead of myself. But as I was the only black chairman to serve in such a high-profile role, it had a different resonance, well beyond personal pique. It resonated with all the racist deprecation that black Americans experience and, frankly, find so intolerable.

Reflecting back from this distance in years (our committee closed its doors thirty-seven years ago at this writing), I think the media simply was not up to showing me the respect they would have shown a white chairman. African Americans had asserted themselves as competent and able in some regions of the nation's mindset, but hardly in all—still the case, most unfortunately, even now. Back then journalists were simply not able to fit the concept of black intellectual and organizational ability into their mentality. The media wasn't up to that level of understanding. Sports fans will recall that only a short time ago it was not accepted that black professional football players could make equally good quarterbacks as whites or equally competent coaches. The default mainstream thinking was that they did not have the analytical ability or mental adeptness for those roles. These kinds of stereotypes die hard and they die slow. They leave their mark. They have left their mark on my generation, and I am in no way exempt.

I was elected fifteen times and served for thirty years. I represented various elements of Cleveland's multiethnic community, but my power base was in the predominantly African American neighborhoods of my district. My strength there derived largely from the Twenty-First District Caucus, and also from the black ministers who were so instrumental in supporting my reelections and so responsive when I needed their backing on issues.

For three decades the spotlight was on me as Ohio's first black congressman. That meant I had to set the standard. I had to create a model for representing the district in such a way that when I left, those following me would have to demonstrate a high level of service to the district's people. I believe I succeeded in doing that, and the proof has been in those who have come after me.

Stephanie Tubbs Jones, who was elected after I retired, had been a protégé of both Carl and myself. In Congress Stephanie quickly established herself as a leader, and she had already made a strong reputation for herself before her tragic, far-too-early death. She had become the first black member of the Ways and Means Committee. She had chaired the House Ethics Committee and co-chaired the Democratic National Committee.

With her unexpected passing, Marcia Fudge was appointed to the district seat. Marcia had been Tubbs Jones's first chief of staff, then she was elected as the first female mayor of the town of Warrensville Heights. Since succeeding Tubbs Jones, Marcia has won four elections to Congress. She too has a record of accomplishment there, serving with distinction on several committees and as chairwoman of the Congressional Black Caucus.

I take a good deal of pleasure in watching how Marcia has embraced the traditional Labor Day Parade, which after almost forty-five years is still a major event in the life of Cleveland's black community and very much the district's political fulcrum. Marcia (and Stephanie before her) has built the parade into something even more significant than it was in earlier times.

Stephanie Tubbs Jones took office in 2001 and Marcia Fudge in 2009 as young leaders in Cleveland's political life. But the city has had a long tradition now of powerful black politicians. My friendship with two of the most important in Cleveland's history sustained me both politically and personally for more years than I care to count. Arnold Pinkney and George Forbes were powers to reckon with in Cleveland's political and civil life—Arnold until his death in 2014, George, still at this writing going strong at the age of eighty-four.

Arnold was a brilliant politician. His great talent was in running political campaigns. He helped elect judges in Cleveland, Ohio governors John Gilligan and Richard Celeste, Carl in his second campaign for mayor, and my own first and second campaigns for Congress. He was Jesse Jackson's campaign manager in his run for the presidency and Hubert Humphrey's deputy campaign manager in his.

Arnold's skills didn't work well for himself, though. He ran for mayor twice and twice lost. He and I had our falling out over the Twenty-First District Caucus, but we made that up and I worked hard for him in his first mayoral campaign. "You worked harder for me than you did for yourself in your own campaigns," he told me.

Arnold was not just my campaign manager; he was a warm personal friend. After I won my first election I was able to persuade him to stay on with me for a while. He came to Washington to organize my office there, then he organized my Cleveland office.

Two of the people he hired for me turned out to be two of the best staffers any leader has ever had. Jewell Gilbert had been a secretary in the law office I established with my brother Carl, Carl Character, Sam Perry, and our other colleagues. When I won my initial race Arnold brought Jewell to Washington. She served on my staff throughout my entire congressional career, which meant she worked for me for thirty-three years, eventually taking over as my chief of staff. The other was Jackie Jenkins, who served with me for twenty-some years. Jackie too was an absolutely superb aide, selfless, intelligent, and invariably steady and responsible.

Arnold was the best in the country in managing political campaigns. But I was also fortunate to have a lady by the name of Lynne Gertrude Powell, one of the feistiest people I've ever known, but also politically brilliant. Lynnie Powell made people think that she was tougher than she really was; in actuality, beneath her tough veneer lived a very soft-hearted and sensitive lady. But she was a talent. Her political skills were similar in many ways to Arnold's; she was, simply, a great organizer with a sure feel for election priorities. The combination of Arnold Pinkney and Lynnie Powell gave me what I considered the most effective campaign people anywhere.

Arnold Pinkney was the kind of friend you want to have, not just for the personal connection, but because he was someone who inspired admiration and respect. When he passed, his wife, Betty, told me that Arnold wanted me to represent all of the public officials at his funeral. So at the conclusion of our long and meaningful friendship I had the honor of helping eulogize one of Cleveland's best.

My relationship with George Forbes goes back at least as far as my relationship with Arnold. Whenever I speak of George I'm reminded of our breakfast meeting when we were opponents in the 1968 race for Congress, when he told me, "Lou, you can't win," and for more than a moment I believed him. George was a man who loves and practices politics in the way it should be practiced, with skill and strength. He was a member of the city council for twenty-seven years and president for sixteen of those. In that position he wielded great power; many people feared as well as respected him. He ran the council with a strong hand; in the eyes of most people, George Forbes ran the city.

George and I always had respect for each other, even during our differences over the Twenty-First District Caucus when he and Arnold took their people out. But just as Arnold and I healed our friendship, George and I did as well. In the one primary where I faced a stiff challenge, George and

Arnold both stepped in and helped me emerge with a victory. On occasion, the three of us, George, Arnold, and I, have been accused of thwarting the progress of younger politicians, but that was never true. We were all secure enough in our positions that we never had to stop anyone's growth. On the contrary, we felt it important for younger colleagues to make progress in their careers, and we did what we could to mentor and advise.

George and his family and I and mine have enjoyed close personal relationships over our long lives. Along with Arnold, George and I have more than once been referred to as "the Mount Rushmore of Cleveland politics." I'm not quite sure how to take that, but each of us certainly exercised enduring power in the city's political life. Our friendship endured as well, and that has given me both strength and comfort throughout these many years.

Friendships are a pillar of the fulfilled life. So is meaningful work. The third pillar is family. Jay and I have been married now for fifty-five years. We have four children and seven grandchildren. We are intensely proud of them all, but I cannot think of them without reflecting on the spiritual strength Carl and I received from our own mother. I know she infused that strength into us, and I see the values she lived by and embodied in the lives of our families' children and grandchildren as well.

She worked, of course, as a domestic, after coming up to Cleveland out of Georgia's cotton fields. She continued working long after Carl and I were able to support her. She was not one to slack off just because she could. She lost her much-loved husband early, but her maternal care for us never wavered for a moment. Over and over she insisted to Carl and me that we needed to "be somebody," that we needed to educate ourselves in order to grasp onto a better life, one not consumed by drudgery and hard physical labor. She gave us the grit to overcome our poverty and the lure of the streets. She was determined, and we drank in her determination.

Long ago I came across a poem by the great African American poet Langston Hughes titled "Mother to Son." Reading it, I was overwhelmed by the feeling Hughes had captured, so very close to how my own mother might well have spoken to me. My life, says the mother in the poem, "ain't been no crystal stair."

> Well, son, I'll tell you:
> Life for me ain't been no crystal stair.
> It's had tacks in it,
> And splinters,
> And boards torn up,

And places with no carpet on the floor—
Bare.
But all the time
I'se been a-climbin' on,
And reachin' landin's,
And turnin' corners,
And sometimes goin' in the dark
Where there ain't been no light.
So boy, don't you turn back.
Don't you set down on the steps
'Cause you finds it's kinder hard.
Don't you fall now—
For I'se still goin,' honey.
I'se still climbin,'
And life for me ain't been no crystal stair.

The poem epitomized her to me. I think about that poem and go back to it often. It speaks to me of my mother's life and of our lives, and the deep life lessons she taught us.

On my mother's last day I took her to a service at Olivet Institutional Baptist Church. The Rev. Jesse Jackson was the guest pastor that day. My mother liked Jesse, and of course he was a friend of mine. We were looking forward to hearing him preach.

Olivet was one of Cleveland's most historic churches, a place where the black community often gathered for rallies and other events. Reverend Otis Moss Jr. was pastor then. He had succeeded the Reverend O. M. Hoover, who had been one of Martin Luther King's best friends. Hoover had marched with King, and Olivet had served as Dr. King's headquarters whenever he came to Cleveland. Rev. Hoover's daughter, Carole, was also close to the King family. She had worked for Dr. King and later became a close companion of Coretta Scott King. Carole was (and still is) an important figure in her own right, a major business presence in Cleveland, and a person I have turned to for help many times over the years, which she has always given unstintingly.

The service at Olivet that morning was long. Jesse preached a long sermon, then he "took in" to the church seventy or eighty people, more than I had ever seen at one service. When we finally finished it took a while for me to extricate myself, with so many wanting to say hello and shake hands.

When we finally got away and were walking down the street toward my car, my mother felt faint. The morning had tired her out. It was clear that she needed help, and as we drove up by Miller's Funeral Home on Quincy Avenue, I said, "Let's stop here a moment and let you rest." By then it was obvious she was weakening. We called an ambulance, which picked her up and took her to St. Vincent's Charity Hospital.

I drove behind, but when I got there they had already taken her in to the emergency room. Doctors were working on her, but they wouldn't let me in, and not long afterward they came out to tell me she had passed. Until that day she had been doing fairly well both physically and mentally. But that morning had been too much for her heart.

We held the funeral three days later at St Paul A. M. E. Zion Church. Mayor Dennis Kucinich sent an honor guard of Cleveland police. Jesse Jackson gave a beautiful eulogy. Carl came up from New York and spoke. I couldn't bring myself to speak. I was too saddened. I thought that some of her grandchildren should instead. They had meant so much to her and she to them. Better to let them speak. Shelley and Chuck did. Their remarks were so moving I could not keep the tears from my eyes. When Shelley left the podium and came back to the pew I took her hand and kissed her. When it was over the police honor guard, including mounted police, led the procession away from the church.

The children were wonderful that day. I knew how fortunate I was to have children like that. I had never had to worry a day about them. Never needed to call a lawyer, never had to pick them up from the police, never needed to be concerned about alcohol or drugs. And my pride in them only grew as the years passed. When my mother died Shelley had graduated from Ohio University, then she got a master's degree and eventually went to work for the Howard University library system. Angie, two years younger, won a scholarship to Howard Law School, then she was recruited by Ohio's governor Anthony Celebrezze as a state assistant attorney general. She's been a judge in Cleveland since. Chuck went into television journalism after graduating from Morehouse College and earning a master's degree at Columbia. As editorial director at Detroit's ABC affiliate WXYZ, he has won thirteen Emmys so far and counting. Lori too went into journalism after attending Ohio State and Howard. She is a highly respected journalist and news anchor at WABC TV in New York. Committed to social and civic issues, she has won numerous Emmys and a George Foster Peabody Award for her coverage of 9/11/2001.

But I can't take the credit for the way they have turned out. That goes to Jay, who at the age of twenty-two assumed the job of being mother to three children from another marriage and then melded our fourth seamlessly into the family unit. She spent her life nurturing them, taking them to the doctor when they were sick, being with them when they needed solace or encouragement. Whatever they needed, she was there. She loved them exactly as I did and was the finest parent and partner in raising them that I could ever have hoped for. Given my work schedule, she was truly the one who provided the lion's share of the comfort and guidance they needed as they grew. So much of the time I was out in the community, lawyering, being a congressman, doing everything I could that the community called on me to do. And all that while she was there with our children day and night.

When I look back on the fifty-five years Jay and I have spent as husband and wife, I can hardly believe my good fortune. My children, my grandchildren, my inspirational wife—all of whom have made my life the happiest in the world. All I can say is that I have been more than fortunate; I have been blessed.

POSTSCRIPT

FORMER CONGRESSMAN Louis Stokes died only days after finishing work on the epilogue to his book. He was ninety years old. He was beloved by the people of Ohio and by a multitude of others in the country, from both the minority and mainstream communities. His legislative work for the poor and disadvantaged made him a legendary figure in the House of Representatives, as did his skill as chairman of various significant committees and his bipartisan orientation toward members on the other side of the aisle. After his death, his body lay in state at the Cleveland City Hall rotunda where thousands came to pay their respects. His funeral, at Olivet Baptist Church, was attended by Vice President Joseph Biden and other leading national and Ohio political figures.

INDEX

Note: Figures in italics refer to photographs; a general entry for Louis Stokes is included, but readers should refer first to names of persons and institutions.